IMAGES
of America

WEBSTER

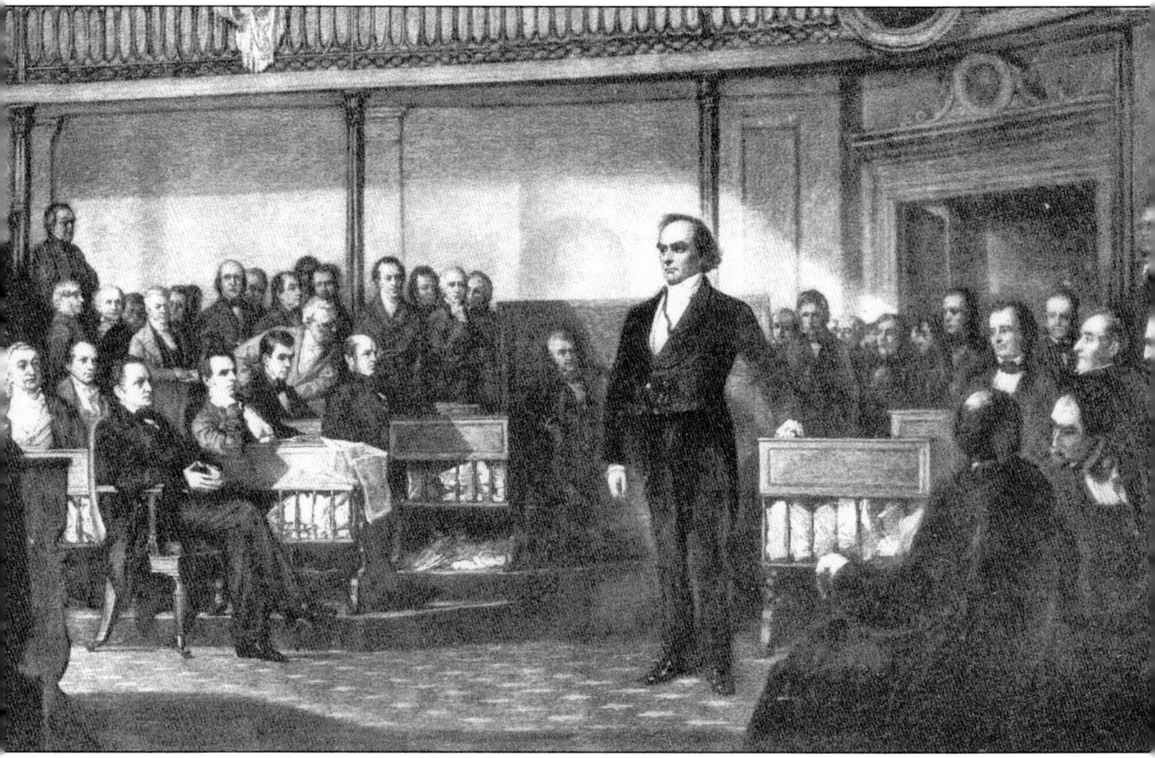

The town of Webster was named for leading American statesman Daniel Webster. Already famous for his many well-conceived public speeches, Webster's "Second Reply to Hayne in 1830" (shown above) is generally regarded as the most eloquent speech ever delivered in congress. In the speech, Webster described the U.S. government as "made for the people, made by the people, and answerable to the people." Abraham Lincoln used this idea in the Gettysburg Address. (Courtesy of *Daniel Webster* by Henry Cabot Lodge.)

On the Cover: This is a George Wall *c.* 1900 photograph from a glass plate negative of apple pickers in Webster. (Courtesy of the Webster Historian.)

IMAGES
of America

WEBSTER

Lynn M. Barton, Joan E. Sassone,
and Mary Hasek Grenier

ARCADIA
PUBLISHING

ISBN 978-0-7385-7254-3

Published by Arcadia Publishing
Charleston, South Carolina

Printed in the United States of America

Library of Congress Control Number: 2009936090

For all general information contact Arcadia Publishing at:
Telephone 843-853-2070
Fax 843-853-0044
E-mail sales@arcadiapublishing.com
For customer service and orders:
Toll-Free 1-888-313-2665

Visit us on the Internet at www.arcadiapublishing.com

Dedicated to the former Webster Town and Village Historians, who have documented and preserved much of our local history

Contents

Acknowledgments

This book would not have been possible without the work of former town and village historians including the following: Thomas Wright, Thomas Gaffney, George Curtice, Esther Dunn, and Richard Batzing. We have based much of the information in this book on the written and oral histories they organized, and we have done our best to be as accurate as possible. Any photographs that do not have acknowledgments are courtesy of the Webster Town and Village archives.

Many Webster families have contributed photographs and family histories. Our thanks to the Arbor, Barringer, Merz, Reiber, Longrod, Schlegel, Holt, Burkhardt, and Henry Zimmer, Thomas Gosnell, and James Gleason families. Additional thanks to John VanAlstyne, Carol Reitz, Nancy Rosin, Richard Crittenden, Robert Holtz, Kenneth Kittelberger, Pat Maracle, Mark Aldridge, Jan Naujokas, Dr. Robert and Kathleen Brennan, Thomas Pellett, Edward and Lorrie Jones, Dolores Maas Zimmer, Lois Metcalfe Bircher, and Theresa Young. We received valuable assistance from the Rochester Museum and Science Center, the New York Public Library, the Denver Public Library, the Rochester Rundel Library local history department, Webster Library, Dr. Richard Laub and Wm. Parsons at the Buffalo Science Museum, the Webster Museum photograph collection, the Town and Village archives, Pat Wayne, the Irondequoit Town Historian, and the Webster Masonic Lodge No. 538.

Special thanks to Rebekah Collinsworth, our editor at Arcadia Publishing, and Carol Saylor and Lisa Fox and Jude Lancy, who provided additional research and support.

With love and gratitude to our husbands Robert Barton, Michael Sassone, and Michael Grenier, for their patience and to Michael, Robert, and Nicholas Grenier for technical support. A huge thank you to Michael Grenier, whose computer skills saved the day many times.

Introduction

The town of Webster, New York, occupies the northeast corner of Monroe County. It is bounded on the west by the tall, wooded bluffs flanking the Irondequoit Bay. Webster's long northern coastline is the dramatic shore of Lake Ontario, one of the Great Lakes. Pleasure boats of all sizes—moored, motoring, or sailing on a summer day—bring a nautical signature to the town. The winding Lake Road that hugs this shore has mansions, cottages, beaches, woods, farms, and parklands along the rolling terrain. This drive along the lake is one of the most scenic routes in western New York.

The east end of town is the County Line Road shared with Wayne County. Webster also shares with our neighboring county the historical thoroughfare that runs through the southern stretch of our town, the old Ridge Road. This road, described as the longest Main Street in New York, is on the high gravel and sand embankment that was formed by wave action from the ancient glacial Lake Iroquois. This ridge is almost continuous through western New York and around Lake Ontario to Toronto, Canada, and beyond. The crest was a natural Native American trail through the deep woods of the area.

The village of Webster has retained many 19th century commercial buildings and several cobblestone structures made from lakeshore, wave-rounded stones. Several buildings are undergoing revitalization, and new construction is bringing new business to the village.

What is today the town of Webster was created in 1840, but had many incarnations before. There were thousands of years of Native American presence. The Paleo Indians, archaic tribes, Hopewell Mound Builders, Algonquin, and Iroquois Seneca were surmised to be here from the tools they left behind.

The French claimed the land in the 17th century, and in 1669, Robert Cavalier Sieur de la Salle, with 21 men and nine canoes, paddled along the shore of Lake Ontario around Webster's Nine Mile Point and through the outlet to Irondequoit Bay. They were searching for the passageway to the Orient. They did not find it, but were credited with being the first Europeans to our area.

The valuable fur trade that passed through our lands and along our lakeshore was the prize that the Marquis Denonville, governor of New France, hoped to secure in 1687, when he led an expedition of French soldiers and allied Miami and Mohawk Native Americans against the Seneca nation. The Seneca had intercepted some canoes loaded with furs headed to Québec. On the Webster sandbar, the site of a small town park today, Denonville set up a staging area for what would become a major event in North American history. Denonville's army marched down the Native American trail, which is today the Bay Road. The battle with the Seneca took place in present-day Victor, New York. Legend has it that the weather was so hot and humid that the marquis was fighting in his underwear.

Nevertheless, Denonville was a distinguished soldier in his native France, and his tactics routed the Seneca. The French then proceeded to destroy the Seneca villages, which were wisely deserted when the army arrived. The Seneca thereafter allied with the British, who were the victors when the French and Indian War ended in 1763. The British then claimed our Webster land. The British colonies of New York and Massachusetts both had claims on our land. In 1786, Massachusetts was allowed to purchase the Native American lands in western New York as long as the Seneca would relinquish their title to it. The state was short of funds so Oliver Phelps and Nathaniel Gorham were allowed to buy the land. The negotiation with the Council of Seneca was held at Buffalo Creek. Phelps agreed to build a sawmill and a gristmill, so corn could be ground and lumber sawed, but he misled them and claimed that these mills would require an area 12 miles by 24 miles. The Seneca were surprised by this figure, but they had already smoked a pipe of assent, so they agreed.

After the Phelps-Gorham purchase, the land was surveyed and towns began to develop. In 1794, the town of Northfield was formed, which consisted of present-day Irondequoit, Brighton, Pittsford, Henrietta, Perinton, Penfield, and Webster. In 1808, we were called the town of Boyle. Penfield separated from Boyle in 1810, and the northern part of that town became Webster in 1840. The southern boundary of our town was set by Gov. William Seward when he signed a bill creating the town of Webster.

This Arcadia book is a picture window on the first 100 years of the town of Webster, ending with the centennial celebration of 1940. The fruit orchards, flower farms, wheat fields, and dairy cows that comprised the more than 400 farms in Webster are highlighted. By 1850, the nursery business was part of Webster's horticultural life. Many greenhouses were constructed, and these glass buildings were a sparkling addition to the landscape. Webster had many flower farms. Henry and Ella Zimmer and their family grew chrysanthemums and orchids at their 733 Hard Road homestead. Some of the other families involved in the nursery business were the Edward Wood family on Maple Drive, the Ernisse family on Klem Road, the Steinorth family on Bay Road, and the Kittelberger family on North Avenue. Vorndran Nurseries specialized in rhododendrons; the Nelson Hallauers grew alpine, herbs, and rare plants from around the world; and the Gent family grew African violets. Both the Froniear and Grineff families grew many varieties of gladioli.

Pictured are some Webster locals whose contributions helped the growth of the town and others who shared their talents or served our nation in early wars. This volume looks at the homes and businesses that were built—some are still with us and others have given way to new endeavors. It pictures the trains, trolleys, wagons, horses, cars, and trucks that made our commercial growth possible.

Pictures that celebrate the lake and bay waters that drew people to Webster for pastimes such as swimming, fishing, and boating are featured.

The town of Webster today is the fastest growing town in Monroe County. We have many beautiful, new suburban houses, excellent schools, thriving churches, champion sports teams, many businesses, and major industries. By looking back at the early days of Webster, the connections to the present and the future are strengthened.

Webster will continue to be the town "Where Life Is Worth Living," our town motto.

One

The Early Days

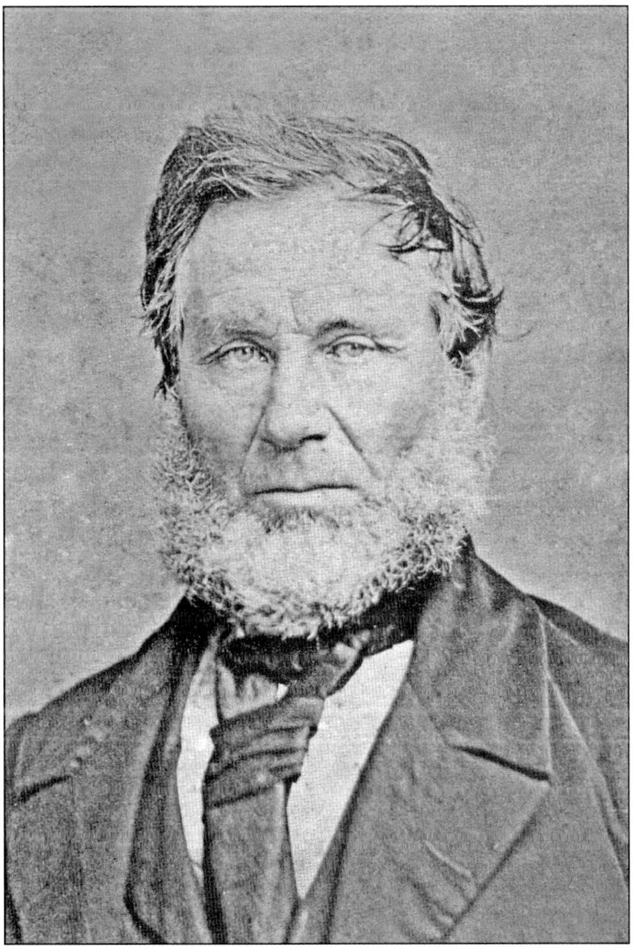

In 1840, a petition with the signatures of 324 inhabitants of North Penfield was presented to the New York State assembly in Albany asking for the creation of a new town, Webster, New York. Gov. William H. Seward signed the bill that created the new town. The first town meeting was held at the Letts Tavern. Byron Woodhull, shown, was elected supervisor of the town of Webster, he also served as supervisor for four later terms.

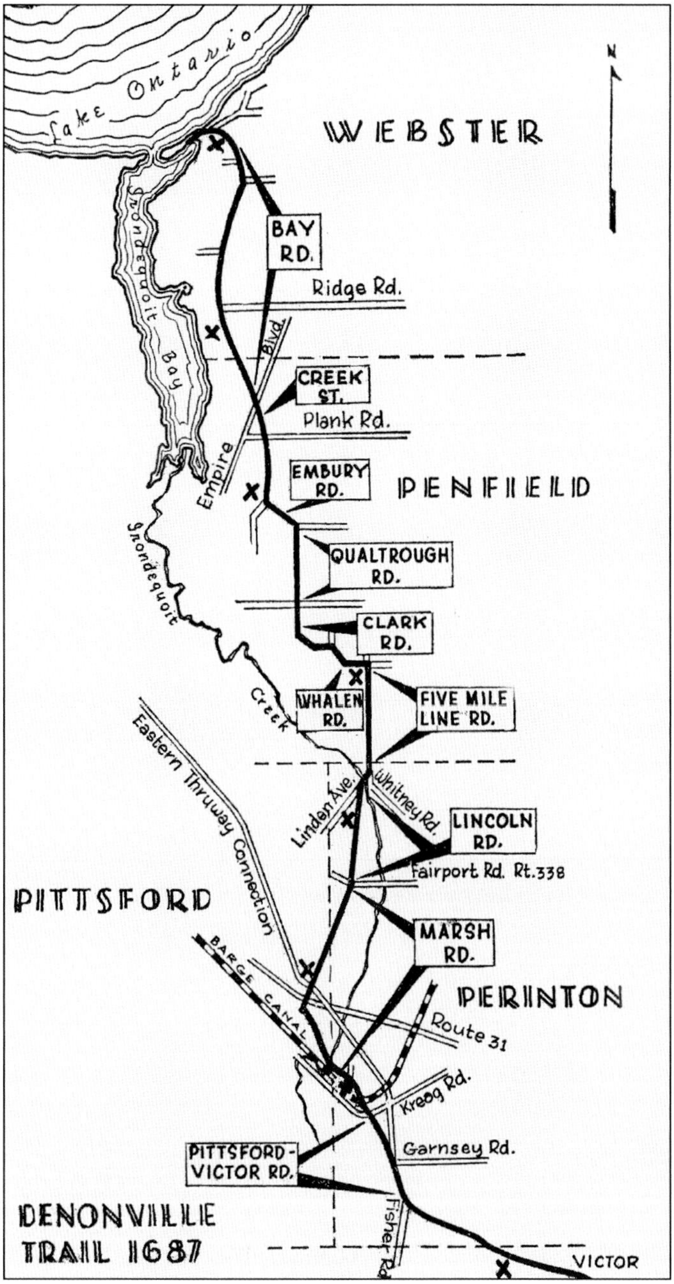

In 1687, the Marquis Denonville, governor of New France—which Canada was called at that time—planned to weaken the power of the Seneca Nation. His army sailed down the Saint Lawrence River, along the shore of Lake Ontario, in 200 wooden, flat-bottomed boats and landed on the sandbar east of the Irondequoit outlet in Webster. Hundreds of trees were chopped down to make pointed pales, which were driven into the sand to build a 10-foot-tall stockade fort. About 400 soldiers remained on the sandbar, and the rest of the army marched south along the present-day Bay Road, which was a narrow Indian trail. The battle took place in the present-day town of Victor with a Seneca ambush. When the Rome, Watertown, and Ogdensburg Railroad was built, many relics were dug up at the fort site, including gun barrels, bullets, axes, and two skeletons.

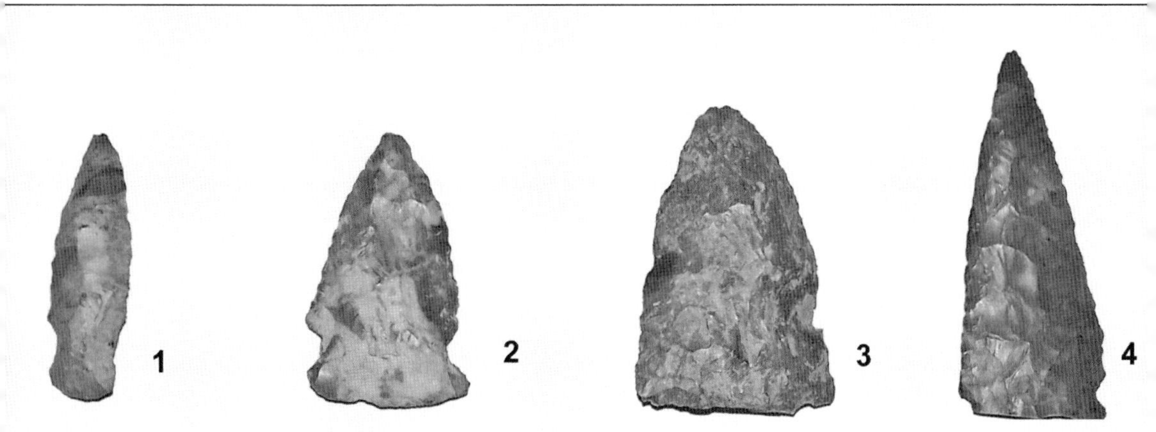

Many Webster farmers have collections of arrowheads found on their farms. These points are from the Rudolf Burkhardt farm and represent 5,000 years of Native American presence. Each point is from a different culture. No. 1 Lamoka, No. 2 Brewerton, and No. 3 Genesee are large, thick points of hunter-gatherer peoples who lived from 3500 BC to 900 BC. No. 4 Susquehanna broad point, No. 5 Orient Fishtail, and No. 7 Meadowood were made by Native Americans who farmed corn, beans, squash, and had villages from 1700 BC to 500 BC. The No. 6 Hopewell point is made of flint from Ohio, not the New York State chert used for the others. These Hopewell people were the Mound Builders, and there are two recorded mounds opened in Webster near the bay from 200 BC to 500 AD. No. 8 Madison Point is from 1350 to 1700 AD. These small efficient arrowheads were used by the Seneca, members of the Iroquois Nation.

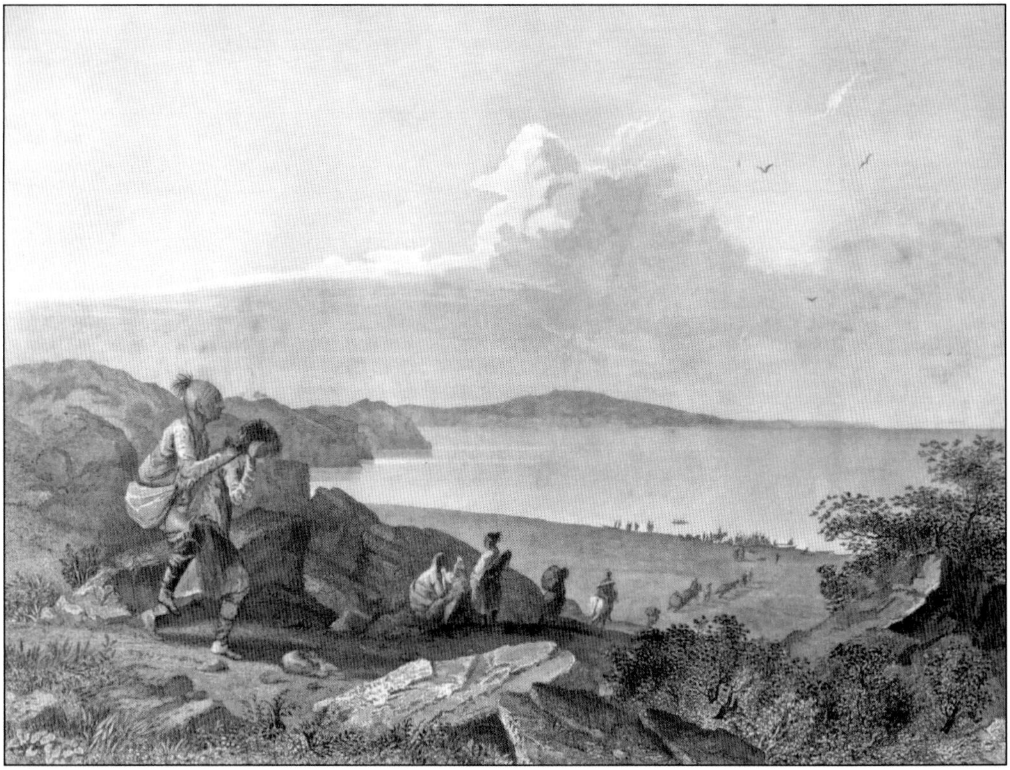

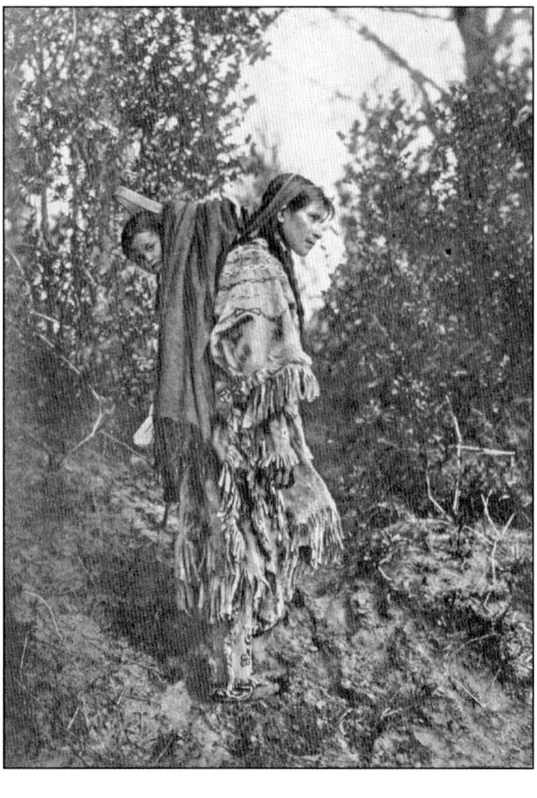

From approximately 1819 to 1860, a band of Missisauga Native Americans had a village in West Webster, south of the ridge, a mile from the Irondequoit Bay near Ship Builders Creek. They were an Ojibwa people and part of the Algonquin language group. Originally from Ontario, Canada, they settled here when the British government took over their lands. When they left Webster, they went to the First Nation Reservation on Rice Lake in Canada, directly across Lake Ontario from Webster. This engraving above was done in 1819 by noted naturalist from New York Henry Schoolcraft. His wife was a Native American of the Objiwa Tribe. (Photograph above, No. 33829, courtesy of the Denver Public Library; at left courtesy of the National Geographic Society.)

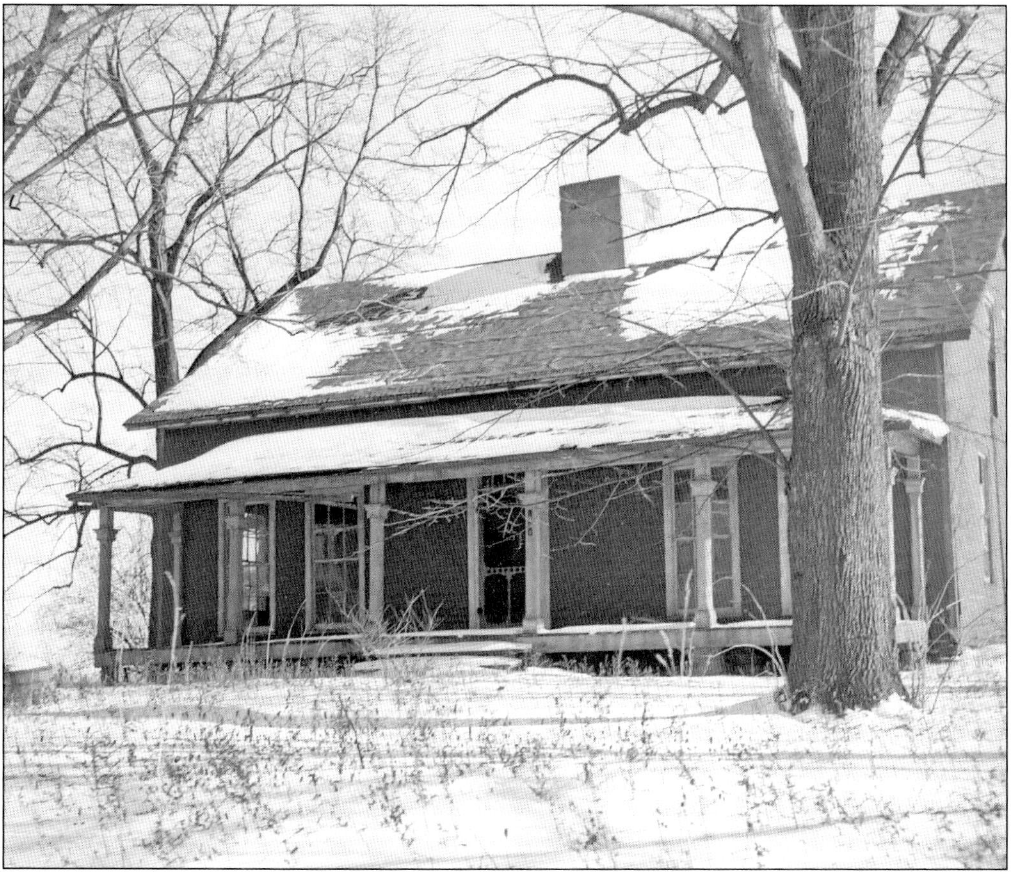

In 1805, Caleb Lyon bought 960 acres of land and built a saw and gristmill on the Four Mile Creek. He had great plans to lay out streets for a village and develop a harbor at the mouth of the creek. However, these ideas never materialized. Dea. Abram Foster, who had met Lyon in the town of Palmyra, New York, decided to move his family to Lyon's Point, as it was called in 1806. Deacon Foster resided there until his death at 89 years of age in 1859. Below is a picture of his son and daughter-in-law Charles and Julia Wooden Foster, the great-grandparents of Earl and Erva Wright of Nine Mile Point. (Photograph below courtesy of the Webster Museum and Historical Society.)

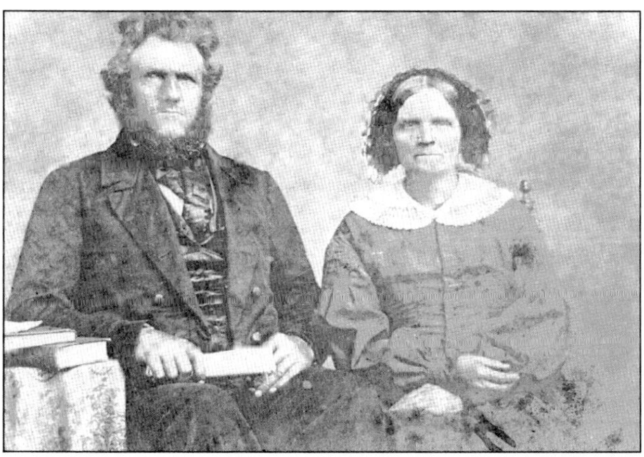

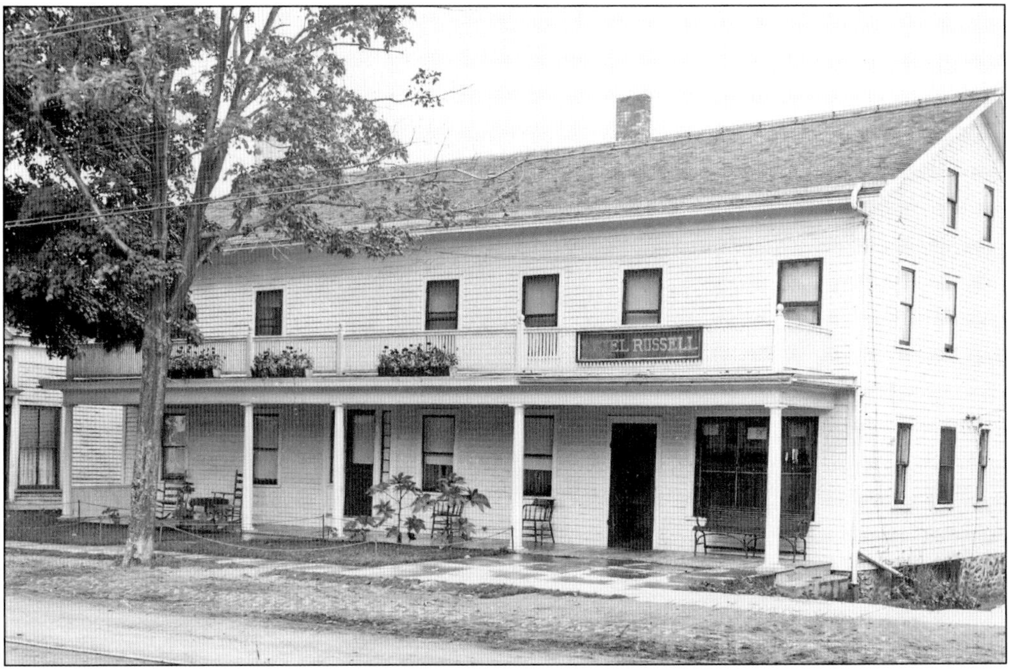

James Spear built the first frame building on West Main Street around 1812. It was a large tavern and stagecoach stop. Alexis Russell purchased the tavern and named it Russell Hotel. After Russell died, his family moved in and conducted a boardinghouse. The hotel would change hands, eventually being known as the DeField Hotel, and then the Stage Coach Inn.

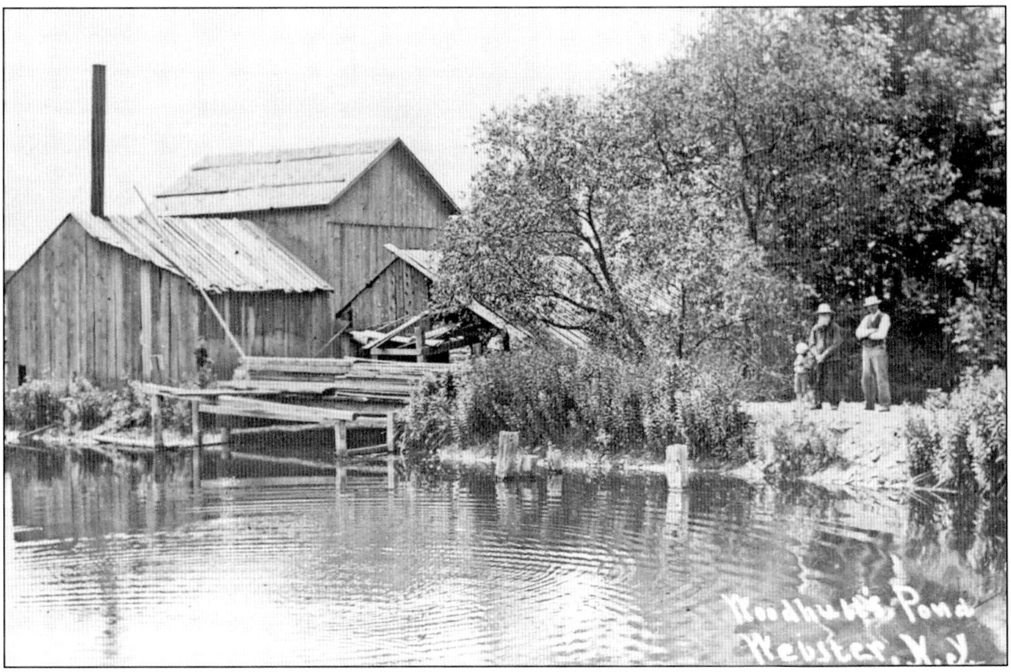

Local mills were important to the early development of Webster. This is a picture of the Woodhull Mill taken by George Wall and located along Mill Creek off Woodhull Road. It was built by Byron Woodhull in 1816 and operated until about 1914.

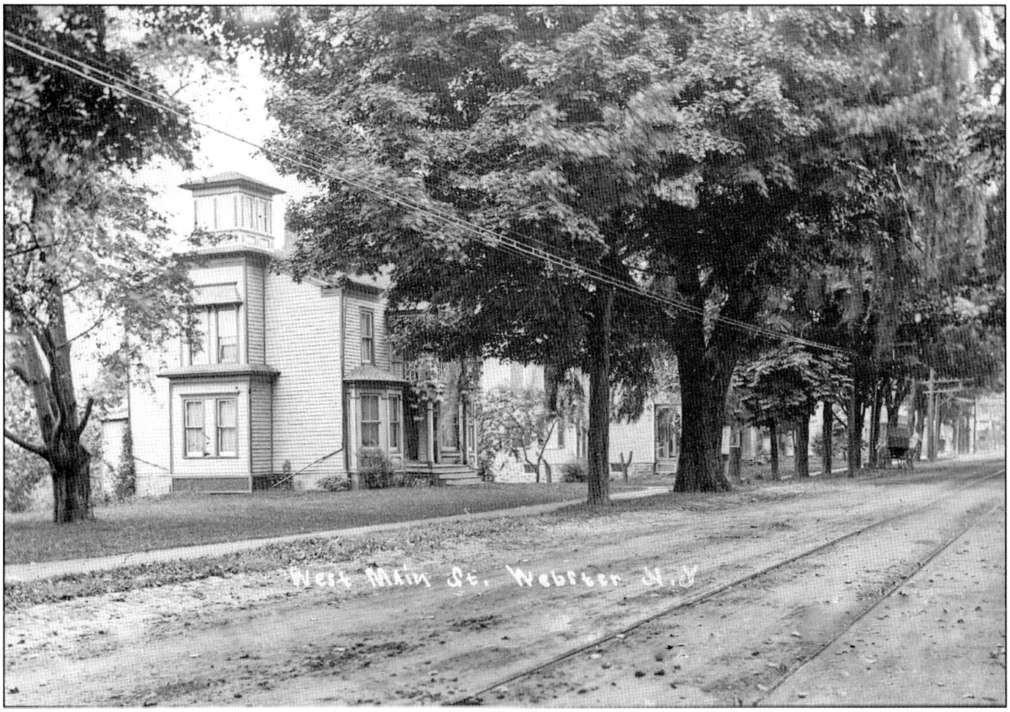

Dr. Oliver Reynolds was a land developer who came to North Penfield in 1817. His home was on West Main Street; it is still standing today. Appointed postmaster for North Penfield in 1834, he was reappointed postmaster of Webster in 1840. He was the originator of a patent medicine, Reynold's Lung Restorative, a forerunner of many cure-alls. Dr. Reynolds was a member of the Masonic Lodge No. 538 of Free and Accepted Masons. It received its charter at a meeting on the second floor of Dr. Reynolds store, the cobblestone building once located at the corner of South Avenue and West Main Street. Below is a photograph of a patent medicine package from Dr. O. Reynolds. (Photograph below courtesy of the Robert Holtz family.)

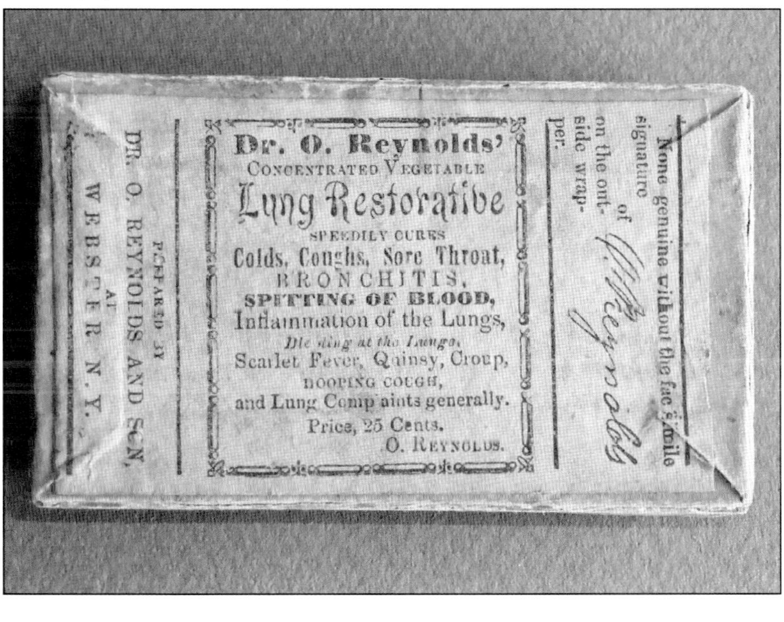

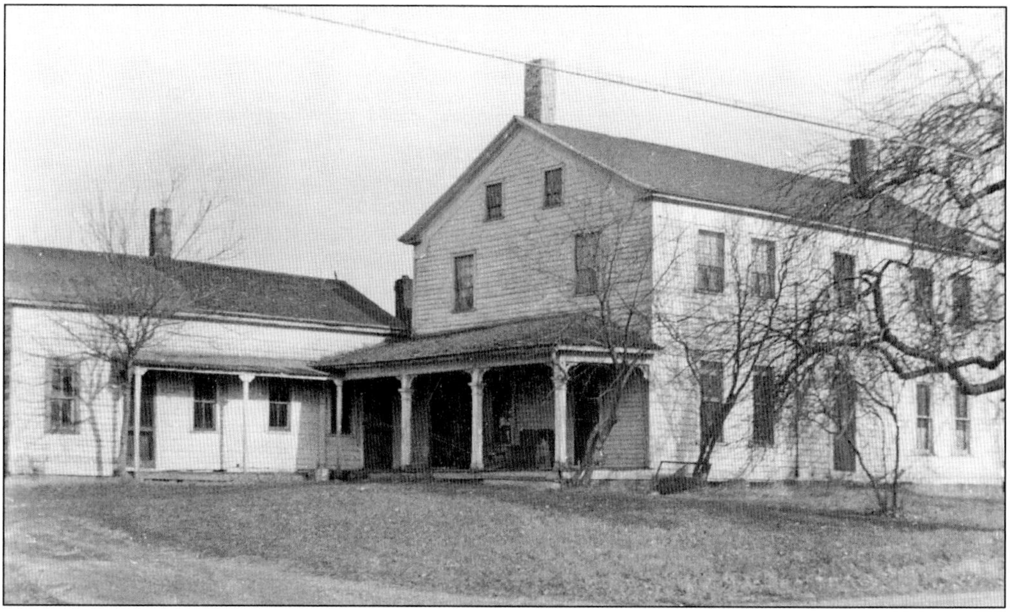

Ebenezer Cook's Inn in West Webster, near the intersection of Empire Boulevard and Old Ridge Road, is one of only two stagecoach stops in Webster still standing. New York State appropriated $5,000 in 1813 to make Ridge Road a passable wagon road, and the stagecoach service began. At the taverns along the way, horses could be changed and passengers could find food and rest.

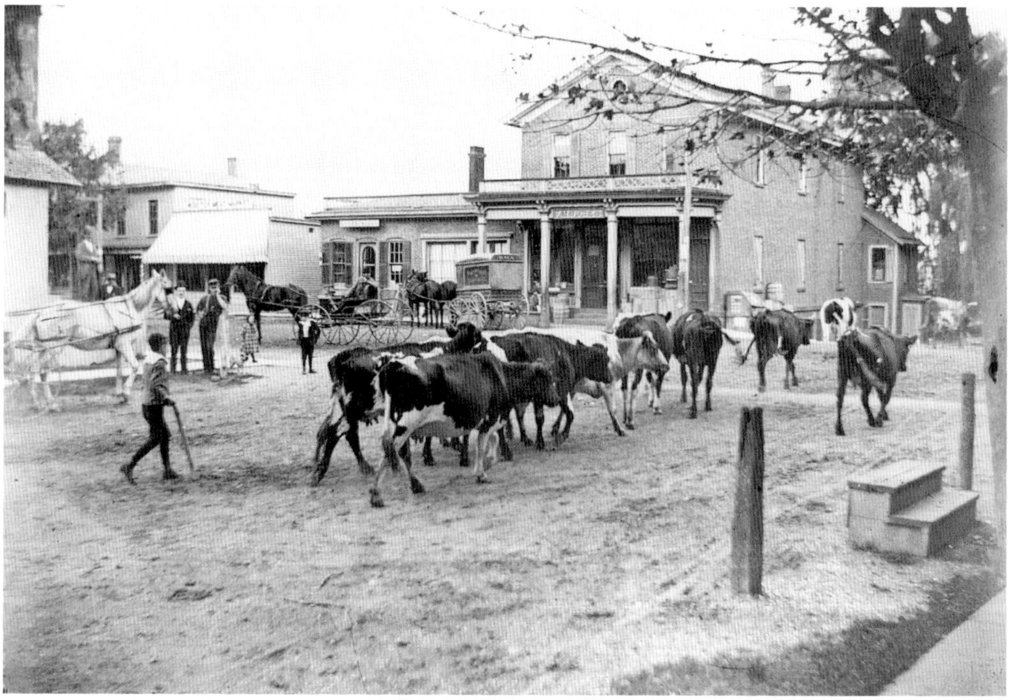

In the early days of Webster, families would keep a cow or two at their homes for milk and butter. Every morning, the boys in the village would round up cows and take them to pastures for the day and bring them back later that evening. This photograph shows cows being driven through the Four Corners, heading north past the Ridge Road.

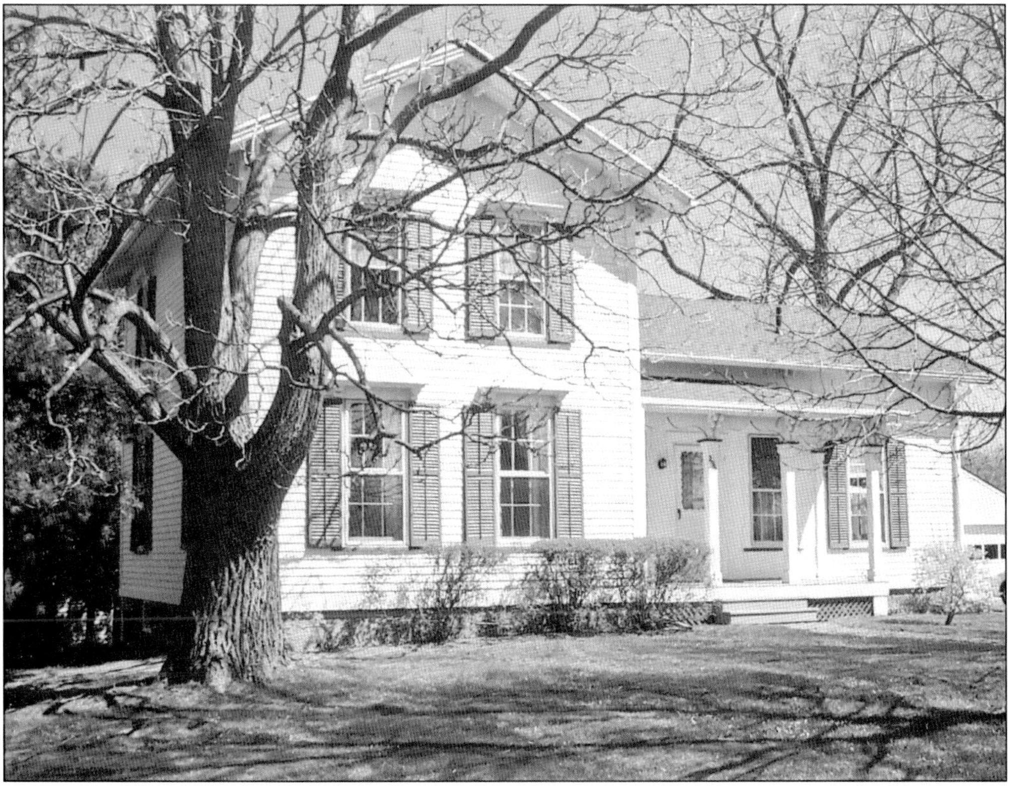

William Wylie built a sawmill in 1825 on the property purchased by Preston Thayer in 1844. Preston added a gristmill, barns, and the house shown above. He was an active member of the Webster community and served as the justice of the peace. The property remained in the Thayer family for over 100 years. The photograph below, taken by George Chapman in 1903, shows the remains of the old sawmill, which was located on the Four Mile Creek that runs through the Thayer property.

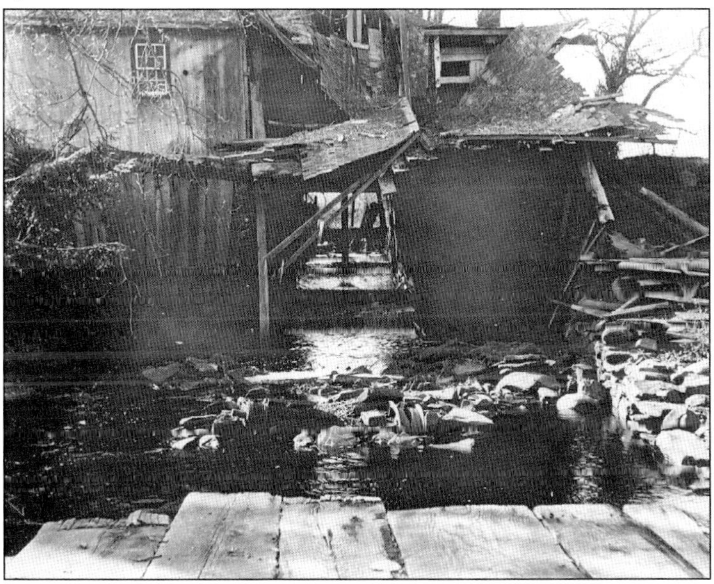

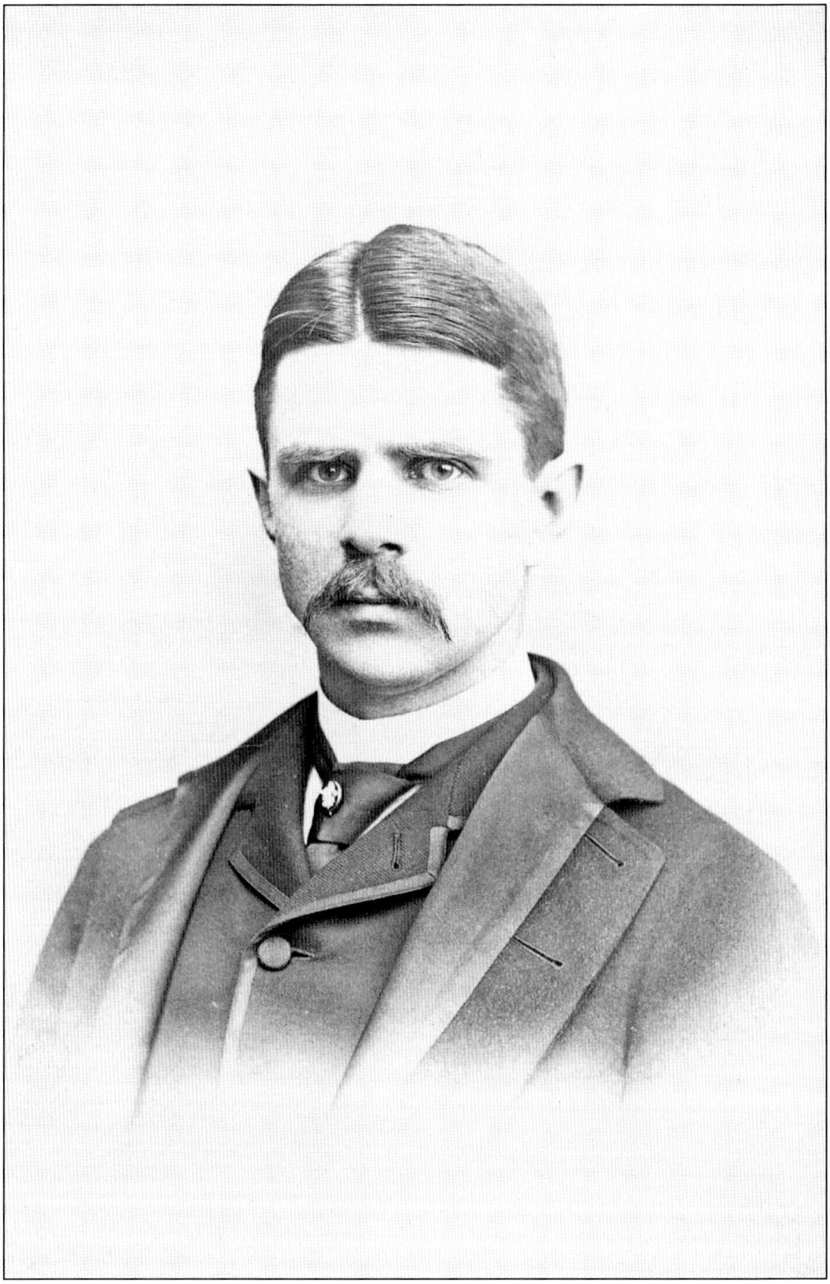

Dr. Luther Emmett Holt, son of Horace and Sabrah Curtice Holt, was born in Webster at the family home on Holt Road in 1855. He was a world-renowned pioneer in the field of pediatric medicine. His book, the *Care and Feeding of Children*, was instrumental in reducing the high infant mortality rates during the early part of the 20th century. Dr. Holt was educated in Webster schools and graduated from the University of Rochester in 1875 at only 20 years of age. His career was spent working in New York City, and he traveled the world lecturing. In a letter to his son in 1913 he wrote, "I have been thinking much of my own boyhood and the old home at Webster, and the discipline and training which the country life of those days—50 years ago—gave. I could wish that you also had something that is quite as good." (Courtesy of the Rosin family.)

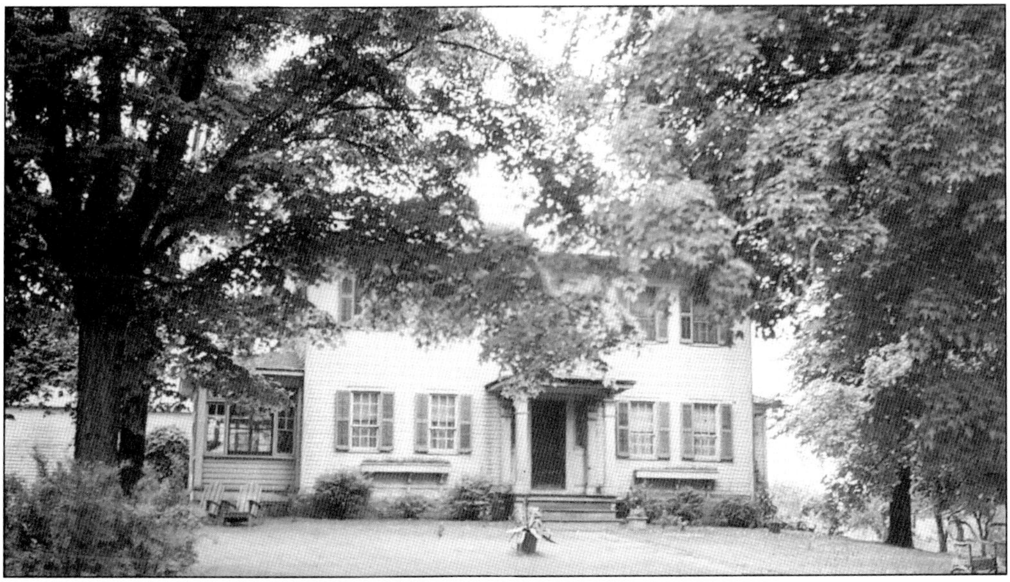

The Holt family homestead, on Holt Road, was built by Constant Holt, who arrived here by oxcart from Connecticut with his wife and cousin in 1812. He cleared the land and built a log cabin. By 1829, he started building a new house. Constant was a farmer and cobbler. He also purchased goods from Rochester and Pultneyville in large quantities and then sold or bartered the items back at home. His son Horace, at right, would later marry Sabrah Curtice and they raised their family at the Holt farm. He was interested in civic affairs, becoming Webster supervisor in 1858–1859. The house stands today, but it is no longer surrounded by the orchards of apples perfected by Horace nor the mulberry bushes where his mother, Polly, raised silkworms. (Photograph at right courtesy of the Rosin family.)

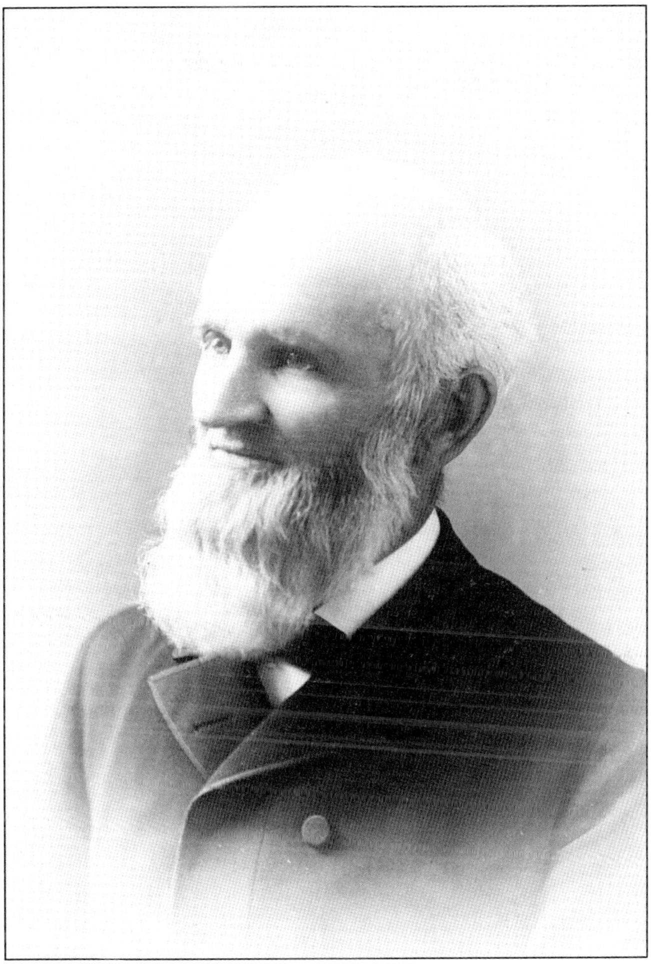

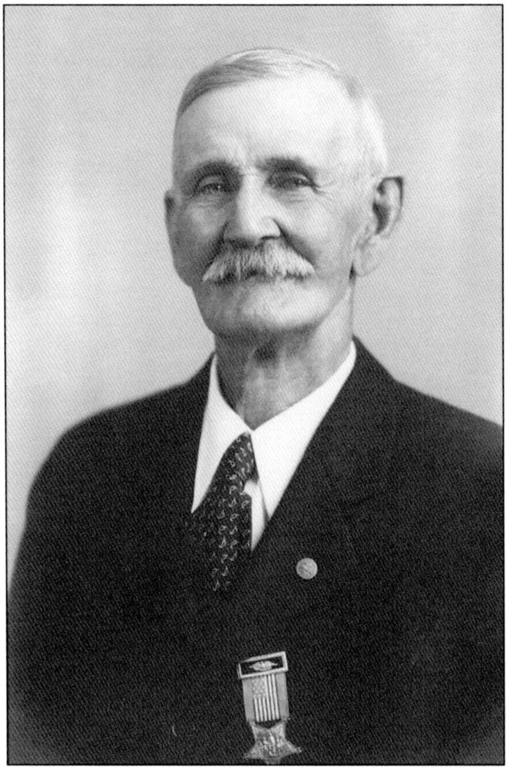

Frank VanAlstyne was the last survivor of the 216 men from Webster who served in the American Civil War; he died at the age of 97 in 1946. He enlisted at 17 in the Battery M of the 2nd U.S. Light Artillery when the unit was recruiting in a tent pitched in front of Reynolds Arcade Building on East Main Street in Rochester. He also served with the 2nd New York Cavalry Company M. He saw service with Gen. Phil Sheridan in the Shenandoah Valley Campagne and also in New York City, quelling the draft riots there. (Courtesy of John VanAlstyne.)

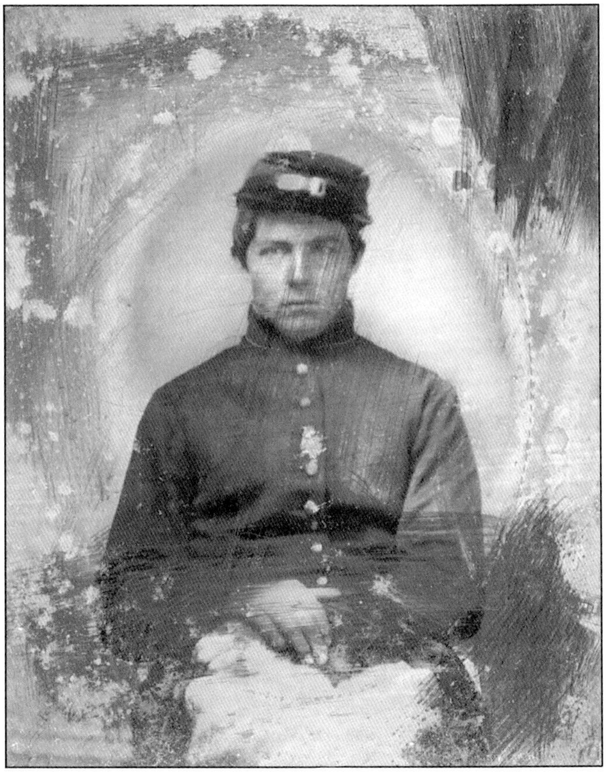

William H. Woodhull, buried in the Webster Union Cemetery, was one of many Webster residents to serve in the Civil War. Born in 1843, Woodhull was a farmer before enlisting in Company A of 108th New York. He was wounded at the Battle of Antietam on September 17, 1862, and wounded again at the Battle of Gettysburg on July 2, 1863. He attained the rank of sergeant and was discharged for his injuries on November 2, 1863.

Two

The Village of Webster

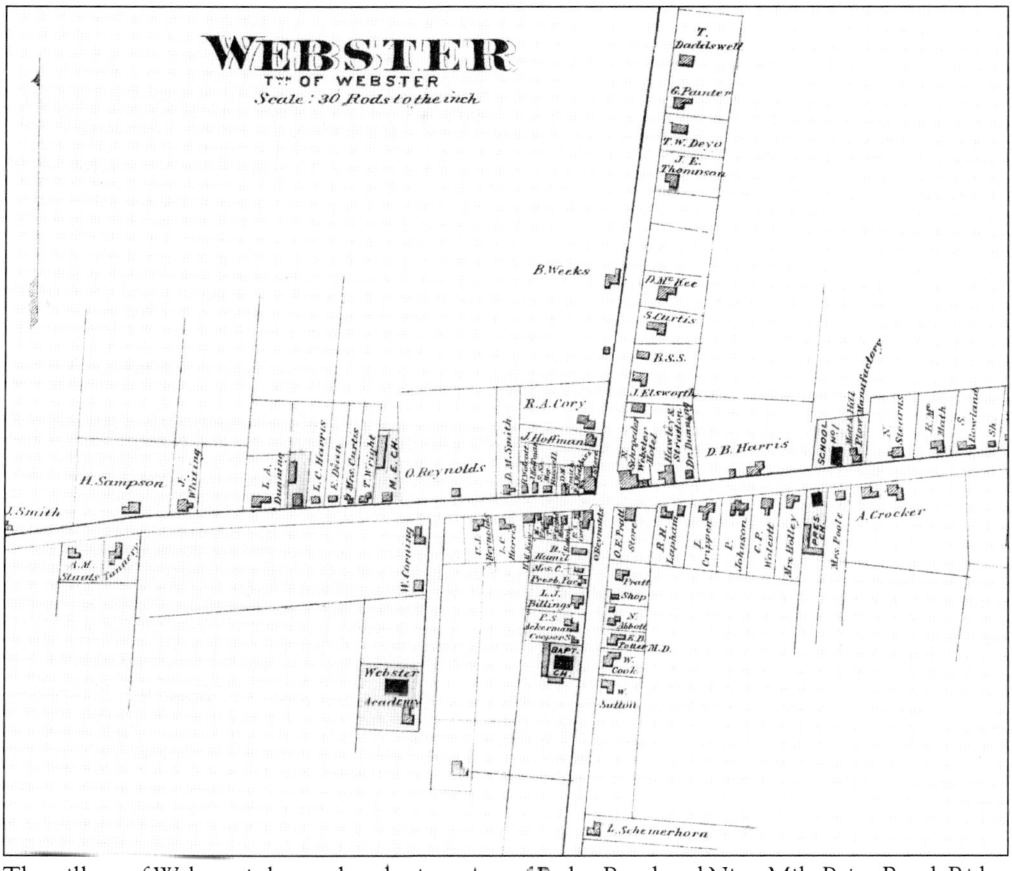

The village of Webster is located at the junction of Ridge Road and Nine Mile Point Road. Ridge Road began as an early Native American trail, which ran along the ridge or shore of what was Lake Iroquois. The area was mostly unbroken forest with a few log structures for a number of years. The mail was delivered by a rider on horseback from Canandaigua, which at the time was the main trading post. The map above is from the 1872 Atlas of Monroe County, New York, by F. W. Beers and Company.

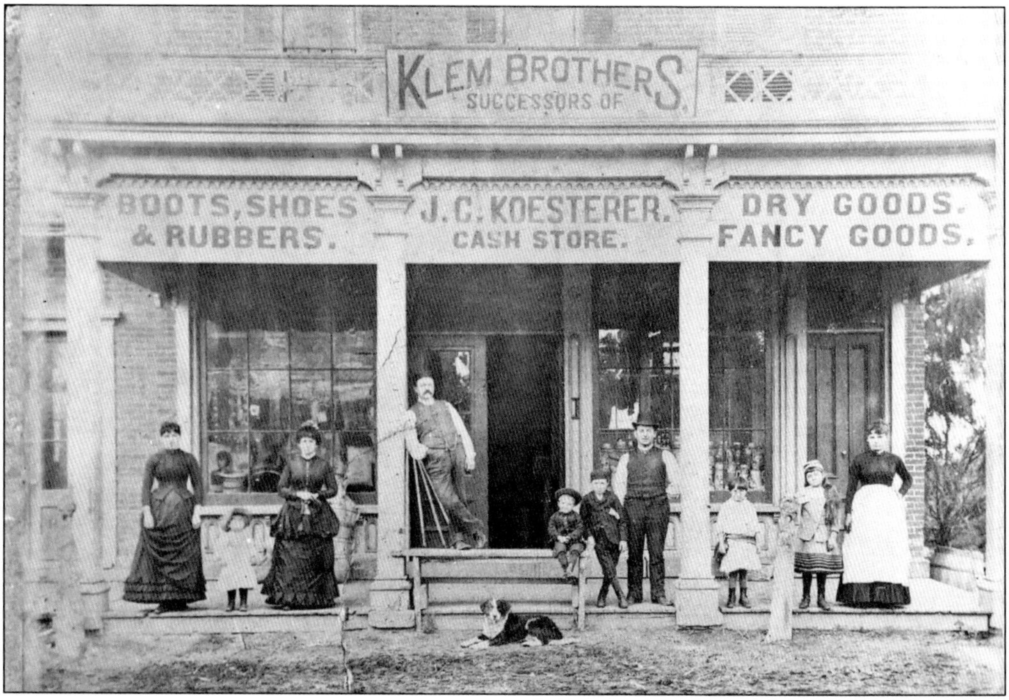

The Klem Brothers store, seen here in 1883, was located on the northwest corner of West Main Street and North Avenue. Pictured are, from left to right, Mary Mertz Klem, Bertha Klem, Elizabeth Knope Klem, Alphonse Klem (the owner), Erbe Klem, Alphonse Klem Jr., Max Hoffman, Carrie Klem Gallagher, Elizabeth Klem Hall, and Jennie Frawley Lieberman.

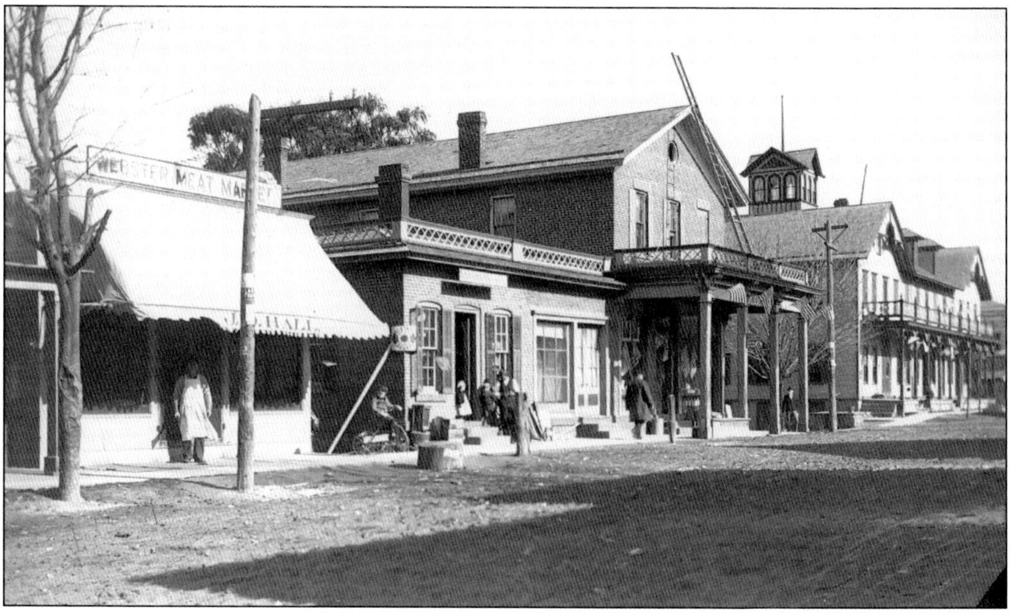

This is the north side of West Main Street, prior to 1898. On the left is the Webster Meat Market of J. D. Hall. The next two buildings to the right were owned by Frank M. Jones and shown before the remodeling of the second story for the Masonic lodge. The building on the far right, across the intersection, is the Webster Hotel.

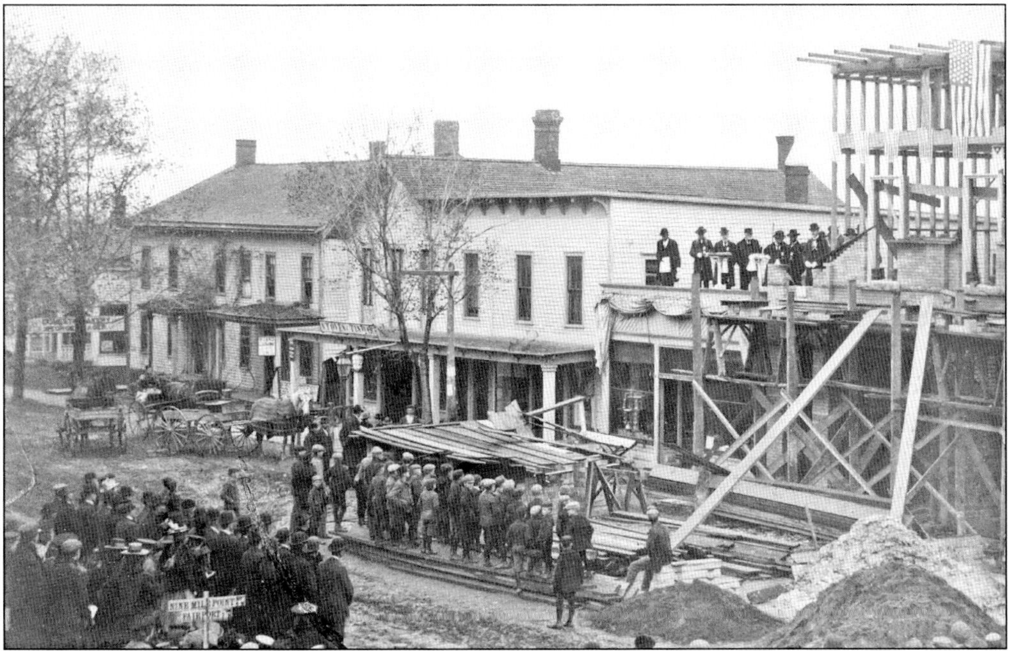

In 1898, Frank M. Jones entered into a contract with the Masonic Lodge No. 538 to have the lodge's meeting hall constructed as the second floor over his general store on West Main Street and North Avenue. The lodge remained there until 1926. In the photograph, the Masonic lodge members are ceremoniously laying the cornerstone for their new building.

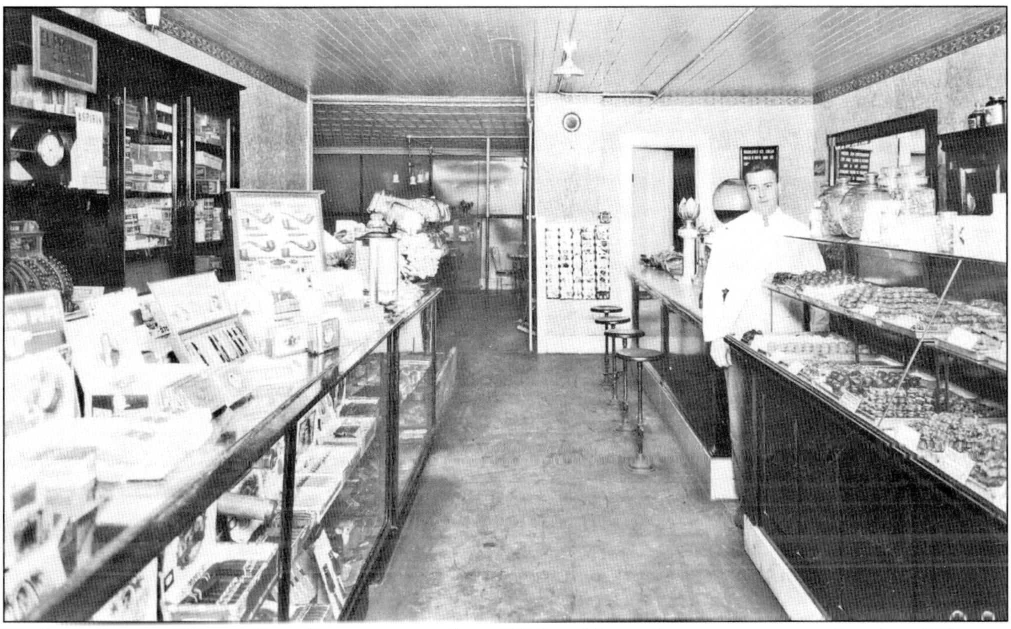

Herbst's Spa on West Main Street, opened in 1923, sold candy, ice cream, and sodas. Tobacco supplies, newspapers, and magazines were also available for purchase. During the 41 years that Henry and Grace Herbst operated the business, the students from Webster High School on South Avenue frequented the store. They would buy a coke and eat their packed lunches while listening to the jukebox, away from the school cafeteria.

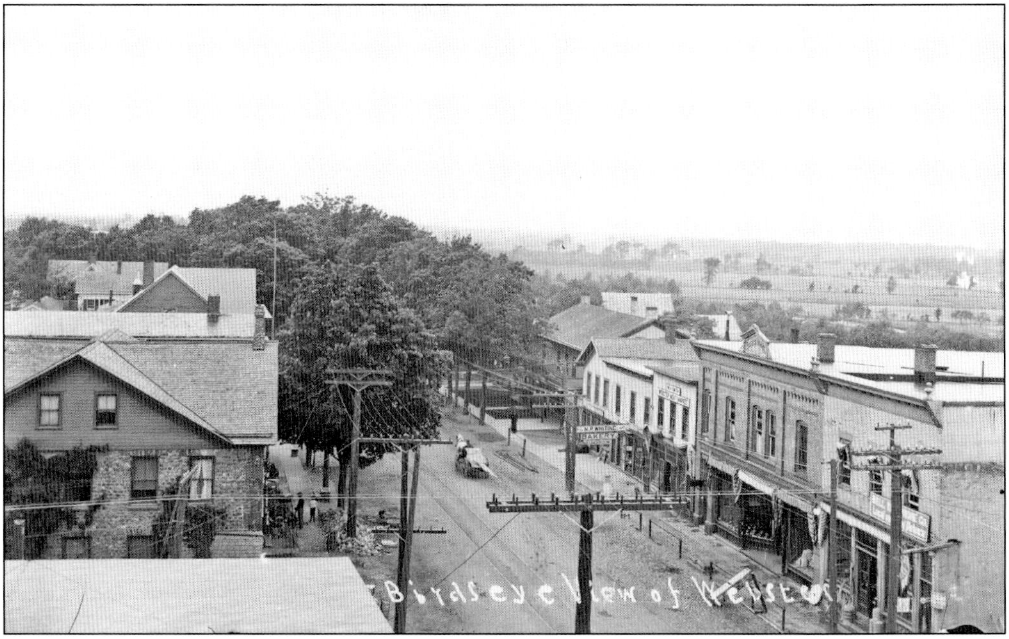

This is an early photograph of The Webster Village taken by George Wall from the third floor of the George Mason building on East Main Street. Looking northwest, you can see early farmland in the distance. Notice the trolley tracks down Main Street.

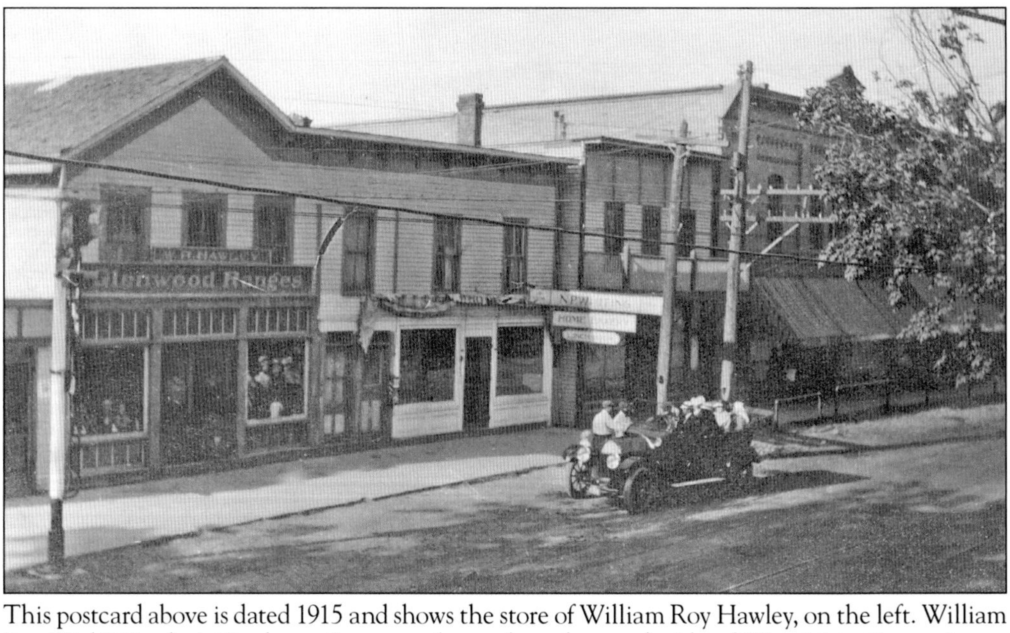

This postcard above is dated 1915 and shows the store of William Roy Hawley, on the left. William Roy "Bob" Hawley's Hardware Store was located on the north side of West Main Street. It was purchased from Harvey Bergh in 1910 with a handshake agreement meaning the new owner would pay as he could. Eventually he moved his business to the new building at the corner of Lapham Park and East Main Street.

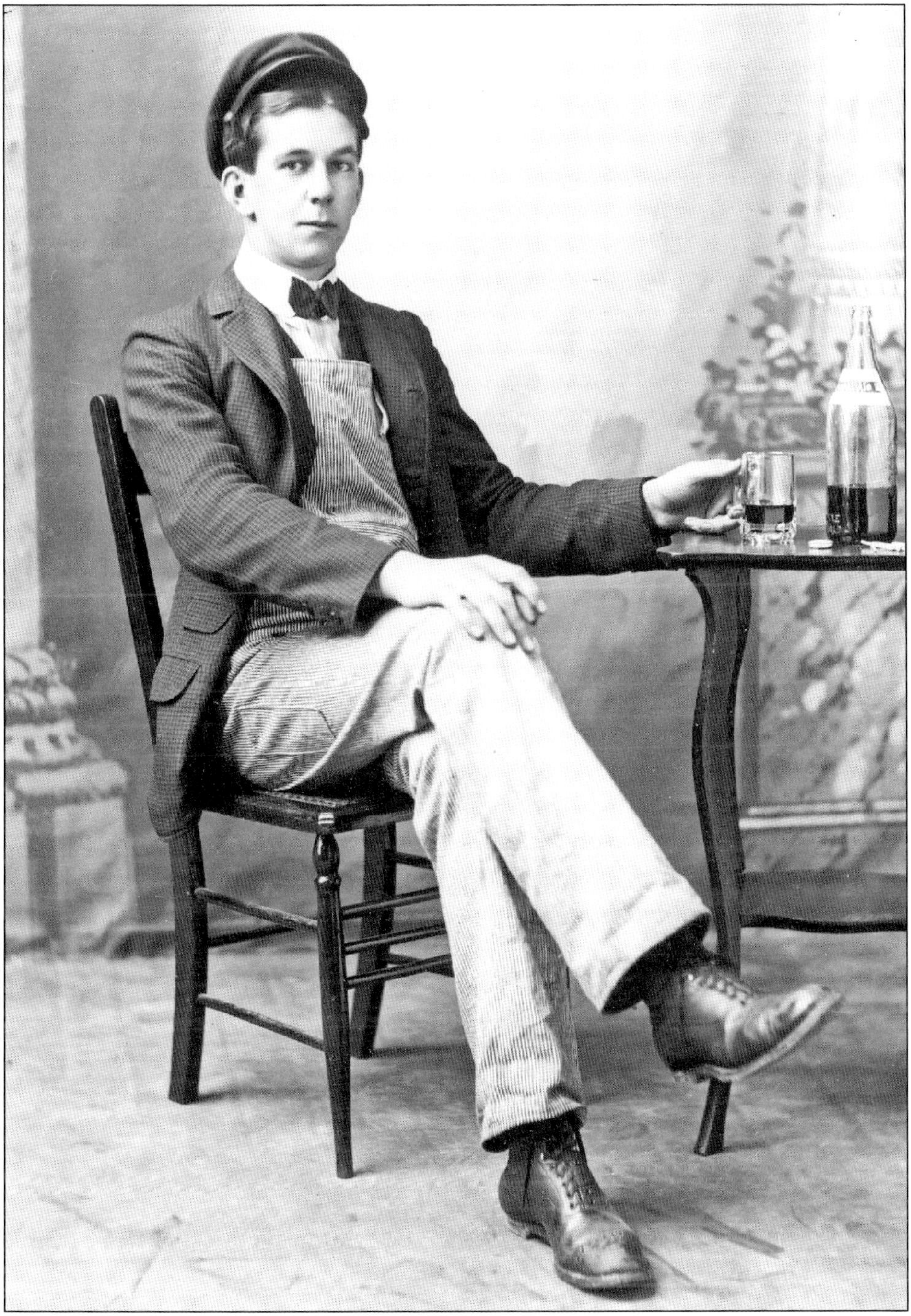

William Roy "Bob" Hawley was mayor of the Village of Webster for 31 years. He was born on the second floor of the Hawley family store. He is shown here as a young man in 1900 wearing a starched collar, bow tie, and overalls, enjoying a glass of ginger ale. As mayor, he saw the village triple in size to approximately 3,600 people. Many innovations were completed during his years in office such as improved streets, a sewer plant, a well-equipped fire department, and an excellent water supply from deep wells drilled into the glacially filled old valley of the Genessee River.

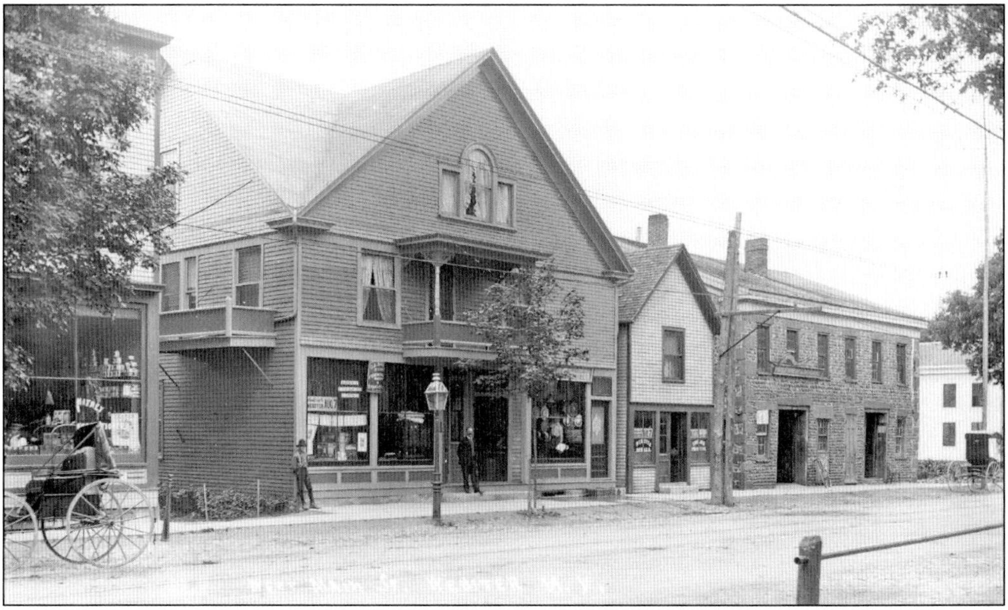

This photograph of West Main Street was taken between 1905 and 1910. The building with the two second-story porches is where George Whitney and his wife conducted a general store, in the left half. Orton Shult had his harness shop in the right. The *Webster Herald* newspaper was located in the next building and operated by Albert "Dad" Andrews. The cobblestone building housed the blacksmith shop of Henry Herman, and later Herbert Wright.

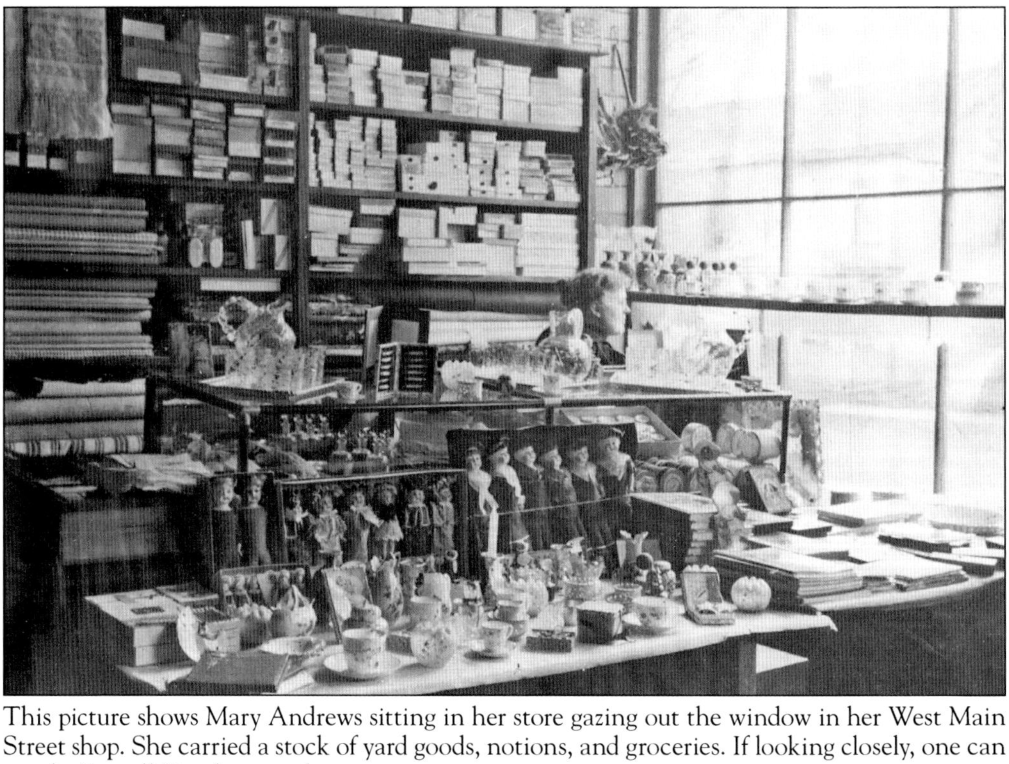

This picture shows Mary Andrews sitting in her store gazing out the window in her West Main Street shop. She carried a stock of yard goods, notions, and groceries. If looking closely, one can see the Russell Hotel across the street.

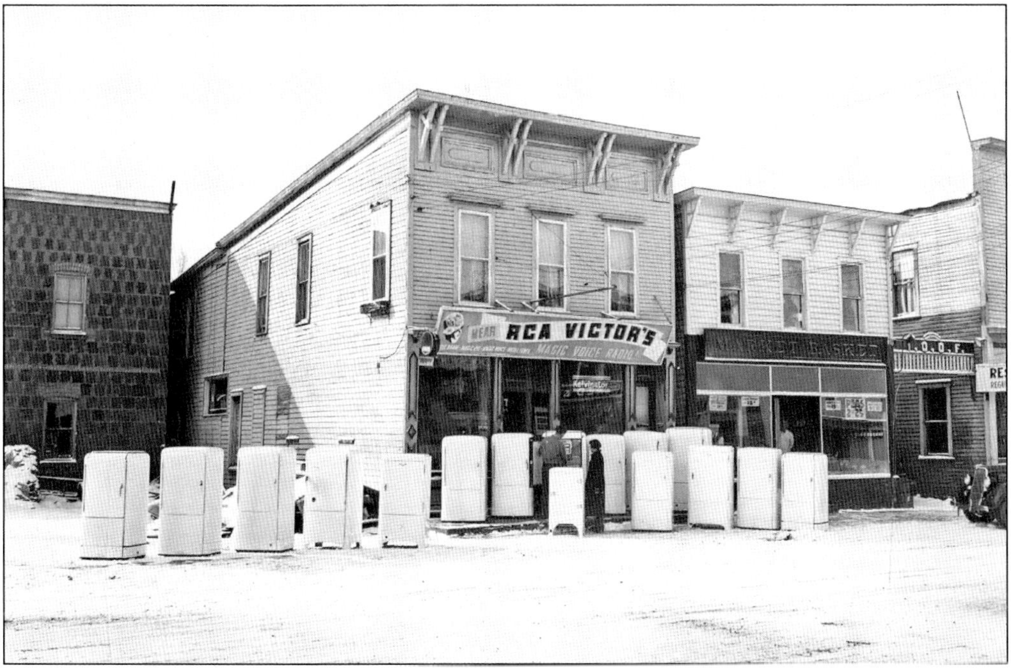

James H. Netzman started an electrical contracting business in 1919. He soon found himself selling and installing electric ranges and washing machines. The first washing machine that he sold was delivered in a wheelbarrow. The picture above is the Netzman's Appliance Store on West Main Street in the Village taken in 1936.

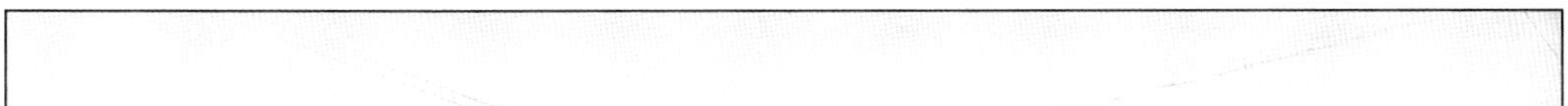

The c. 1906 picture above is showing the southwest corner of West Main Street. The large cobblestone is Hendee's store. The little store next door to the right was a millinery store. Later it was the barbershop of Jess Robson. The next store was that of William Wahle, a tailor, with men's furnishings. The next store was operated by Mary Andrews, and just beyond was Selleck's barbershop.

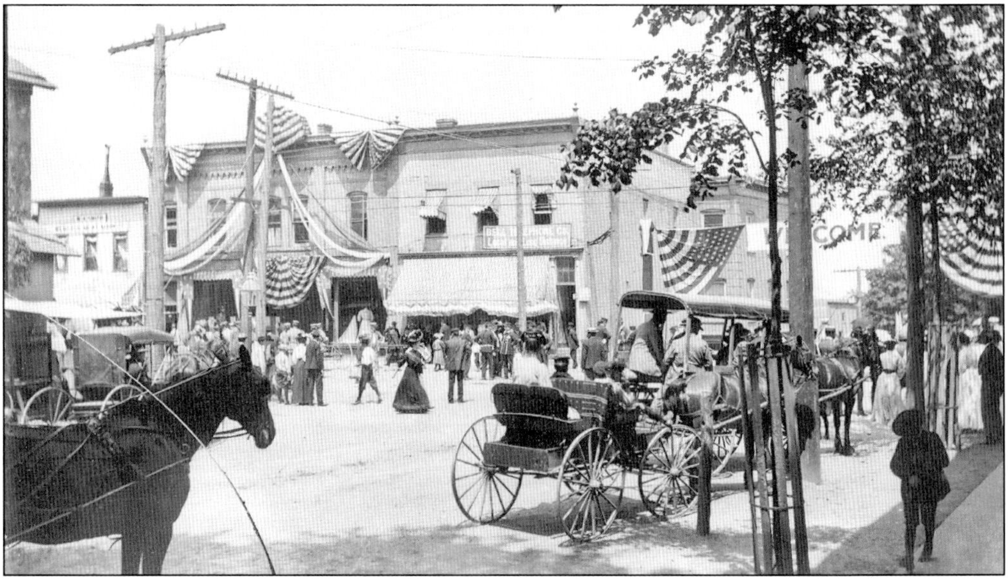

This summer scene of the four corners in the village shows residents dressed in their Sunday best. Note the Bell Telephone Company sign on the corner building, their exchange was located in the back room on the second floor. Note the gas streetlight by the two poles. A lamplighter made the rounds at dusk to turn on the lights and at midnight to turn them off, unless some unruly youth shut them off first.

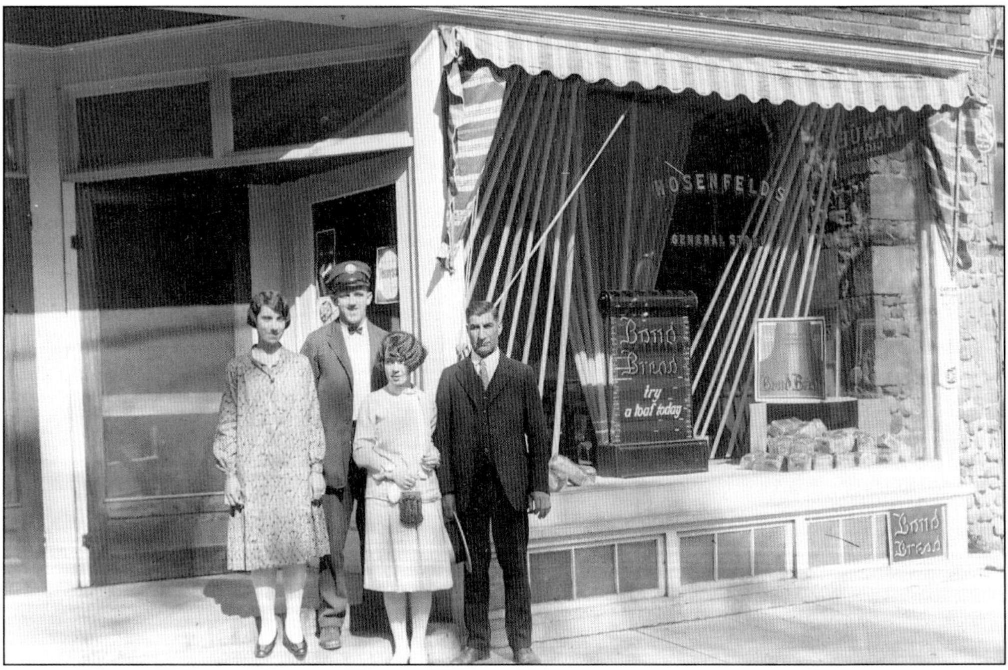

Located on South Avenue, just behind the cobblestone building on the corner of West Main Street, is the Hosenfeld Block, built in 1919 by Frank Hosenfeld. It was a general store that offered groceries. From left to right are Eva Hosenfeld—daughter of Frank, Merle Sweet—the Bond Bread deliveryman, Stel Kime, and Frank Hosenfeld. Hosenfeld always had a large wooden barrel of pickles for his customers.

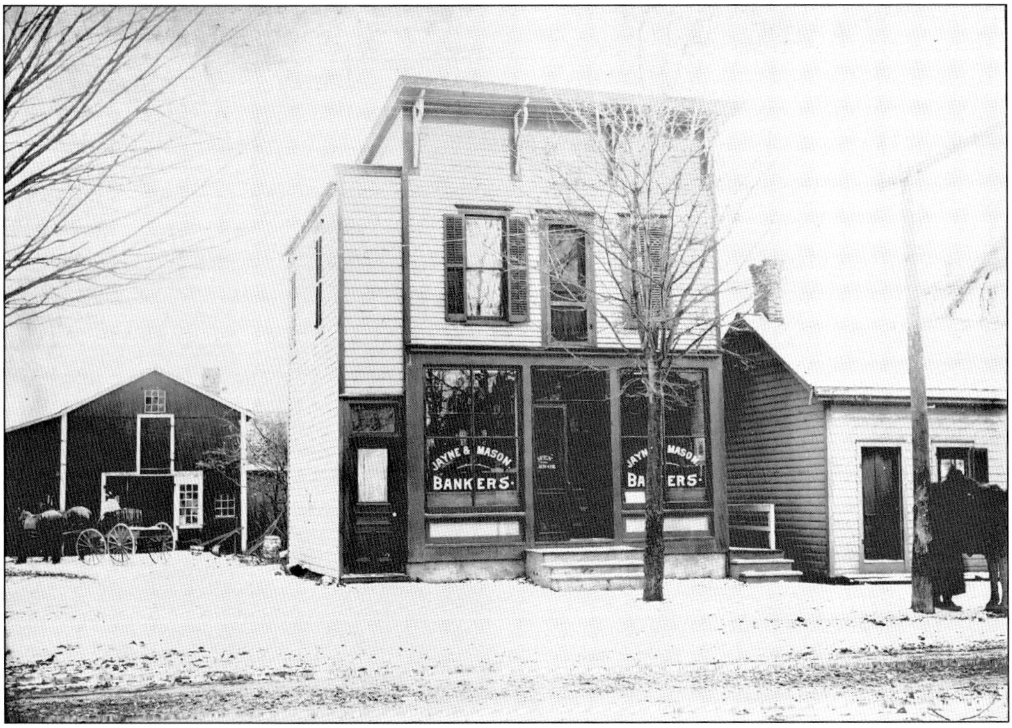

In 1900, William C. Jayne and George G. Mason of Webster started a private bank. It was located on the west side of South Avenue near the four corners. They started with $5,000 capital. It became a great success with customers from all neighboring towns who opened accounts and did business there. They remained there until 1906, when they constructed their brick building on East Main Street. (Courtesy of Granville Chambers.)

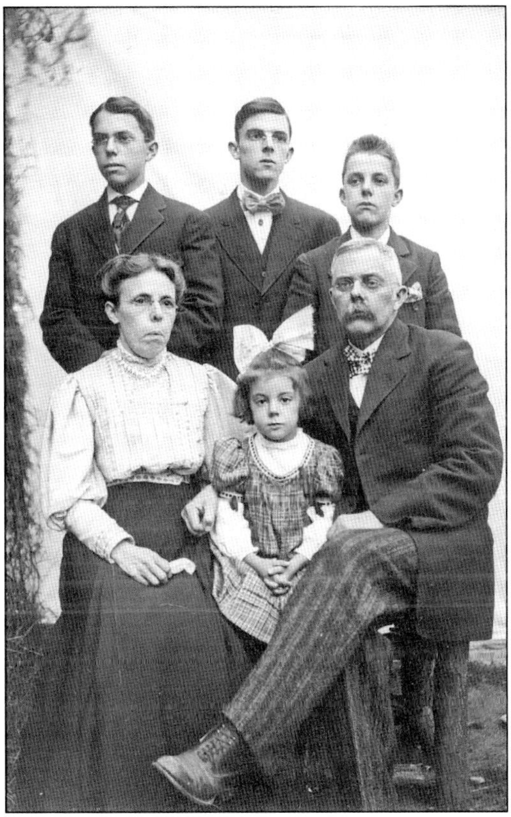

This photograph is of the Wall family. From left to right are (first row) Ida, Evelyn, and George; (second row) Hollis, Osmond, and Roger Wall. Many of the photographs seen in this book were taken by George Wall.

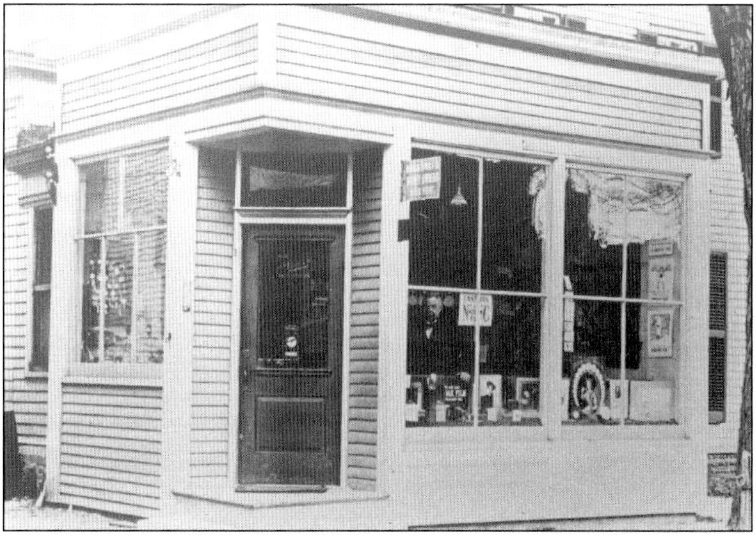

The "Little Shop Around the Corner" was located on South Avenue in the old Timothy Corning house. George Wall bought this house and built an addition around 1906. This gave him more room for his watchmaking, optometry, and photography business. He remained in business until about 1925.

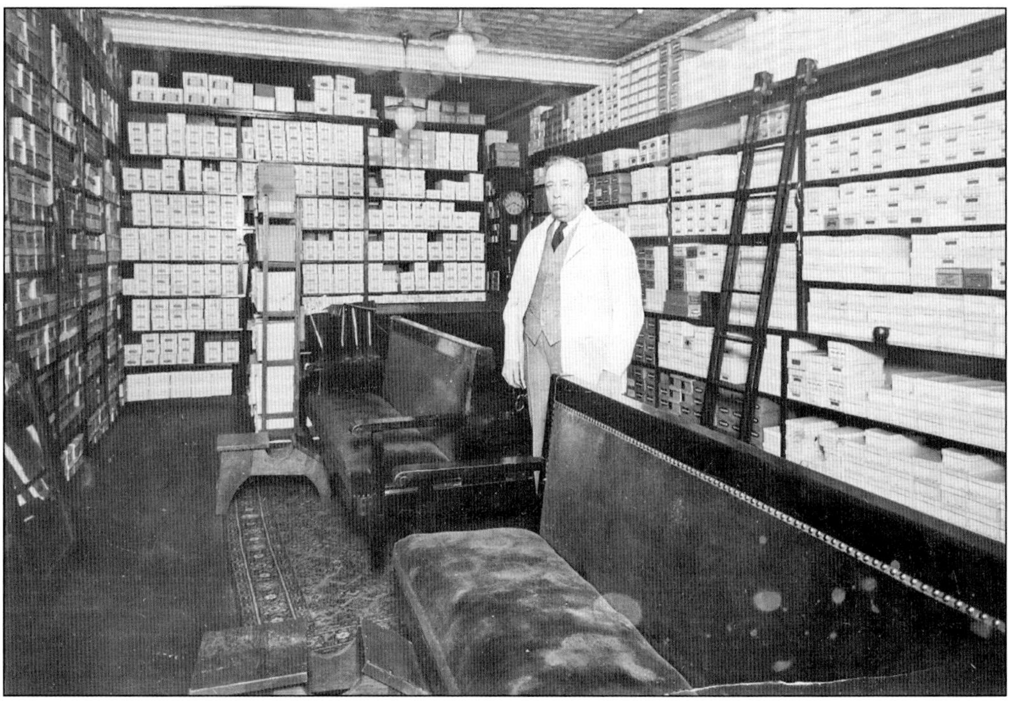

By the 1930s, William Kime purchased the home and shop of George Wall on South Avenue and moved his family and business, Kime's Boot Shoppe, to the new location. Kime had started selling boots and shoes part-time from his home on East Main Street. He relocated the business to South Avenue on the west side, the Hosenfeld building, before purchasing the Wall property across the street. The picture above was taken in 1937 at his new location. (Courtesy of the Kime family.)

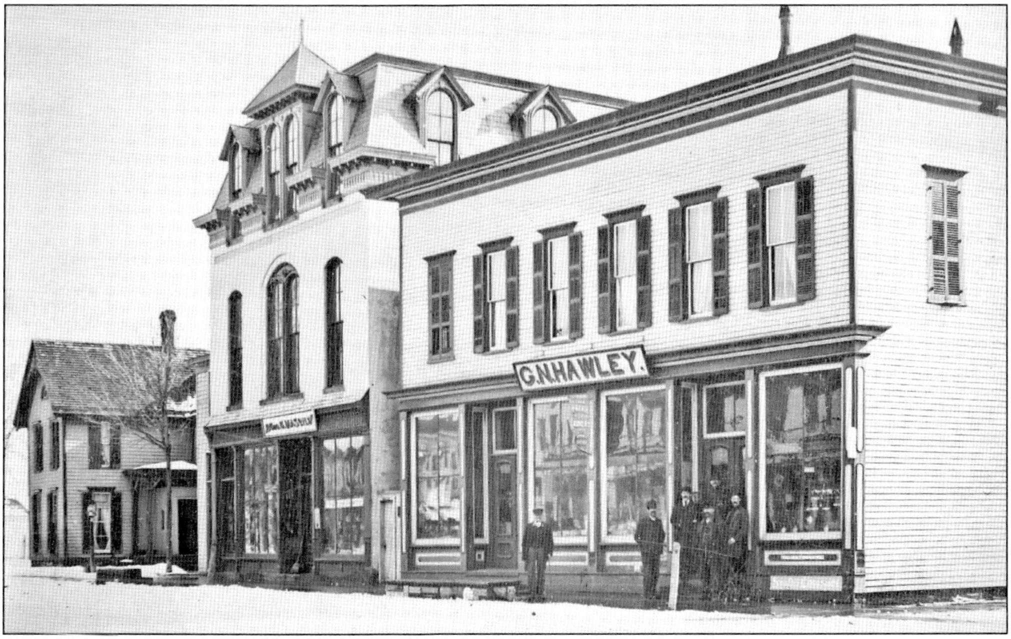

George N. Hawley built this well-stocked general store on the corner of East Main Street and South Avenue around 1881. Previously, he had operated the old Corning Store on the north side of East Main Street from about 1870 to 1880. Hawley sold the building to George H. Witmer about 1907. The door on the right opened to the part of the store described in the picture below.

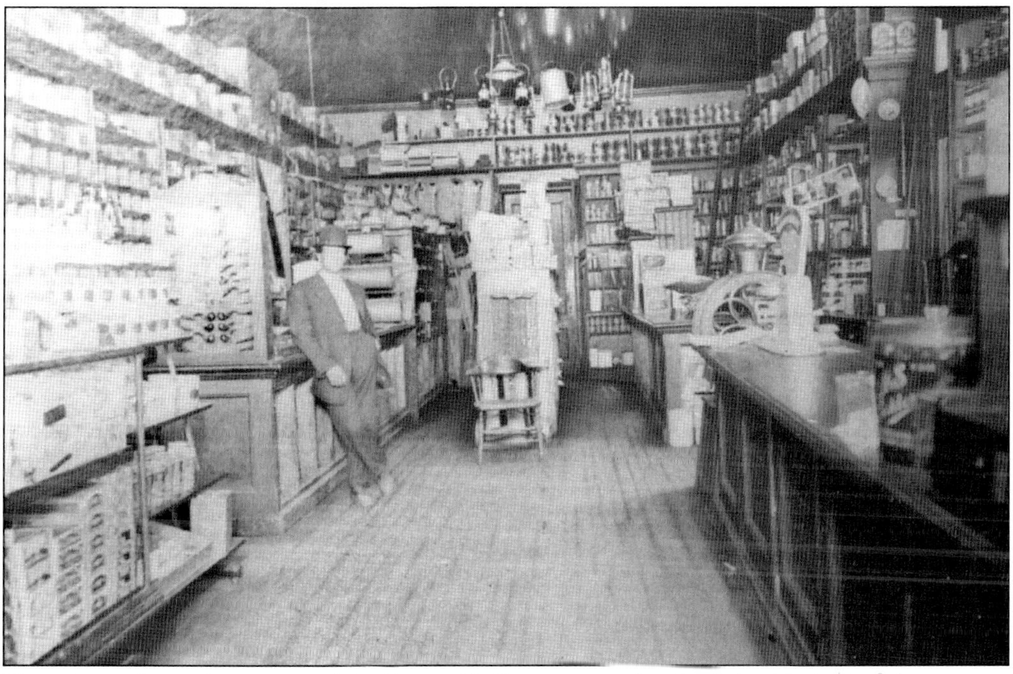

This picture shows the interior of the George N. Hawley store. On the right side, behind the counter, was the stock of groceries. Beyond the coffee grinder was the paint department, and the counter on the left, in front, held a large supply of tobacco, pipes, and cigars. The back section, where the man is leaning, was the hardware department and contained all kinds of nails, bolts, and nuts.

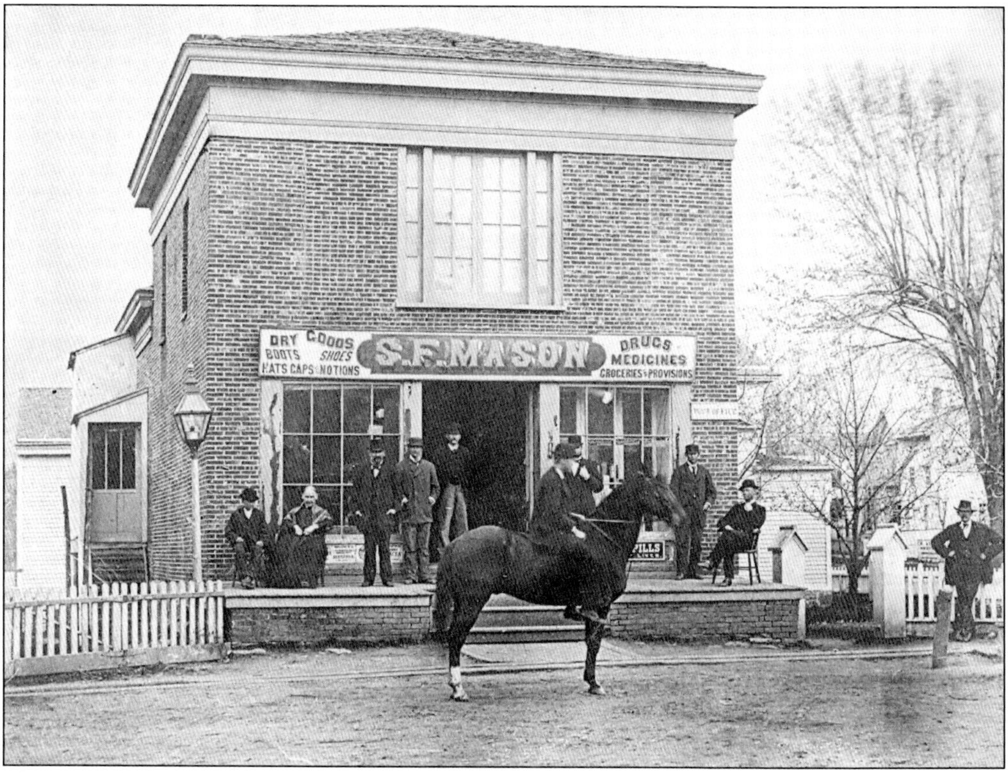

The Safford F. Mason general store was located on the south side of East Main Street. Safford Mason bought the store around 1873 and ran the business until his sons took over about 1885. Eventually his son George bought out his brothers and was the sole owner. He took the old building down and built the new three-story Mason Hall, pictured below. The first floor was a general store, which included a pharmacy, groceries, and clothing. The second floor had a large space where meetings and elections were held. The third floor was called the "Opera House," where musicals and inspirational speakers entertained Webster citizens. The Tausch family owns the building today.

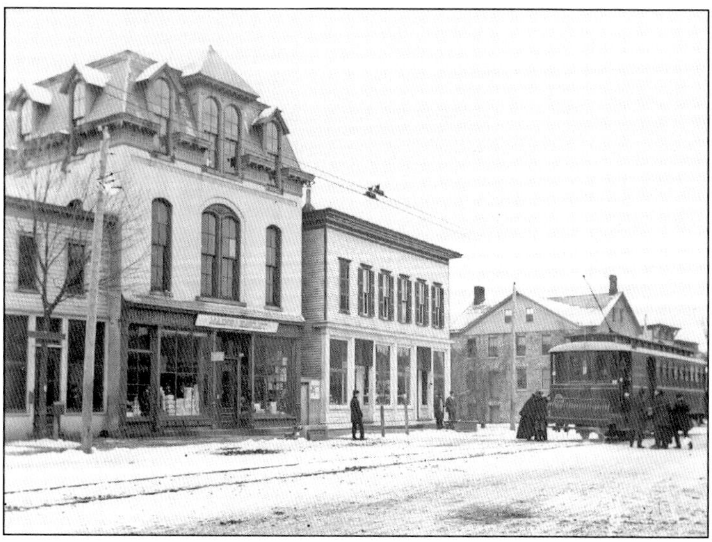

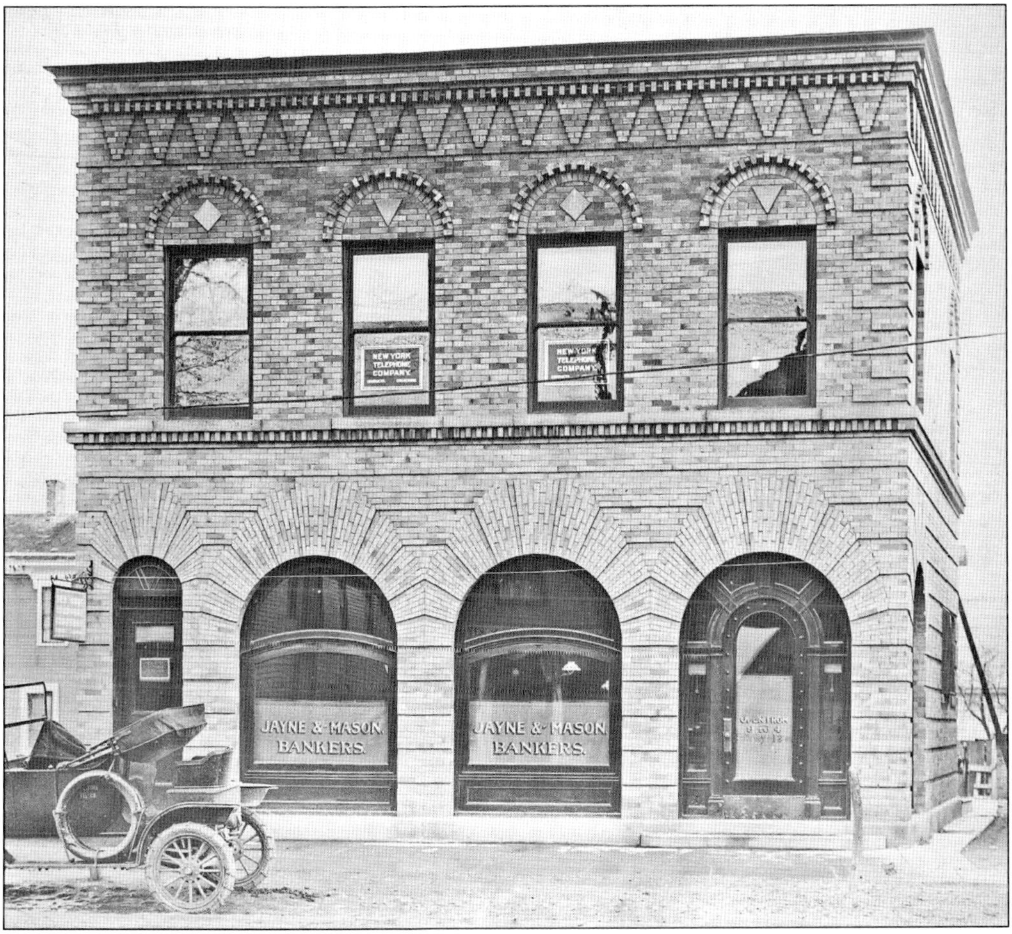

William C. Jayne and George G. Mason built their bank on East Main Street in 1906. Jayne and Mason did general banking, financed and handled all five issues of U.S. liberty bonds during World War I, and had banking connections with the Chase National Bank of New York City. Below is the interior of the bank with George G. Mason standing on the left and William C. Jayne on the right. This building is on the National Register of Historic Places and also was designated a local landmark in 2009.

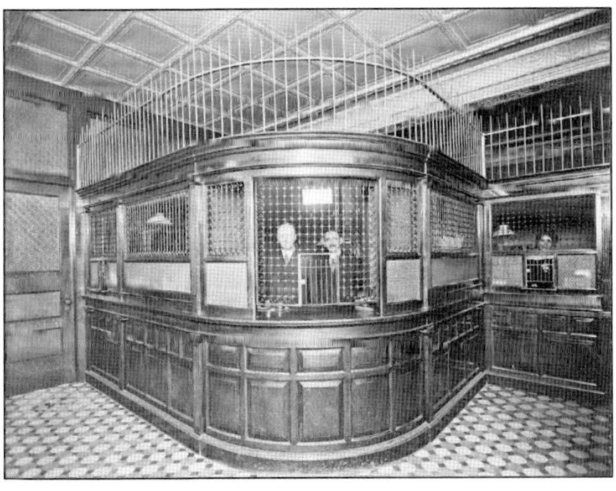

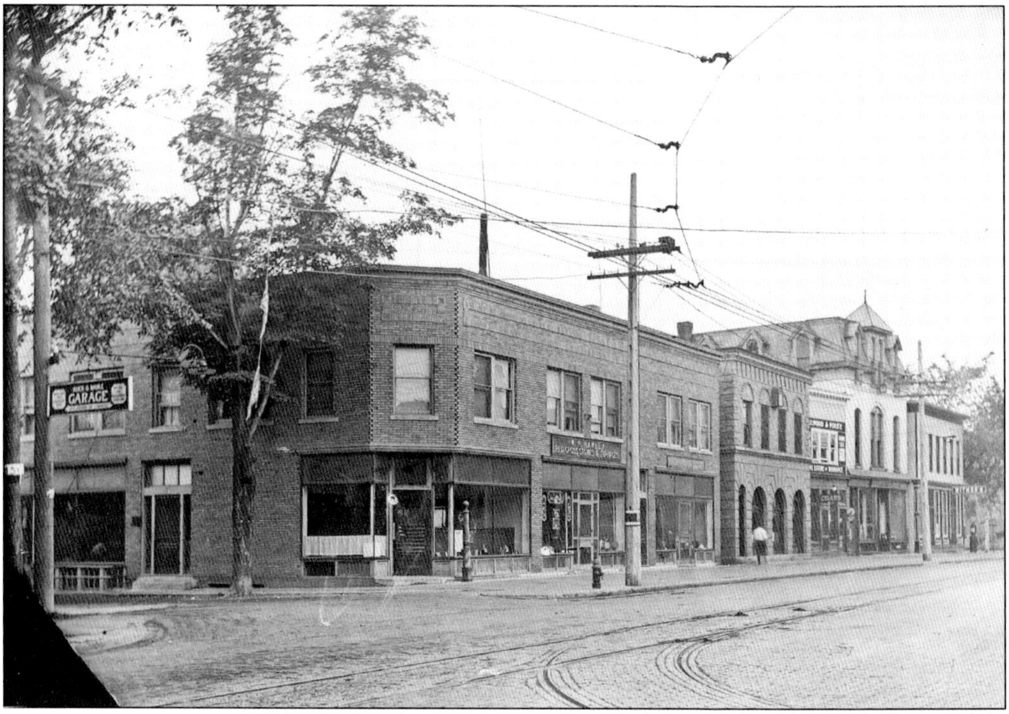

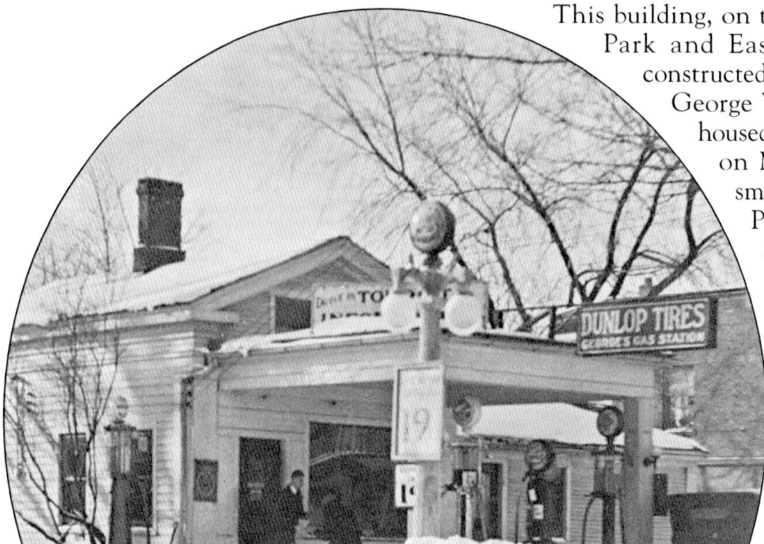

This building, on the corner of Lapham Park and East Main Street, was constructed by Frank M. Jones and George Wiser around 1910. It housed five retail stores, three on Main Street and two smaller ones on Lapham Park, with apartments on the second floor. At one time, a shoe and millinery shop were located in the Lapham Park stores, and in the corner shop, the Webster National Bank was in operation until about 1932. The middle store was the post office and the end shop was the William Wahle Tailor and Men's Clothing Store. Notice the brick road and trolley tracks. The *c.* 1925 photograph at left shows the opposite corner, across Lapham Park, where the Nagle Gas Station stood.

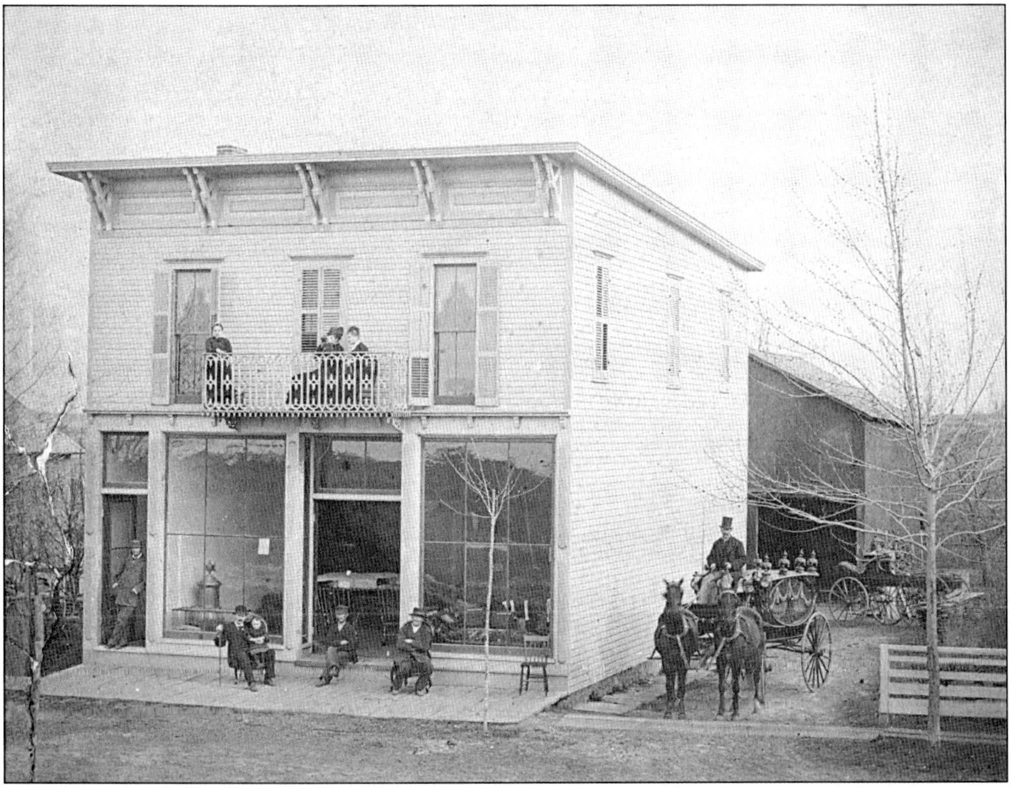

Lewis H. Crippen began a furniture and undertaking business around 1870 located on East Main Street between Lapham Park and Dunning Avenue. Notice the horse-drawn hearse, which was used even after the limousine service had been introduced. There were living quarters on the second floor, indicated by the ladies sitting on the balcony. In the 1920s, it became the Smith and Lotze Furniture and Undertaking Business. The *c.* 1920 picture below shows the interior of the furniture store.

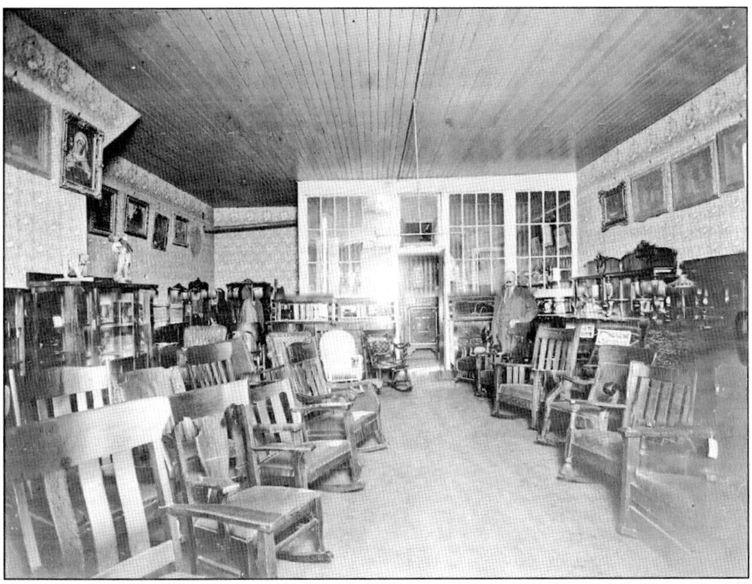

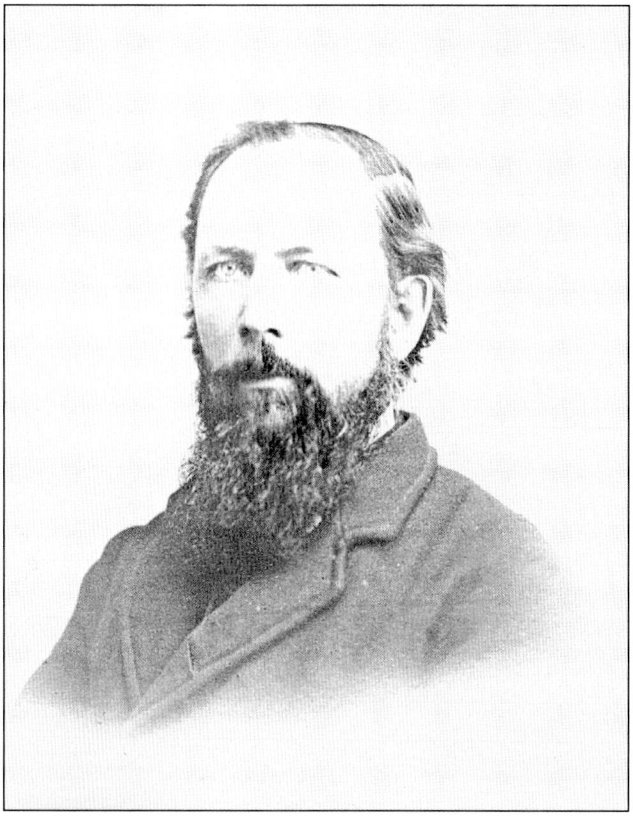

Dr. John D. Dunning is pictured at left. He was the son of Gerald Dunning and Polly Hicks Dunning, pioneer settlers of Webster. He grew up on a farm just east of Holy Trinity Church on Ridge Road. He began his studies with Dr. Ezra Potter of Webster. He attended lectures at the Buffalo Medical School. After graduation in 1852, he worked one year with Dr. Potter before starting his own practice. He was very involved in community organizations, including the presidency of the first board of education of the Union Free School. He resided in the home built by his late Uncle John Hicks, at the corner of East Main Street and Dunning Avenue. When Dr. Dunning died in 1901, he was the oldest member of Webster Lodge No. 538. (Photograph at left courtesy of the Webster Masonic Lodge No. 538.)

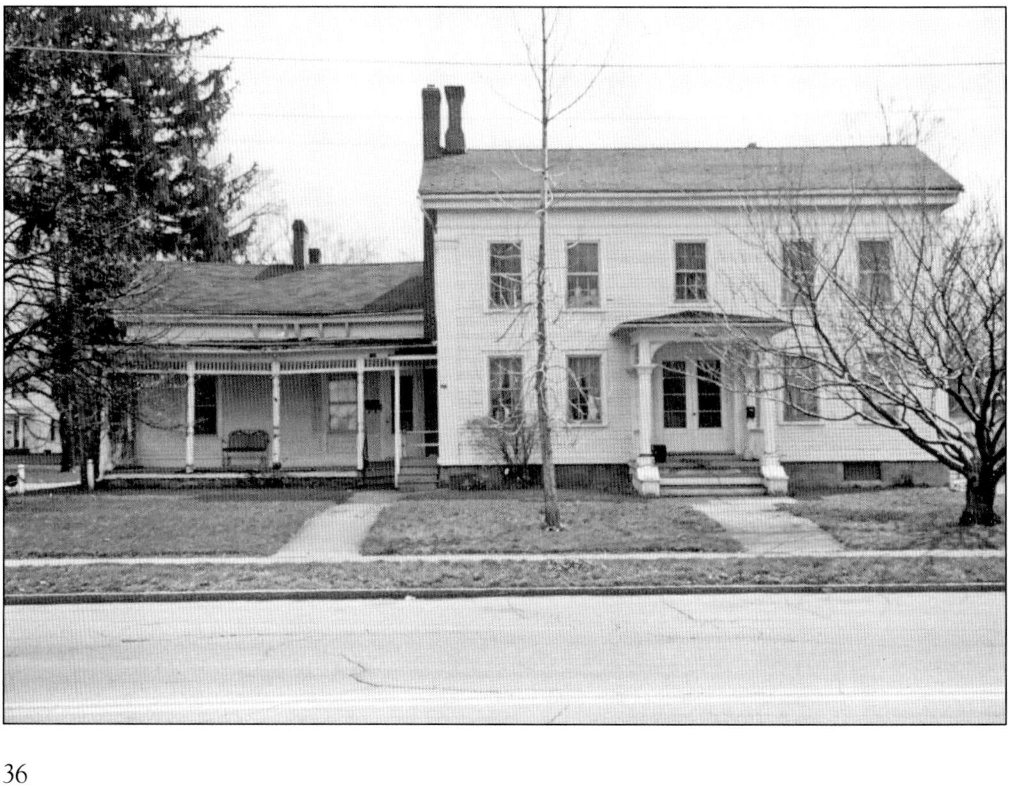

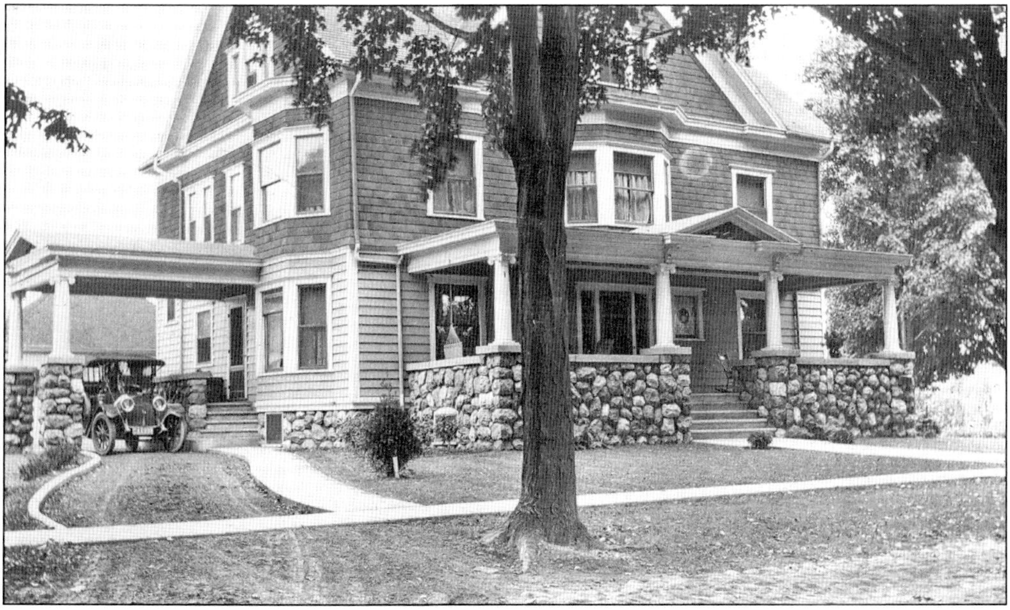

Dr. William Stanton moved to Webster in 1900 and took over Dr. Charles Reitz's practice. Around 1912, Dr. Stanton built this lovely home at 121 East Main Street, where he continued his practice until retiring in 1917. He joined the U.S. Medical Reserve Corps, commissioned as captain. As lieutenant colonel, in 1927, he declined a recommission. He sold his home in Webster about 1919 and moved to Buffalo, where he specialized in the care of asthma patients.

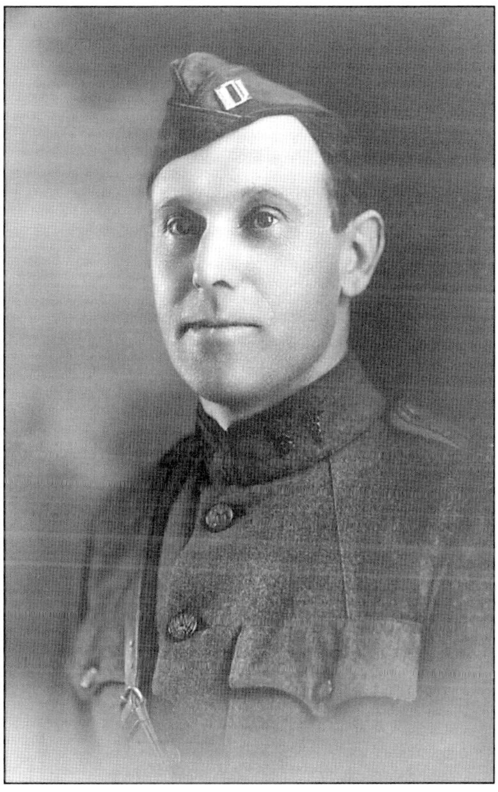

Dr. James B. Foster of Webster practiced medicine with Dr. Maine for 10 years before joining the U.S. Army medical department and serving overseas in World War I. In a letter written to the grange in 1917, he wrote that he was a transportation officer with an animal-drawn field hospital. He was taking care of 36 mules and 24 horses. He returned to Webster in 1919 to continue his practice. (Courtesy of the Foster family.)

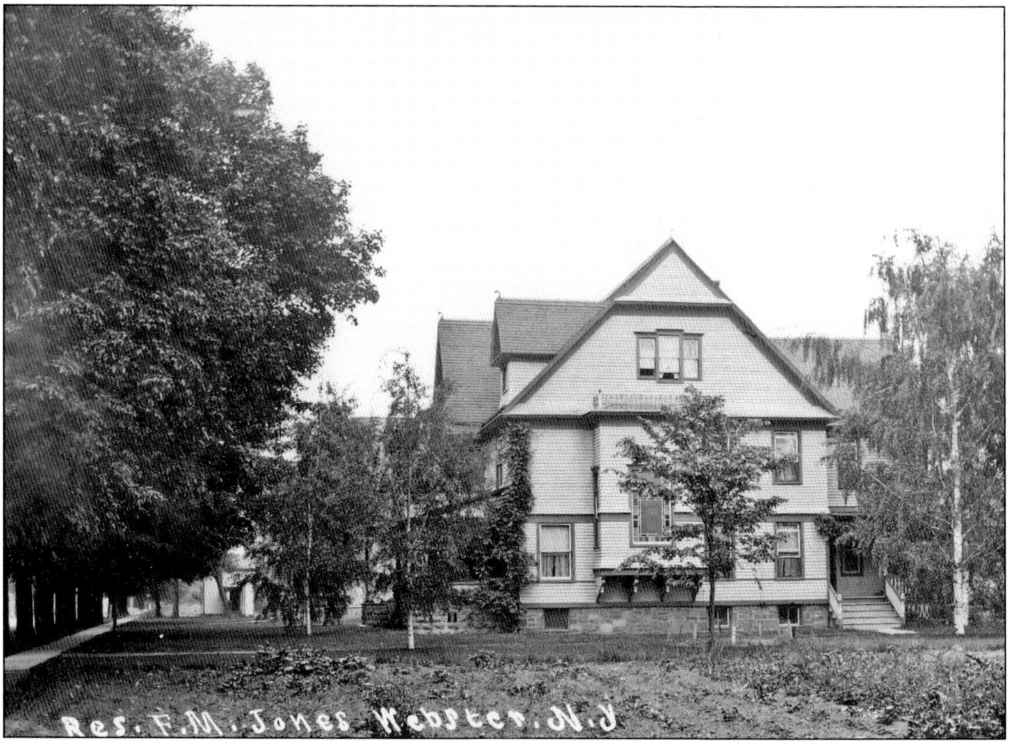

Mr. Frank M. Jones moved to Webster from Union Hill in 1890. He was a very successful businessman and took an active interest in the progress of his community. He built his home at 135 East Main Street *c.* 1890. By 1930, the property was owned by Mary Hoffman, who had opened her home as a hospital. The hospital could handle eight patients at a time, and 114 tonsillectomies were performed, along with major and minor surgeries. They handled a lot of accident cases, pneumonia patients, and one for hypothermia. Over the years, 194 babies were born there. The bill below is for a seven-day maternity stay. The hospital closed in 1937. (Photograph below courtesy of Lynn Barton.)

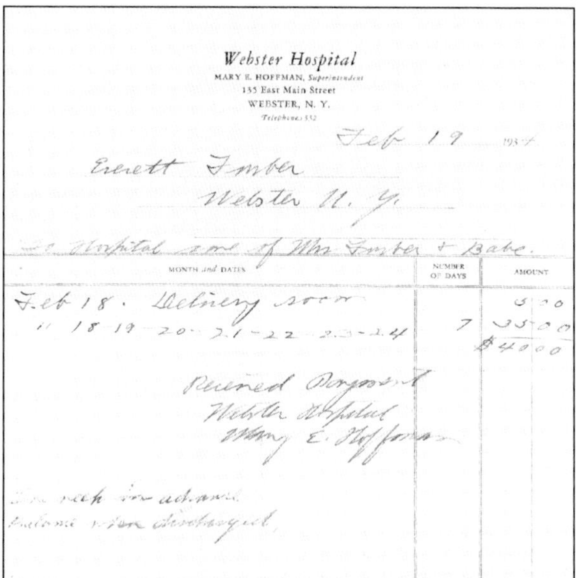

Webster Hospital
MARY E. HOFFMAN, Superintendent
135 East Main Street
WEBSTER, N. Y.
Telephone 532

Feb 19 193

Everett Fmber
Webster N. Y.

MONTH and DATES	NUMBER OF DAYS	AMOUNT
Feb 18. Delivery room		5 00
" 18-19-20-21-22-23-24	7	35 00
		$40 00

Received Payment
Webster Hospital
Mary E. Hoffman

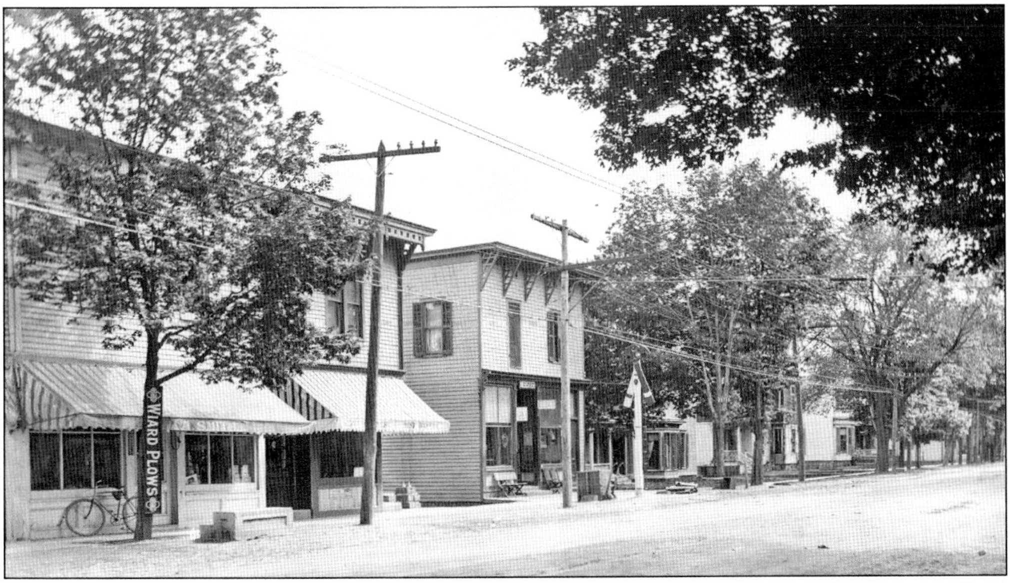

This c. 1905 photograph of East Main Street shows the Anthony Smith Hardware Store (left) operated by his son Paul. This store was founded by the Corning brothers when they came to Webster in the early 1800s. Peter Smith, brother of Paul, had his law office upstairs. The next business is the Webster Bakery, and then the trolley station—with the signal pole with movable semaphore arms—out in front of the station.

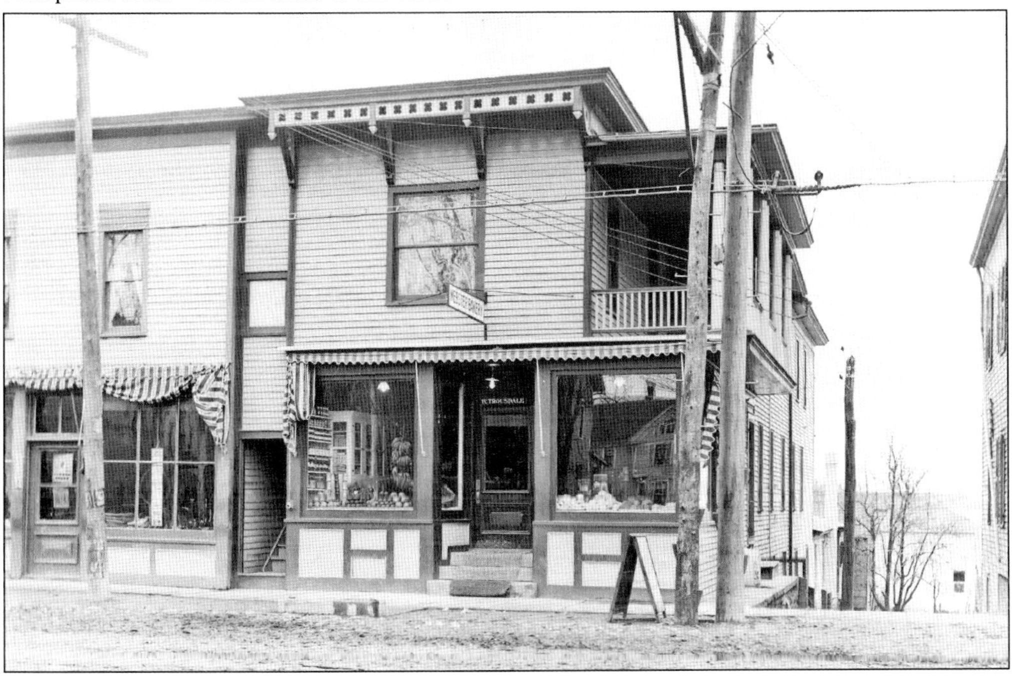

The Webster Bakery, located on East Main Street, was operated by Wesley and Barbara Truesdale from about 1907 to 1929. The bakery had a large wholesale business and shipped boxes packed with 50 loaves of bread to all the towns on the Sodus Bay Trolley line. The baking ovens were in the basement, and it was a favorite place for kids to stop, warm up in the winter, and have a fresh donut.

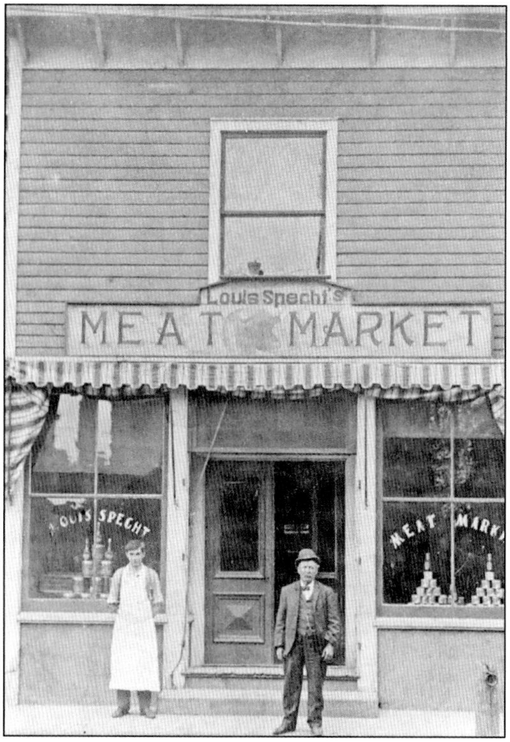

Louis Specht ran a meat market from this building on East Main Street in 1896. It was next door to the Webster Hotel. He was known as an expert butcher and sausage maker. The photograph at left, c. 1905, shows his son Louis Specht Jr., on the left, wearing the apron.

The popular Webster Candy Kitchen was opened in 1908 by Charles, Steve, and their cousin Harry Papapanu in the Specht building. Homemade candy and ice cream were available. In the beginning, only ice cream sundaes and sodas were served. Before home freezers, customers would stop by and pick up a pint or quart of ice cream before dinner. Ice cream was made at the store every Thursday. By 1940, light lunches were served.

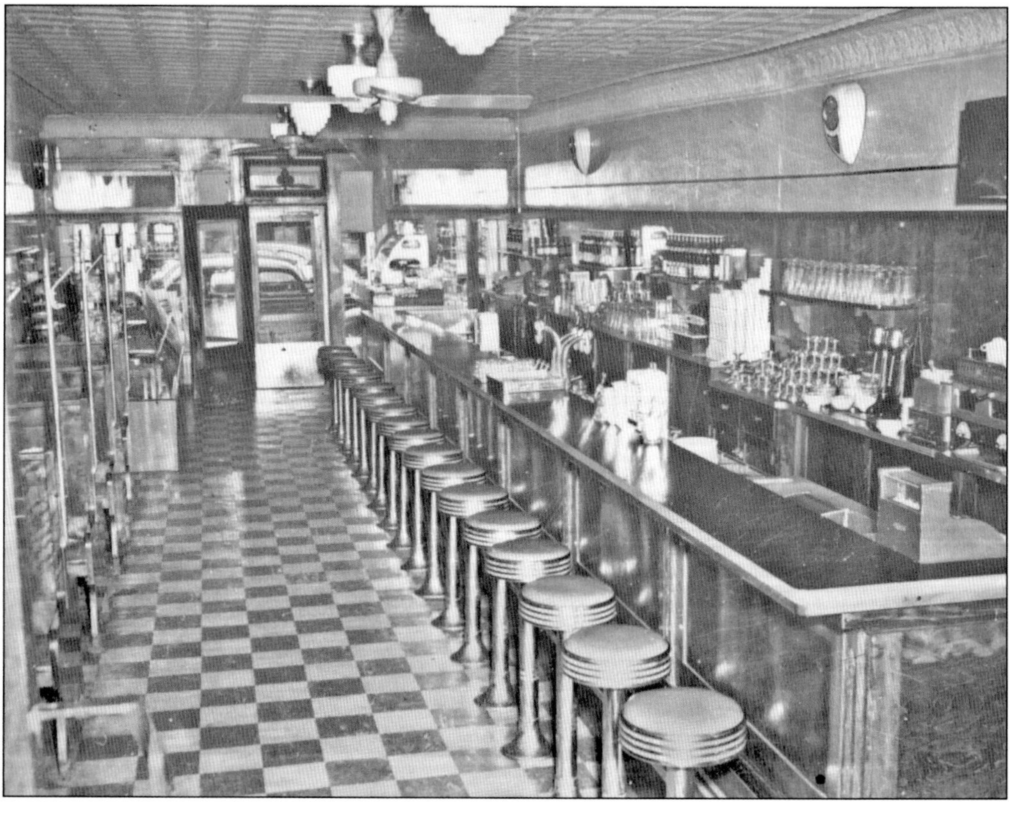

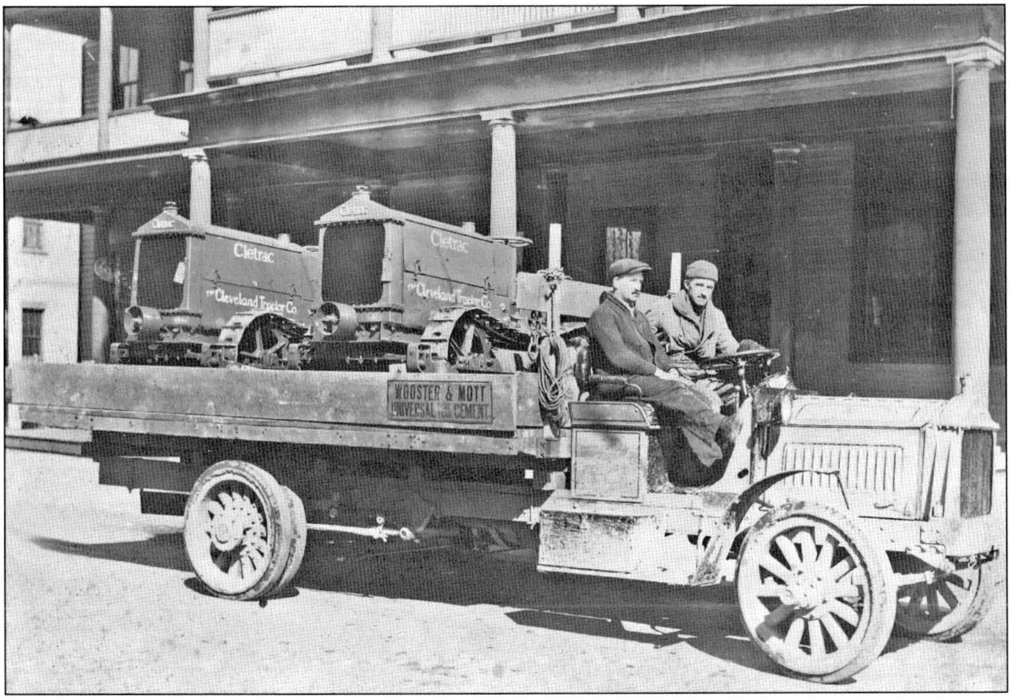

This is a delivery truck from the Wooster and Mott business, located on the east side of North Avenue just south of the train tracks. The truck is carrying Cletrac tractors heading to farms in Red Creek and North Rose. This picture was taken on East Main Street in front of the Webster Hotel.

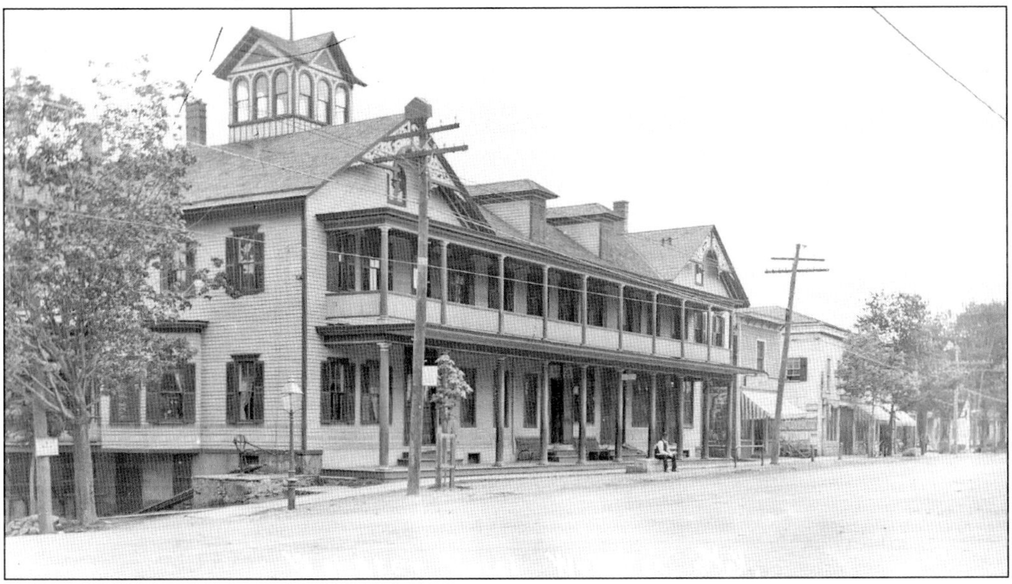

The Webster Hotel was located on the northeast corner of East Main Street and North Avenue. This 19th century building had many owners over the years, until its demolition in 1963. The hotel had 22 rooms, a large dining room, a modern kitchen, and all the modern improvements: heated by steam, electric bells, and it was well lit and ventilated. Many band concerts were held on the upper balcony on Saturday nights and special occasions. During World War II, the cupola on top of the building was used by air raid spotters, who manned a station there.

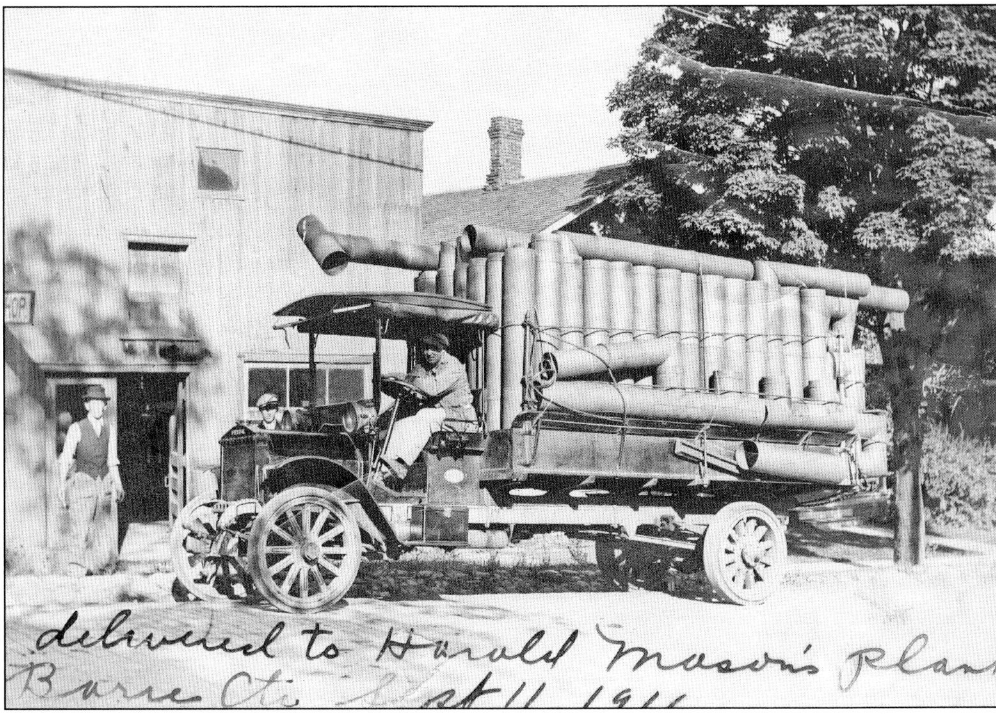

Johnson Brothers Plumbing and Tin Shop was located just behind the corner building at West Main Street and North Avenue. The picture above shows a load of dry house piping and fittings heading to Virginia. The driver is believed to be Roy McGuire. It would not have been a pleasant ride considering that the tires of the day were of solid hard rubber. The photograph below shows the interior of the shop, Frank Prinzing is on the left, Bud Johnson is the little boy, and the gentleman on the right is Reginald Johnson. You can see patterns used for making different types of piping hanging along the wall. The patterns were drawn on flat sheet metal and cut with hand snips. They repaired sprinklers, coffee pots, milk cans, and whatever needed to be soldered that they could repair.

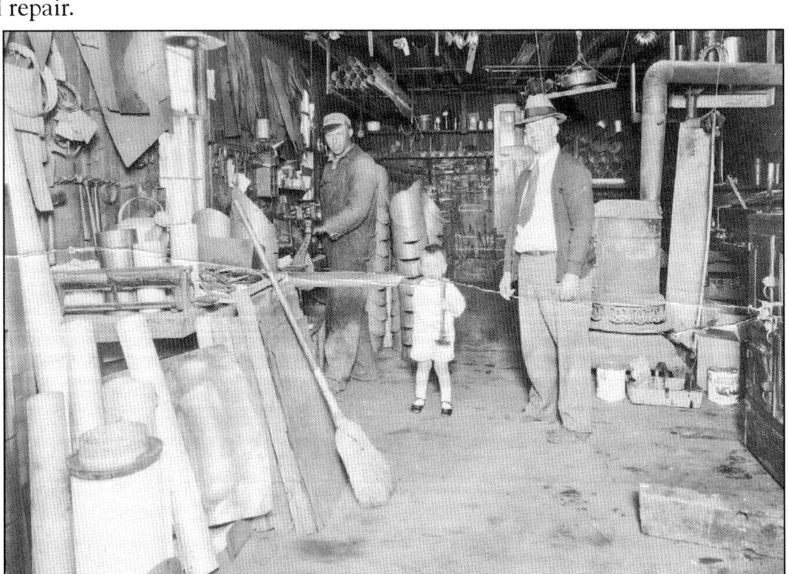

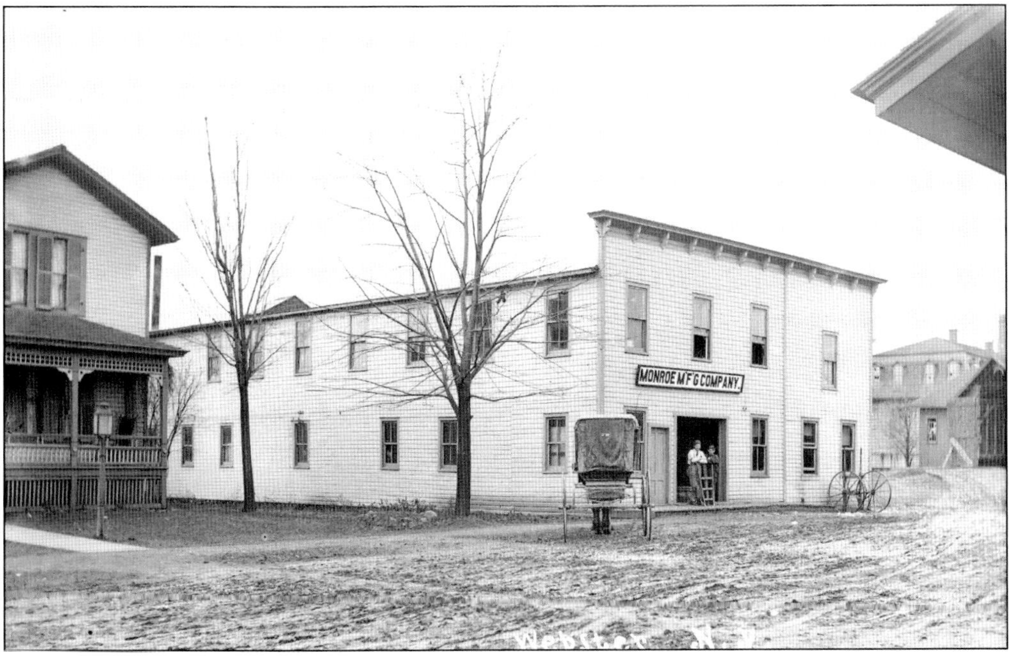

Located on the south side of the railroad station on Railroad Street, Monroe Manufacturing Company got its start about 1892. George H. Curtice started making burial cases and found it difficult to find a craftsman who could apply the covering material to the wooden caskets. Eventually he hired Edward R. Paynter from Franklinville, Cattaraugus County, who had engaged in this type of work. Over the years, the company changed ownership. By 1919, a new partnership was formed between Edward Paynter and Morton Nivison. In 1924, the business became known as the Monroe Casket Company, and by the 1940s, the business was dissolved because of decreased business. The picture below is an early image of the factory. Morton Nivison is thought to be on the right.

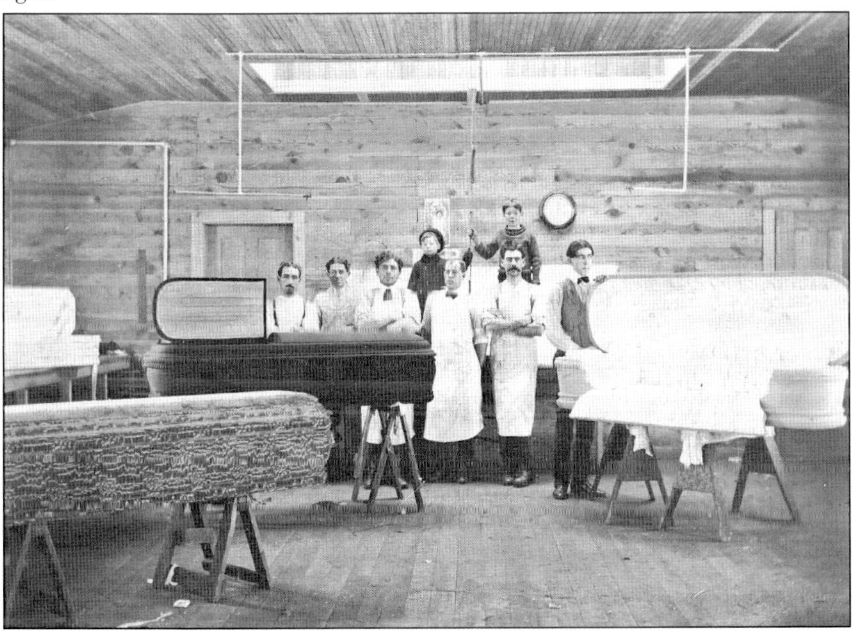

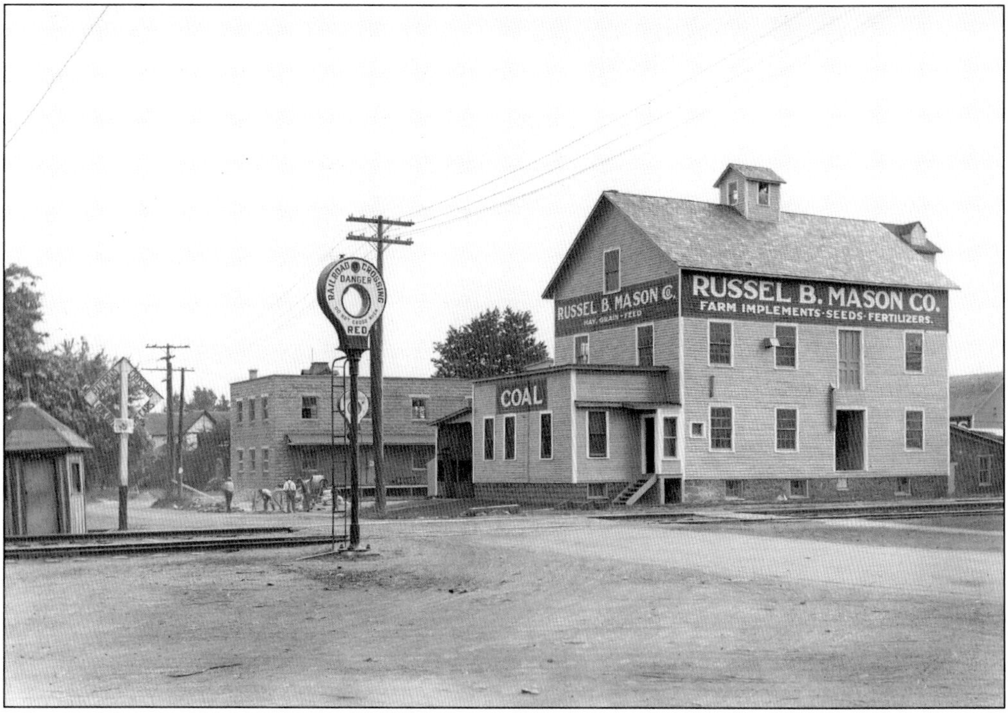

The Russel B. Mason Company on North Avenue, opened in 1923, sold livestock feed, coal, farm supplies, and machinery. Later on, fruits, vegetables, and lawn and garden supplies were sold.

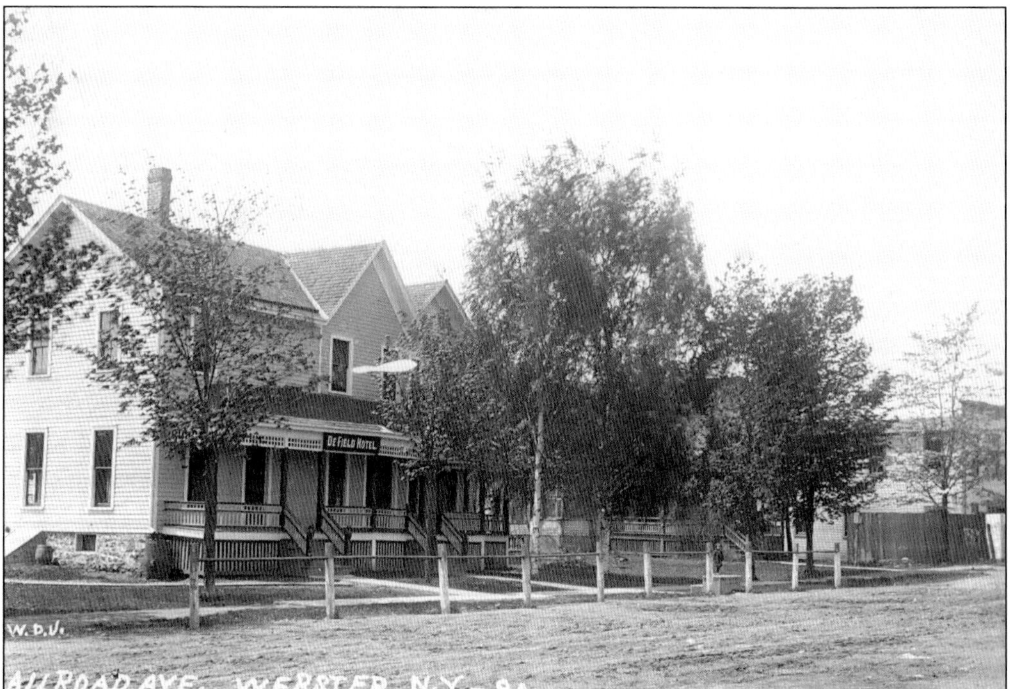

Pictured above is one of two Defield Hotels that operated at one time in the village of Webster. This one was located on Railroad Street across from the train station, on the corner of North Avenue.

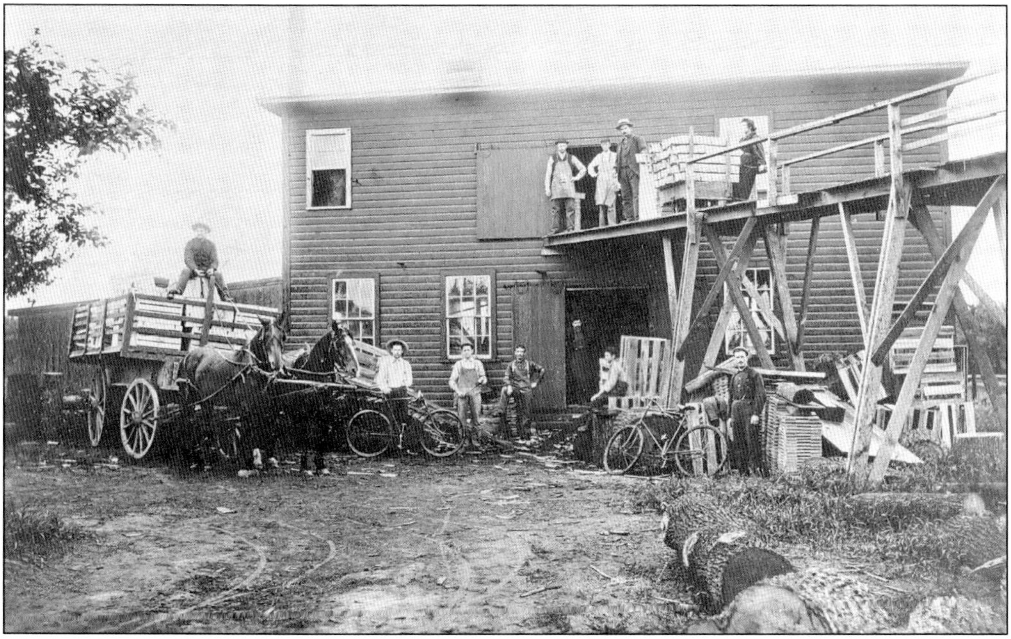

The Kittelberger brothers purchased a small basket factory in West Webster in about 1893. The Kittelberger brothers purchased property on Donovan Street and built a larger factory. In 1912, the business was incorporated under the name "The Webster Basket Factory." The business stopped making baskets in 1969 and continued as a wholesale outlet. A fire in 1977 destroyed much of the factory, and it eventually had to be torn down.

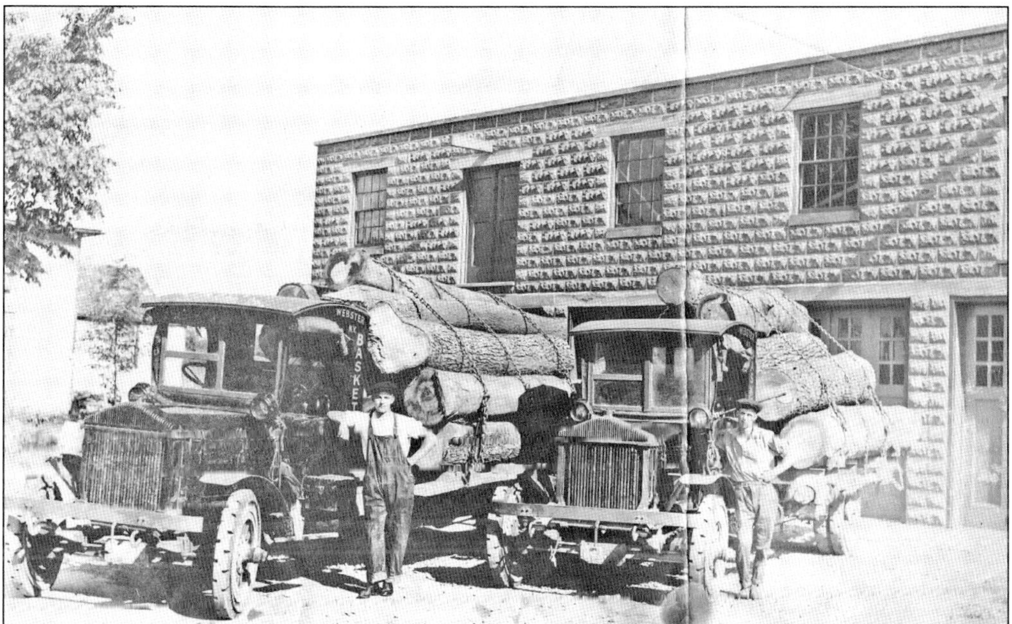

In the early days, basket making required large quantities of timber. It was cut in the winter and brought to the factory in sleds, then during the summer months it was processed for the manufacturing of baskets and crates. Farmers eventually started to cut their own trees and deliver them to the factory to supplement their income.

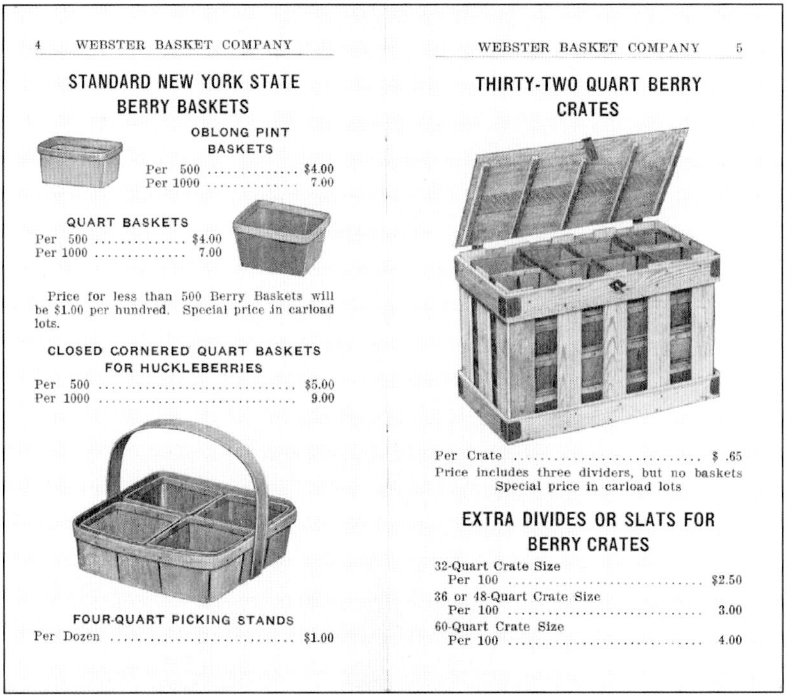

4 WEBSTER BASKET COMPANY

STANDARD NEW YORK STATE BERRY BASKETS

OBLONG PINT BASKETS

Per 500 .... $4.00
Per 1000 .... 7.00

QUART BASKETS

Per 500 .... $4.00
Per 1000 .... 7.00

Price for less than 500 Berry Baskets will be $1.00 per hundred. Special price in carload lots.

CLOSED CORNERED QUART BASKETS FOR HUCKLEBERRIES

Per 500 .... $5.00
Per 1000 .... 9.00

FOUR-QUART PICKING STANDS

Per Dozen $1.00

WEBSTER BASKET COMPANY 5

THIRTY-TWO QUART BERRY CRATES

Per Crate .... $ .65
Price includes three dividers, but no baskets
Special price in carload lots

EXTRA DIVIDES OR SLATS FOR BERRY CRATES

32-Quart Crate Size
Per 100 .... $2.50
36 or 48-Quart Crate Size
Per 100 .... 3.00
60-Quart Crate Size
Per 100 .... 4.00

The Basket Factory produced all types of fruit and vegetable baskets including berry baskets as seen at left. They also produced crates of all types to pack the baskets into for safe shipping to markets. Other popular baskets were the market basket, baskets for clothes, and even Easter baskets that were sold in F. W. Woolworth stores throughout the country.

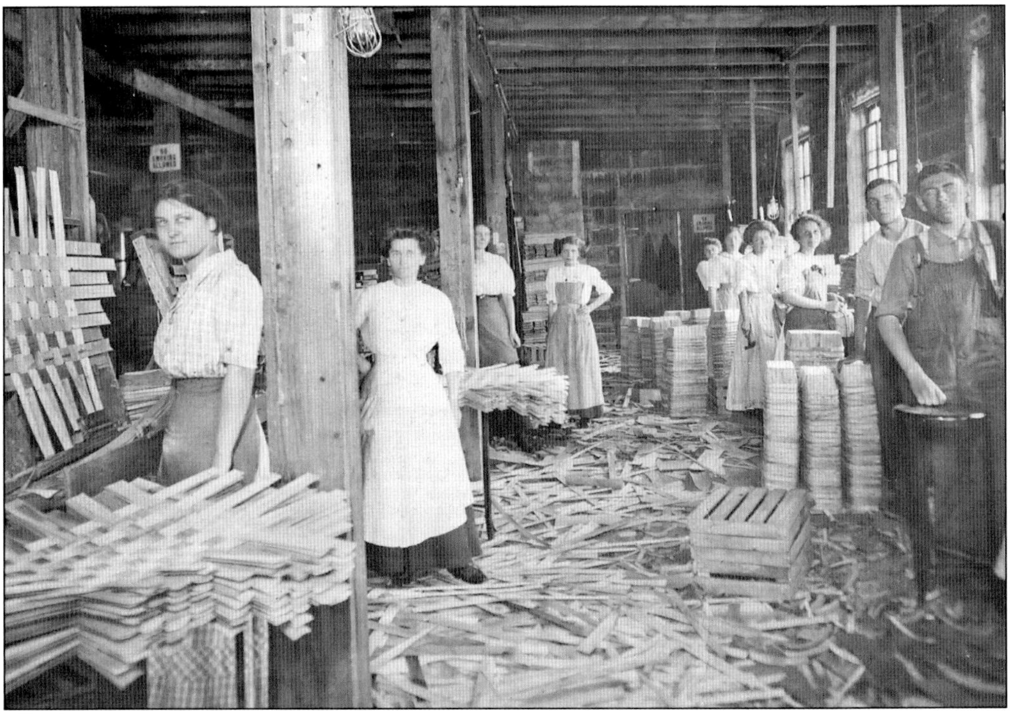

Early baskets were produced by the skilled hands of the workers. The baskets were constructed over wooden forms using hammers and tacks as this picture shows. Eventually modern machinery made the job much easier and tacks were replaced by wire staples. By 1938, over 150 people were employed and produced an average of 5,000 baskets daily.

Three

Fruits and Farms

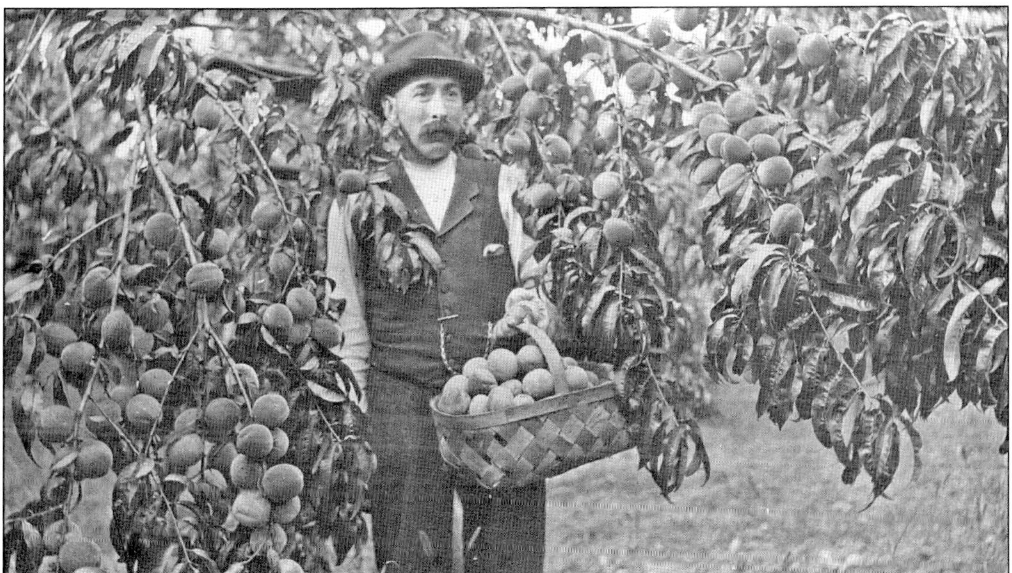

In 1875, the town of Webster had 400 farms, most with orchards growing apples, peaches, pears, and cherries. Farmer George Neubrand is shown picking peaches. (Courtesy of Kenneth Kittelberger.)

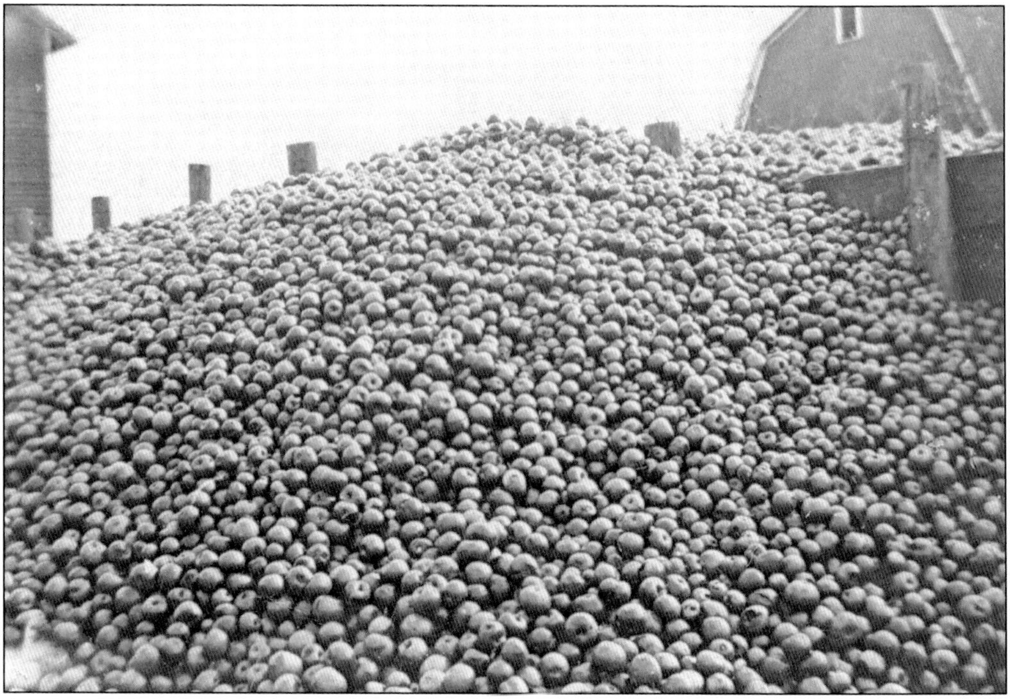

Apple drying in Webster goes back to the 1840s, when residents started drying apples in their kitchens. They would core, quarter, and string the slices on a line to dry. By about 1870, small quantities were dried in the sun for sale to stores and for domestic use. Drying apples would become a very lucrative business for many area farmers. The apples seen above were from the Martin Yaeger farm on Salt Road. (Courtesy of Ann Yaeger Mason.)

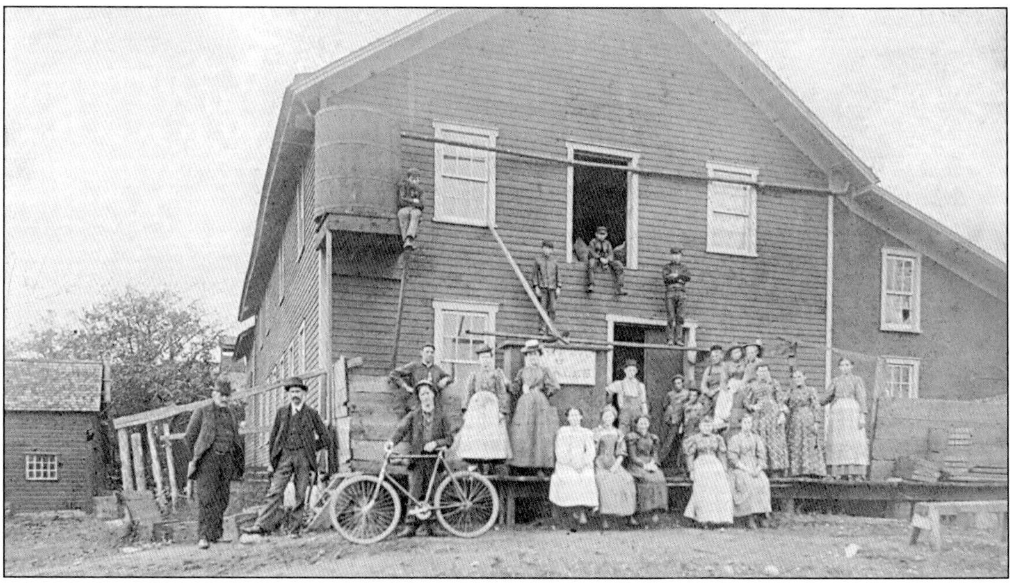

After his marriage to Catherine Hettler of Webster in 1864, John W. Hallauer purchased a farm on Webster Road. Eventually John Hallauer and his family decided to try drying apples. They started out small, and in a short while, they were able to dry over 10 bushels a day. This was the beginning for the Hallauer family business. (Courtesy of the Webster Museum and Historical Society.)

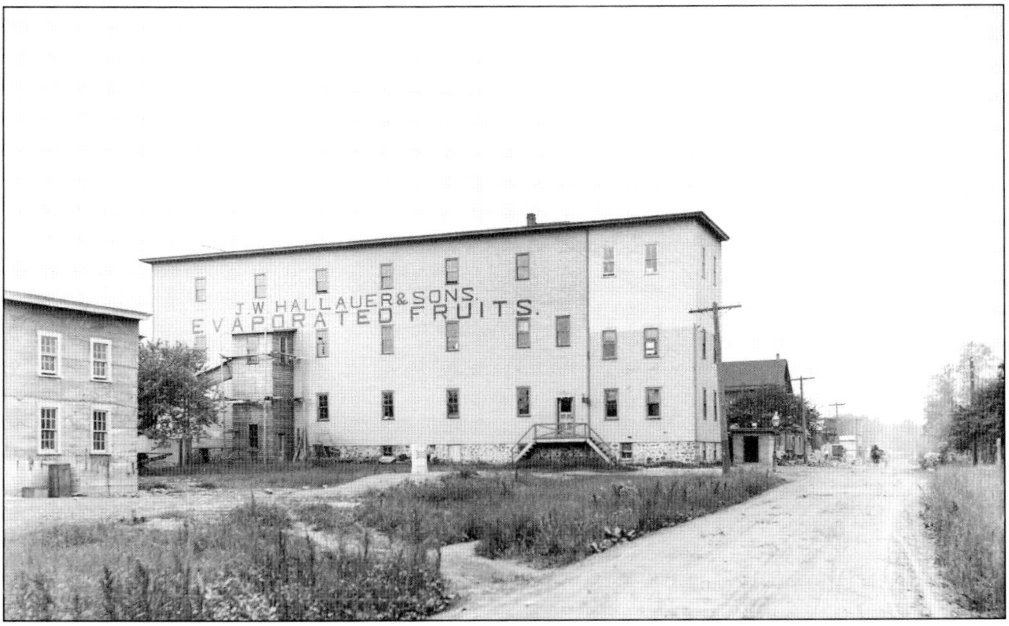

The J. W. Hallauer and Sons Evaporated Fruits was located on the west side of North Avenue, between the railroad tracks to the south and Commercial Street on the north. The Hallauers started to buy apples about 1890, and by 1899, they were in the export business. John W. Hallauer died in 1909, and his sons George and John J. continued the business and were very successful. A large portion of their business was shipping to Hamburg, Germany, and up until World War I, they were one of the largest exporters in the world. Pictured below are ladies at work in the Hallauer plant *c.* 1900.

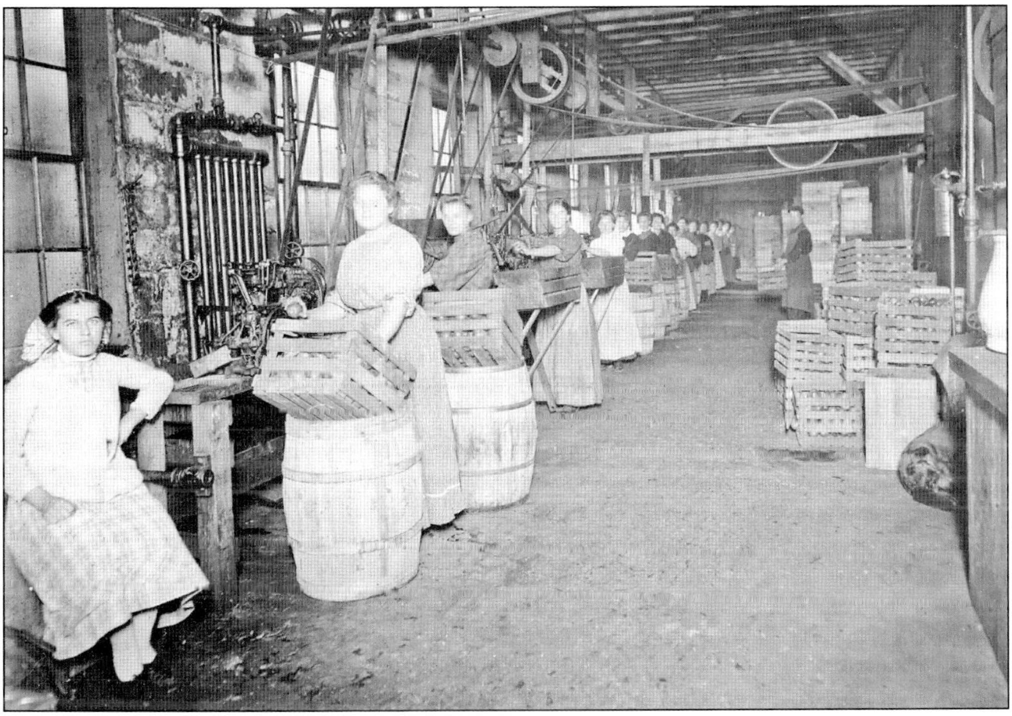

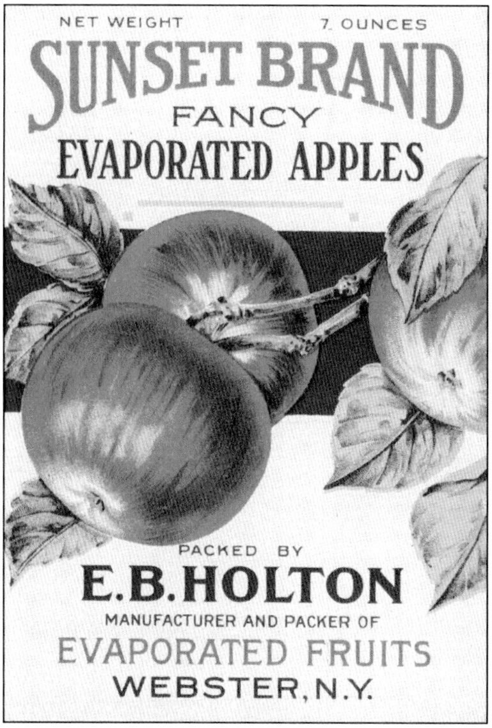

A list of members of the New York State Evaporation Association, published in 1918, includes some 35 firms giving Webster as their home base with evaporators in localities throughout the apple-growing belt of the state. Some of those listed were Fred Hecker, Henner and Pellett, Samuel Brewer, Frank Hosenfeld, Winslow and Merz, Wooster and John Cox, Martin Yaeger, and Frank Yaeger. (Courtesy of the Webster Museum and Historical Society.)

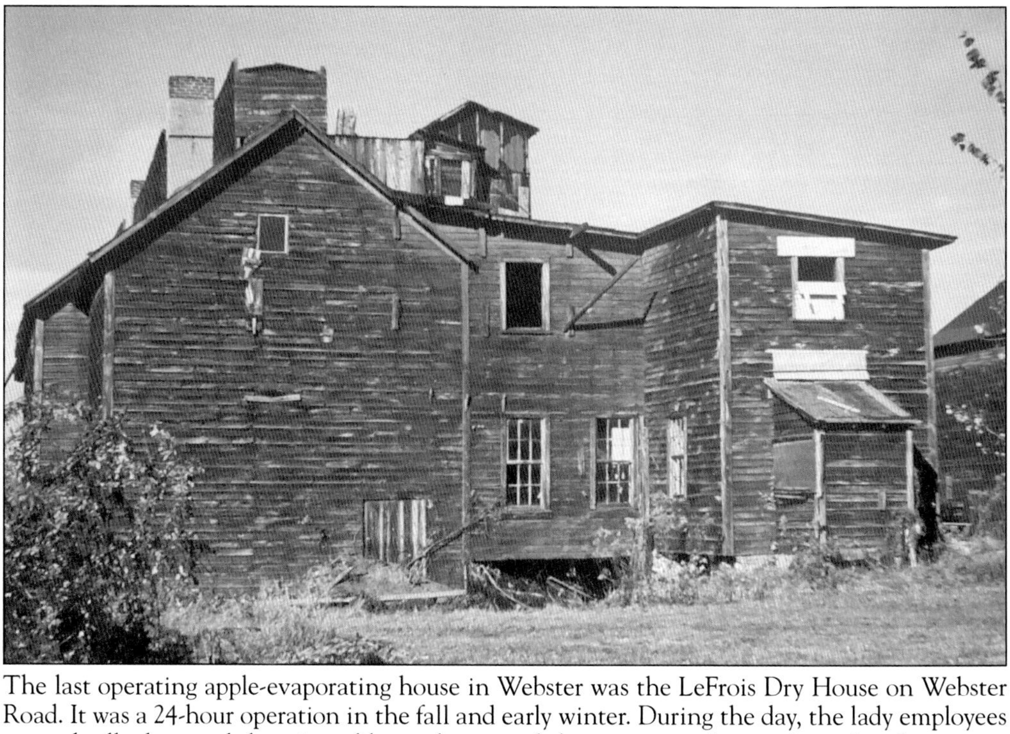

The last operating apple-evaporating house in Webster was the LeFrois Dry House on Webster Road. It was a 24-hour operation in the fall and early winter. During the day, the lady employees sat and talked around the trim tables and operated the paring machines. At night, the owners Corbin Crittenden and Arthur J. LeFrois turned the apples on the drying kilns and kept the fires burning. (Courtesy of Dr. Robert and Kathleen Brennan.)

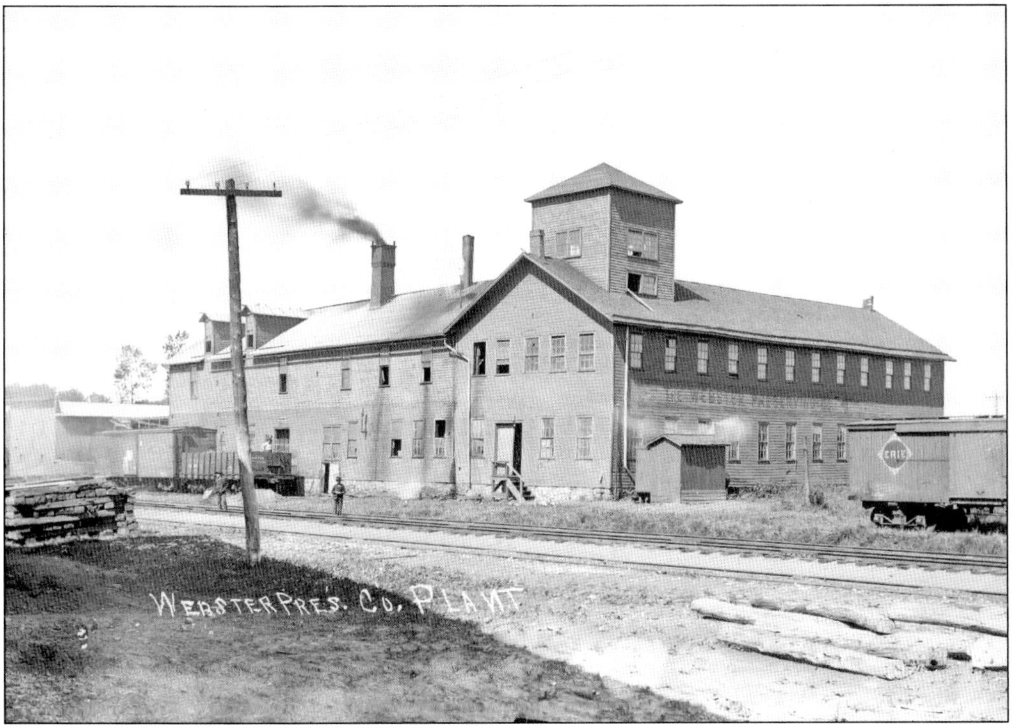

The Webster Canning and Preserving Company was started about 1885, after some leading businessmen and farmers decided Webster should have a canning factory. Operations soon began with the canning of strawberries and cherries. Other fruits—pears, plums, and peaches—followed. In the early days, much of the work was done by hand. Later the "sanitary" can, developed by the Cobb brothers of Fairport, New York, was first used at the Webster plant. The canning of sauerkraut is believed to have been started by the Webster Preserving Company. Sour cherries, tomatoes, tomato juice, apples, beets, and carrots rounded out the product line.

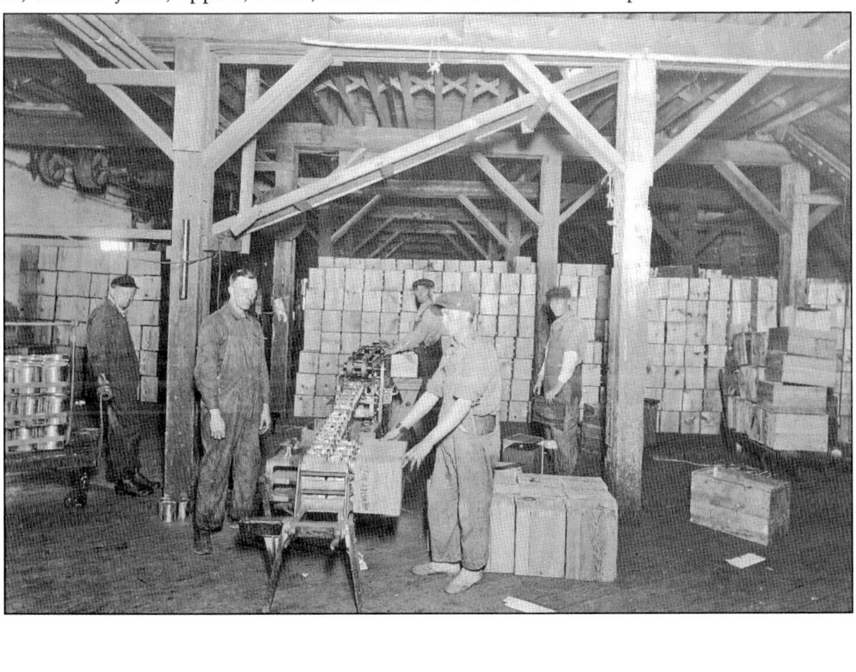

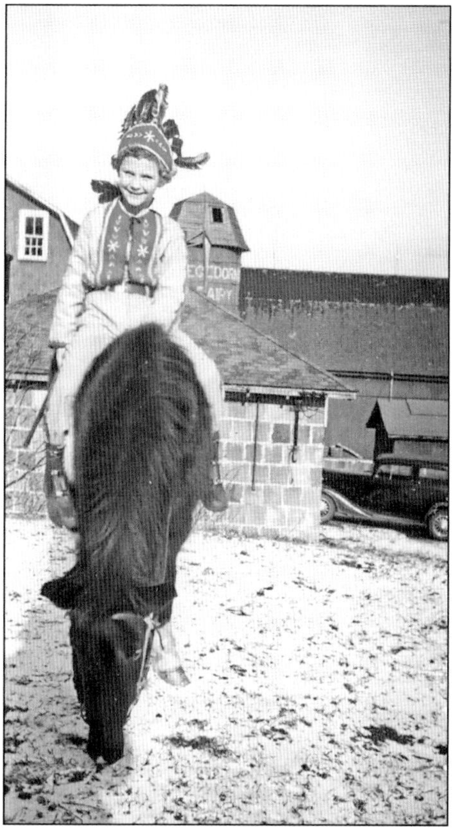

The Hegedorn family had a large dairy farm on Hard Road with 65 acres and about 200 Holstein cattle. They built a dairy store on the corner of Ridge Road and Hard Road. This photograph, taken in 1938, shows Gary Hegedorn on his pony in his Native American outfit. The Hegedorns were early settlers and have been very active in the Webster community. (Courtesy of the Hegedorn family.)

Katherine Simons owned the farm at 692 Maple Drive (Cemetery Road). She was a widow who emigrated from the country of Luxembourg in 1911 with two of her children, Marie and Peter. Daughter Mary Catherine came over one year earlier to work as a domestic and arrange for the family to come. Simons was known for the cats she trained to guard her hens against predators. (Courtesy of the Arbor family.)

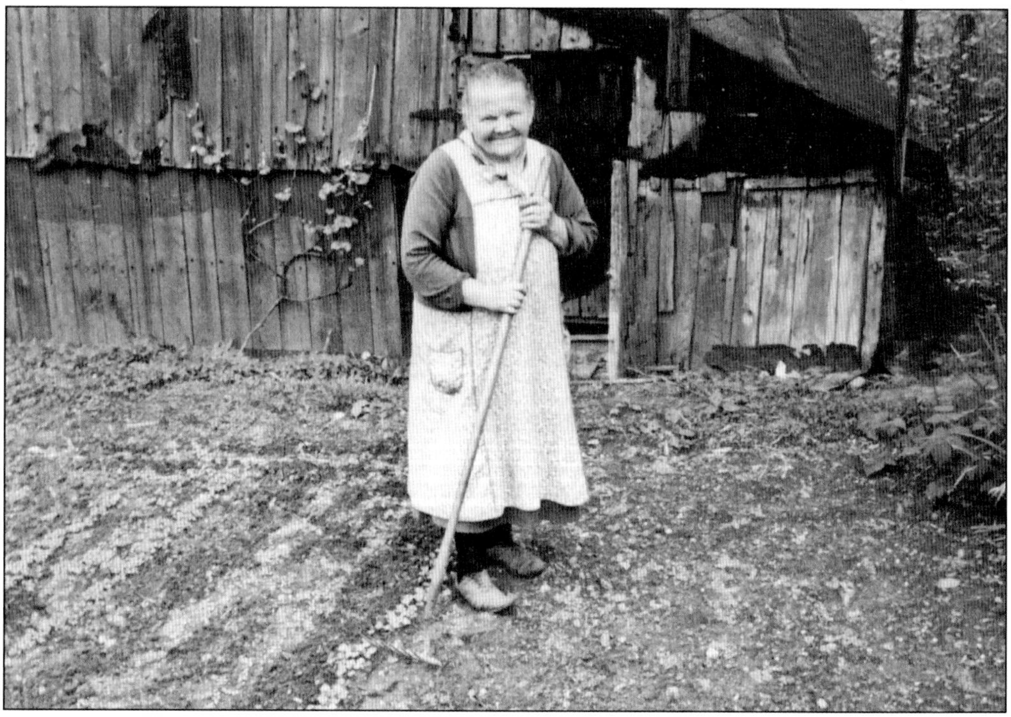

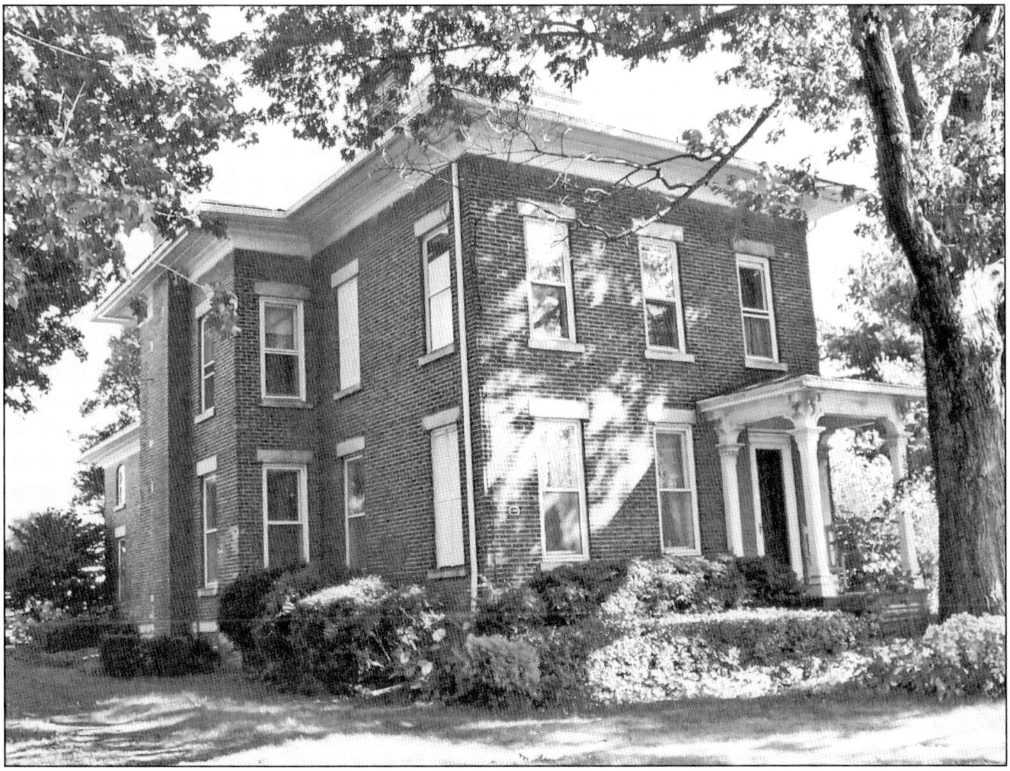

This brick Italianate-style home, located at 394 Phillips Road, was built by Charles S. and Sabrina Robb Wright *c.* 1850. It still has its original cupola or glassed roof pavilion, which was used for ventilation or as a scenic outlook, along with its original finial on top. Charles served as town supervisor from 1864 to 1866 and again in 1868 and was largely responsible for the creation of the Lake Ontario Shore Railroad through Webster.

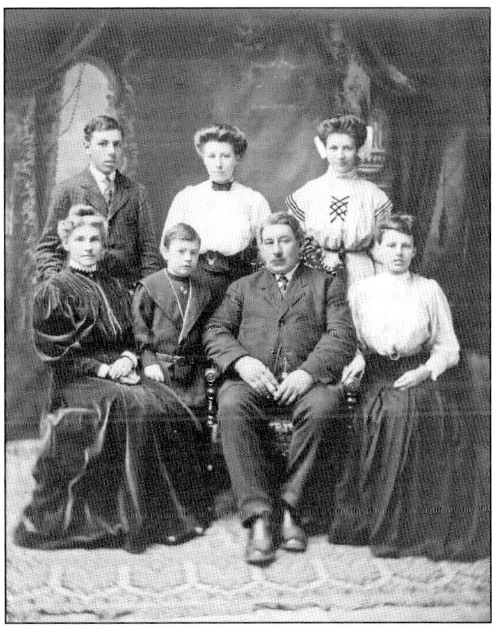

Dufay Wright was born in 1857. He was a 48-year member of the Webster Grange, master from 1896 to 1911. The Wright family shown in the photograph are, from left to right, (first row) Emma, Charles, Dufay, and Rubey; (second row) Wiburn, Ethel, and Pearl. Wright worked with his dad, Charles, until taking over the farm. They threshed oats in July, wheat during August and September, and buckwheat in October. (Courtesy of Patricia Maracle.)

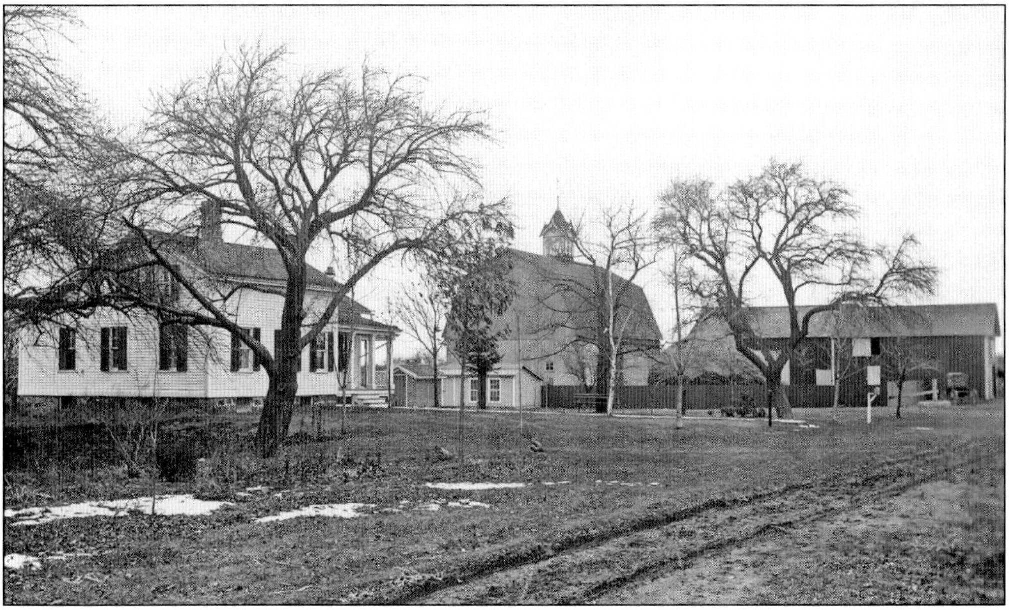

This postcard shows the home of Donat Mayer who arrived in Webster around 1876 and purchased property on Five Mile Line Road from Perry Langdon. He was a farmer who began making apple cider, grinding and pressing his excess apples. Other apple growers soon began bringing apples to Mayer and his son Donat Jr. for processing. Donat Jr. purchased the farm from his father in 1904. (Postcard courtesy of the Robert Holtz family.)

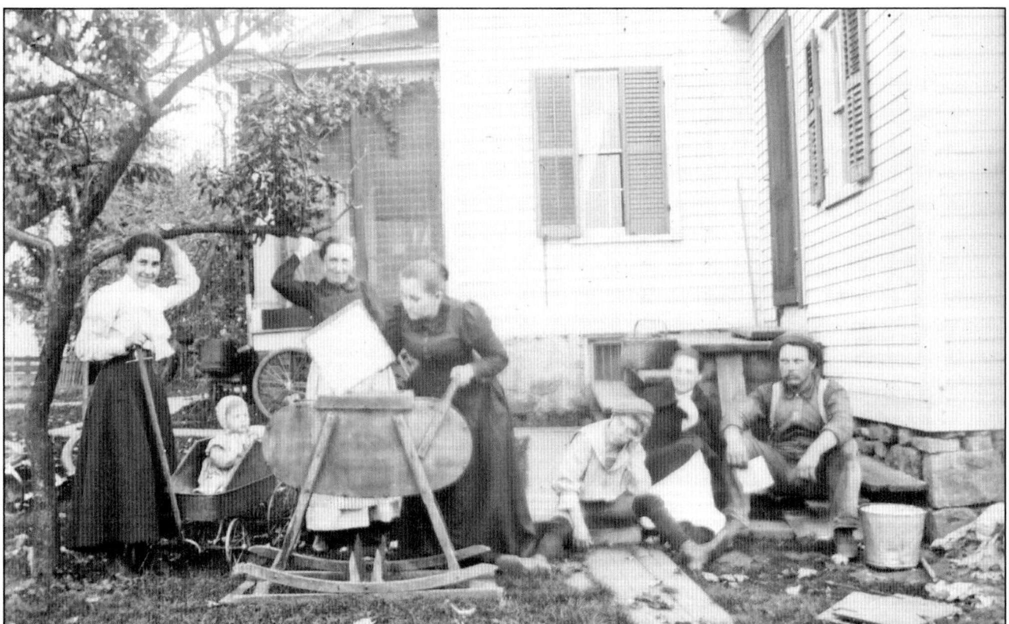

Harvey Mayer is shown as a young boy sitting on the walkway while his mother works with a rocking butter churn as family and friends look on. Harvey was born in 1889, attended Webster schools. Harvey sold the cider mill in 1962 while retaining the family home next door to live in. Of the original 16-plus cider mills in the Webster area, Mayers Mill is one of the very few remaining.

Children are playing on a large dirt pile in a winter scene at the Mayer farm. The barn, which is still standing, had a cupola that was for ventilation.

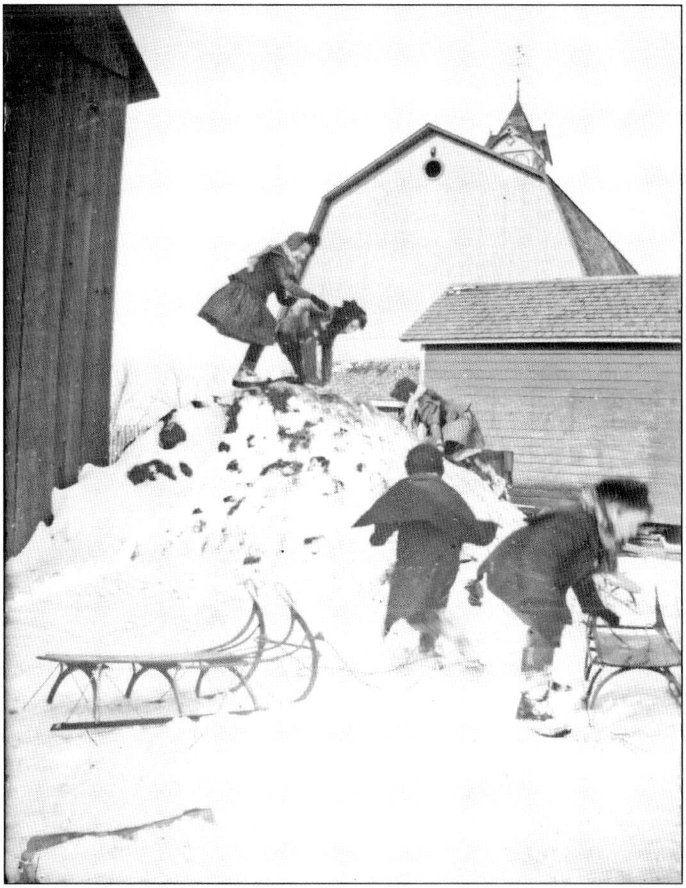

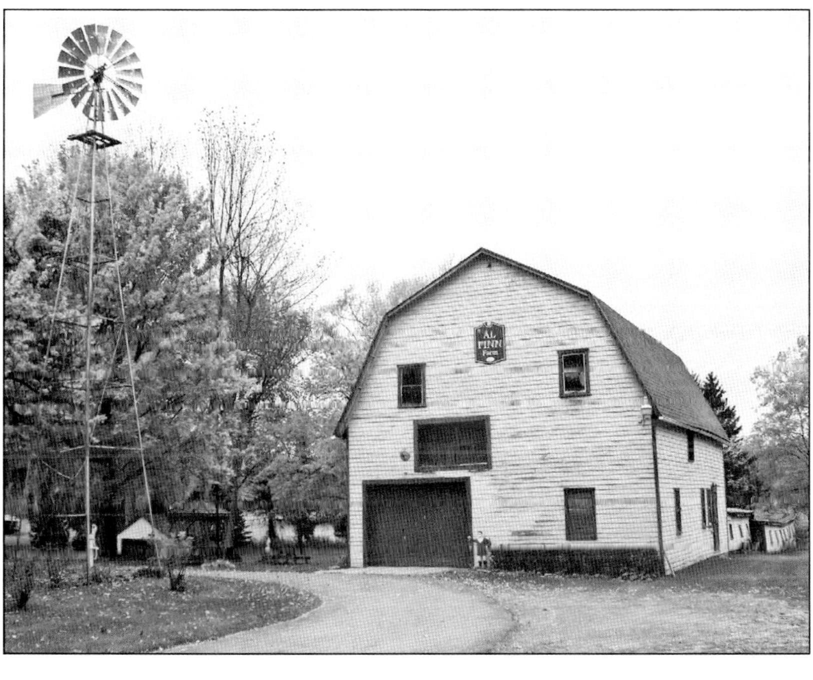

This barn that housed the horses for the Finn homestead on Gravel Road was built in the early 1850s. The windmill was used to provide waterpower for one of the first flush toilets in the town. All but 5 acres has been purchased by the town for a park.

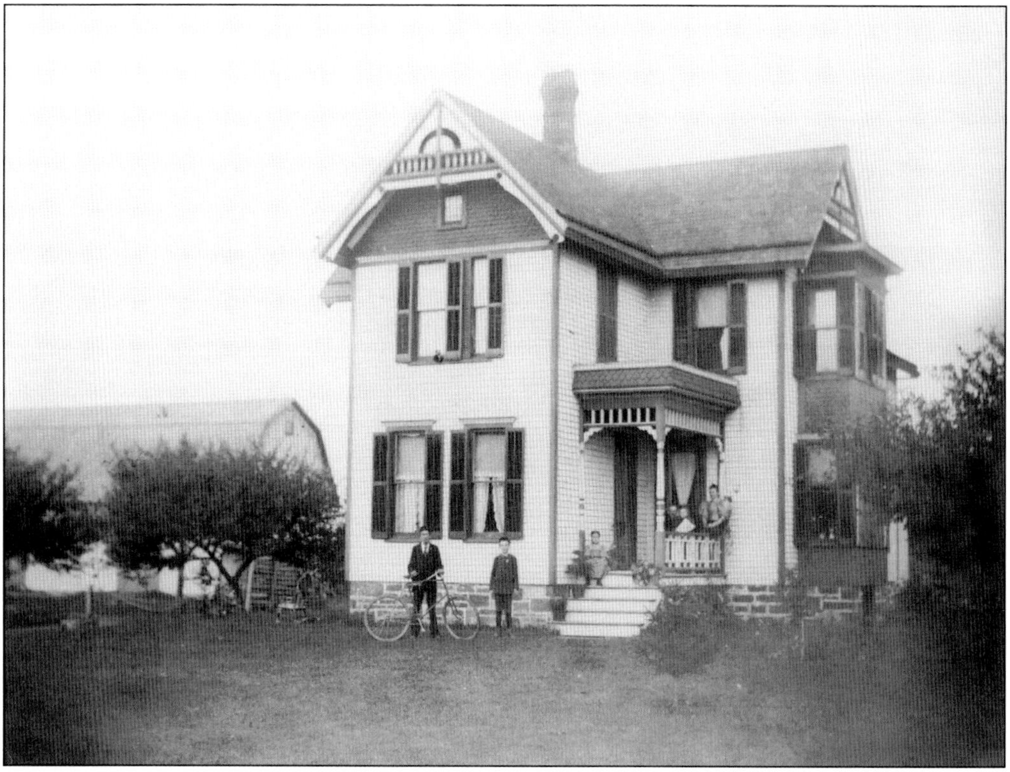

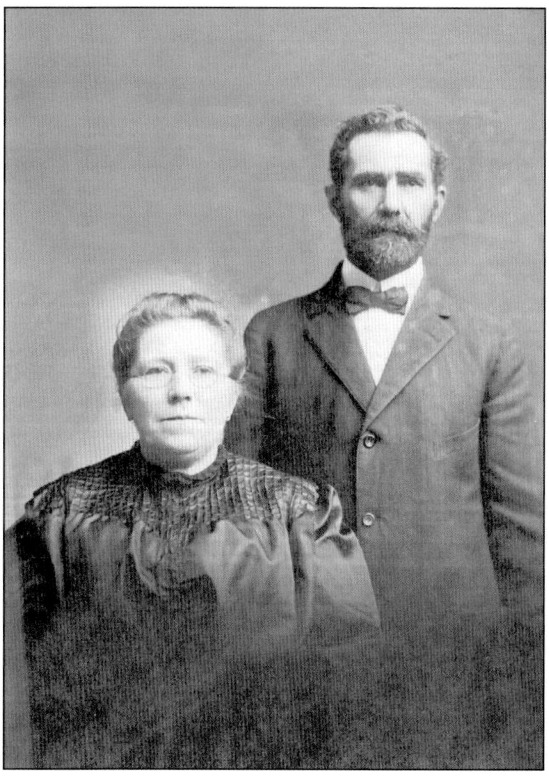

This *c.* 1895 photograph features the Kircher family home at 440 Basket Road. Charles C. Kircher and his wife, Frances A. Bowman, are on the porch with their daughters Helen and Stella M. Sons Charles Arthur, standing behind the bicycle, and Irving H. are in front of the family home. (Courtesy of the Longrod family.)

Prior to 1910, Jacob and Catherine Longrod purchased the Kircher farm at 440 Basket Road. They had emigrated from the Netherlands with their families. They were married in 1883, living in Williamson. Their son William married Nellie LeBar in 1912 and took over operation of the family farm. The farm had apple and cherry orchards, berry fields, chickens, pigs, cows, horses, sheep, and turkeys. Jacob and Catherine are pictured at left. (Courtesy of the Longrod family.)

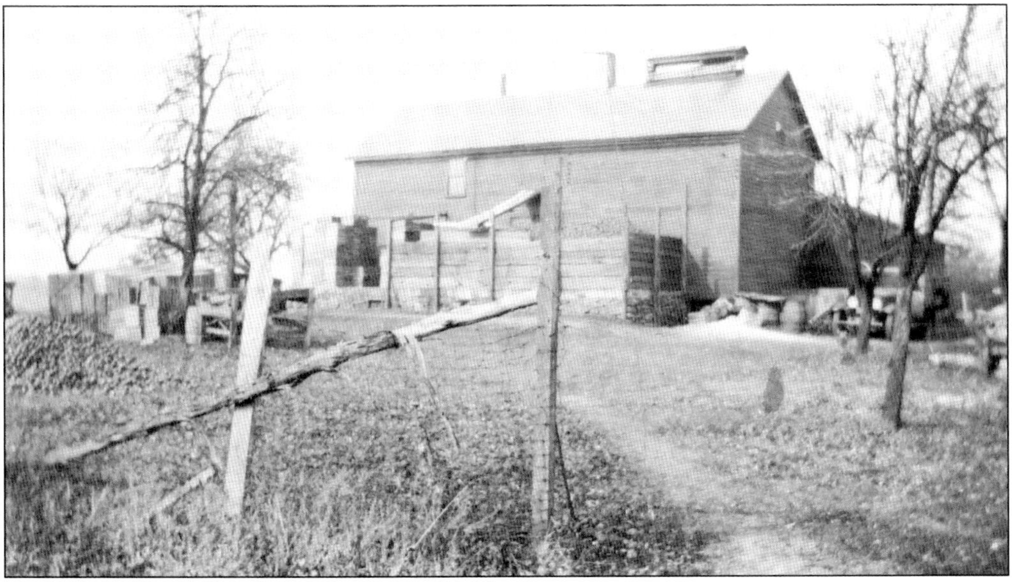

The Longrod farm at 440 Basket Road operated a dry house. Wilbur Longrod, remembers coming home from school and having to work for his dad in the dry house. A stove was used to heat the building. The apple slices were dumped on the floor upstairs. The heated air flowed through floorboards, which had spaces between them, and out a large vent in the roof. It would take 24 hours to dry the apples. The dry house stayed in operation until about 1940. Below is a photograph of berry pickers on the Longrod farm, taken c. 1928. Wilbur is sitting with a baseball bat at the right of the bottom row. His sister Evelyn is standing to his left, and their mother—Nellie, wearing a straw hat with dark trim—is standing behind Wilbur. (Courtesy of the Longrod family.)

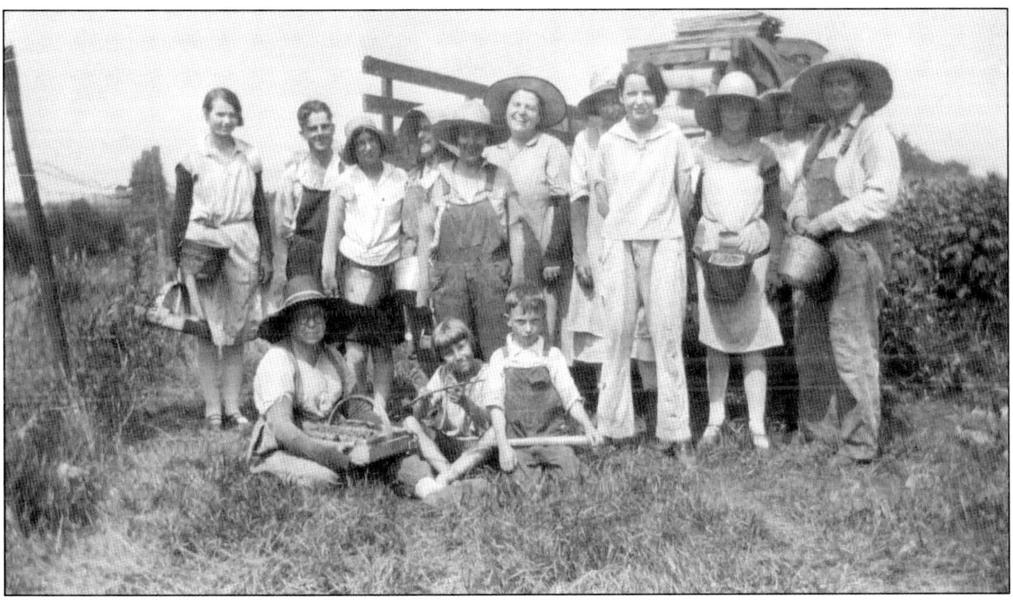

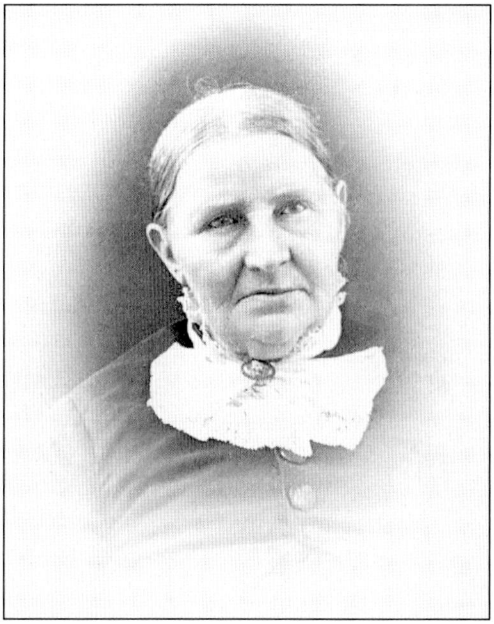 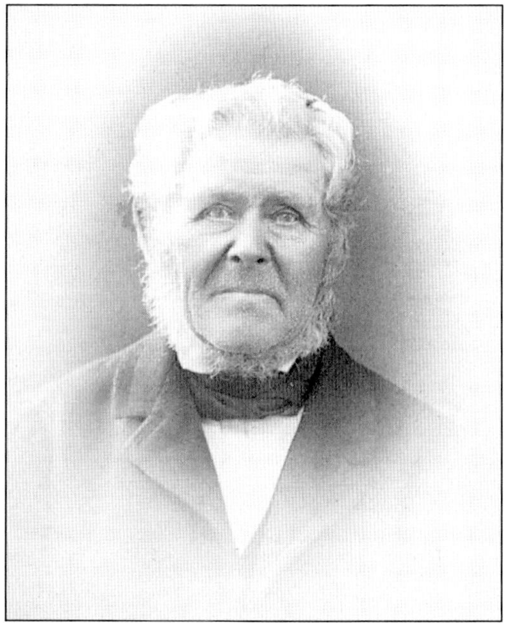

John Maas and his wife, Johanna, came to Webster from Holland in the mid–19th century. They settled on the west side of Salt Road across from where the Webster Golf Club is today. They built a vernacular-style farmhouse and had fields of strawberries and raspberries as their cash crop. (Courtesy of Dolores Maas Zimmer and Teresa Young.)

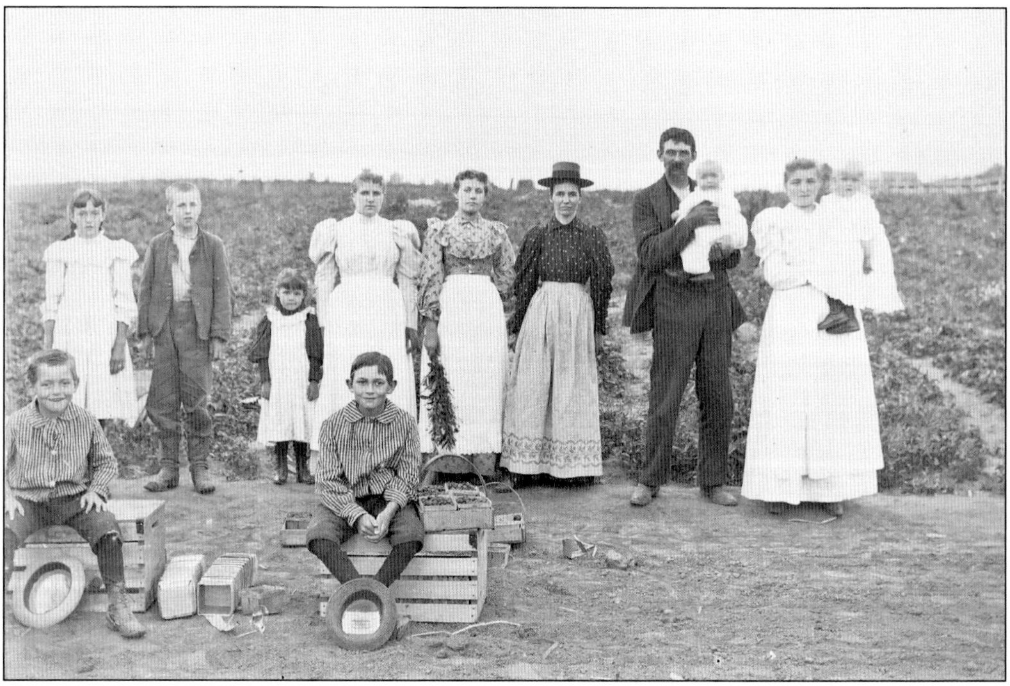

Henry Maas, son of John Sr., is shown holding his son Clarence, and his wife, Eugenia, is holding their son Elmer on the far right of the photograph after a day of harvesting the fruit. The farm had pigs, chickens, and horses, and hay and grain were also cultivated as feed for the animals. (Courtesy of Dolores Maas Zimmer and Teresa Young.)

A second son, John Maas Jr., born in 1850, was an early Webster photographer as well as a carpenter. This glass plate negative photograph shows a self-portrait of John Maas Jr. with two of his nieces Gertrude and Emma Maas. It was taken in his workshop, a building next to the main house on Salt Road. The tools of his carpentry trade surround them. (Courtesy of Dolores Maas Zimmer and Teresa Young.)

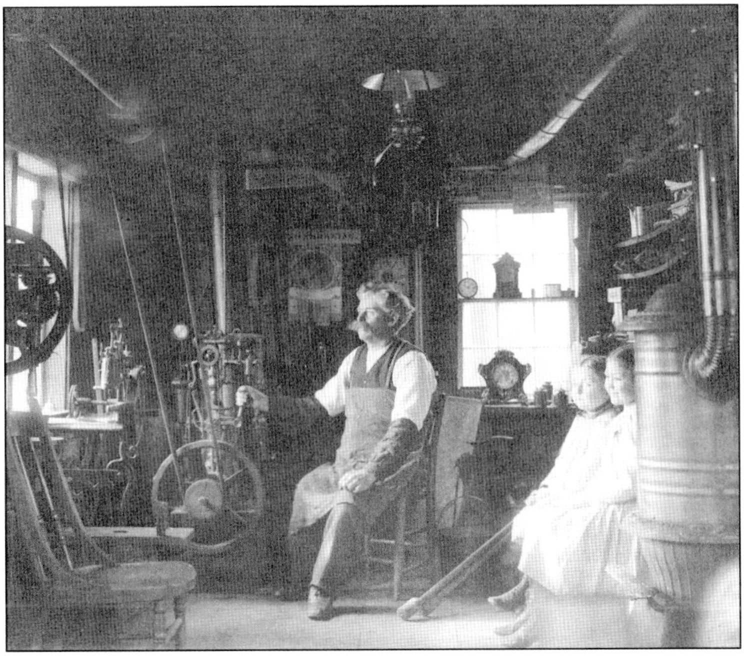

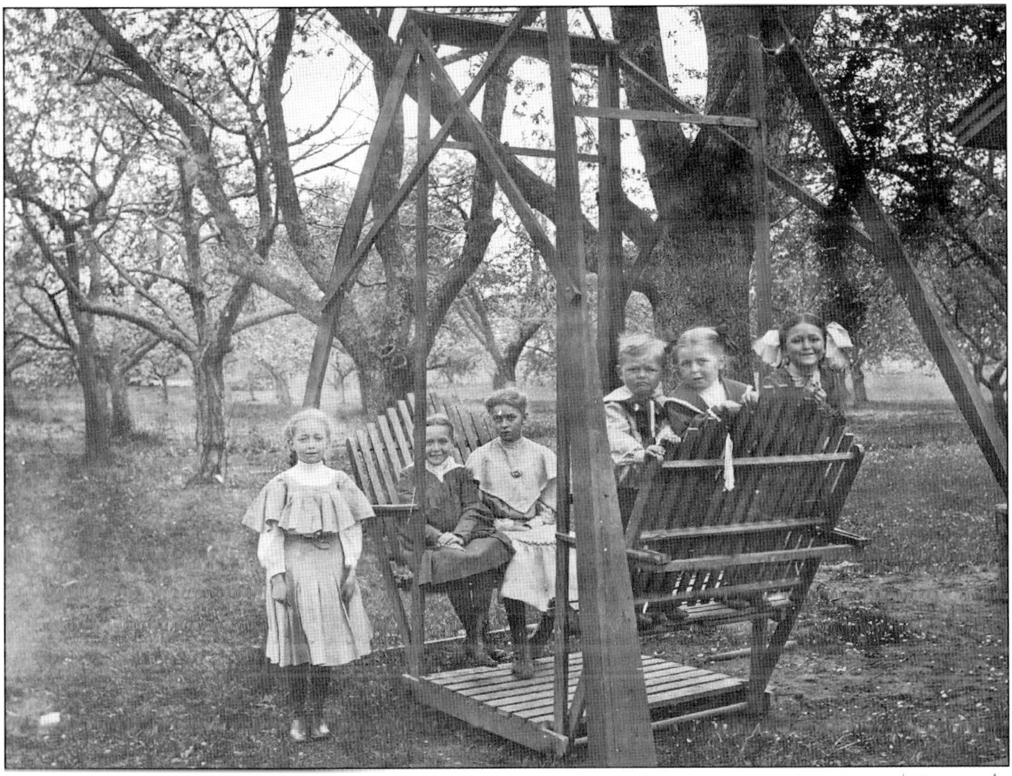

Emma (standing) was born in 1895, and her siblings Mary, Flora, George, Agnes, and Gertrude Maas are the children playing on the wooden swing that John Maas Jr. built on the farmstead. The Maas family operated the farm until 1924. (Courtesy of Dolores Maas Zimmer and Teresa Young.)

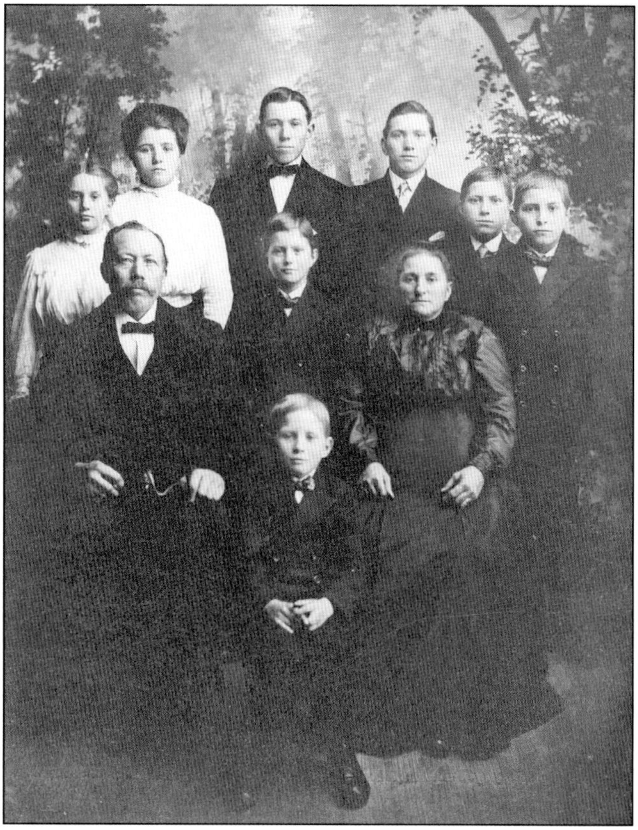

The Anton Bischoping family had moved to Webster prior to 1900 and purchased a farm on Phillips Road with 50 acres. They grew potatoes, tomatoes, and apples. The family portrait shows, from left to right, (first row, seated) John; (second row) Anton, Joe, and Mary; (third row) Elizabeth, Theresa, Fred, Frank, and twins Edward and Albert. (Courtesy of the Bischoping family.)

This photograph, dated 1906, features the August Merz family. Their farm was on Ridge Road, where today the Atlantic Restaurant is located. From left to right are (first row, seated) August and Anna; (second row) children Elmer, Emma, George, Anna, and Clarence. August was a farmer and was known for his apple cider. He bought barrels from a Canadian whiskey manufacturer, and the cider was infused with additional flavor. (Courtesy of the Merz family.)

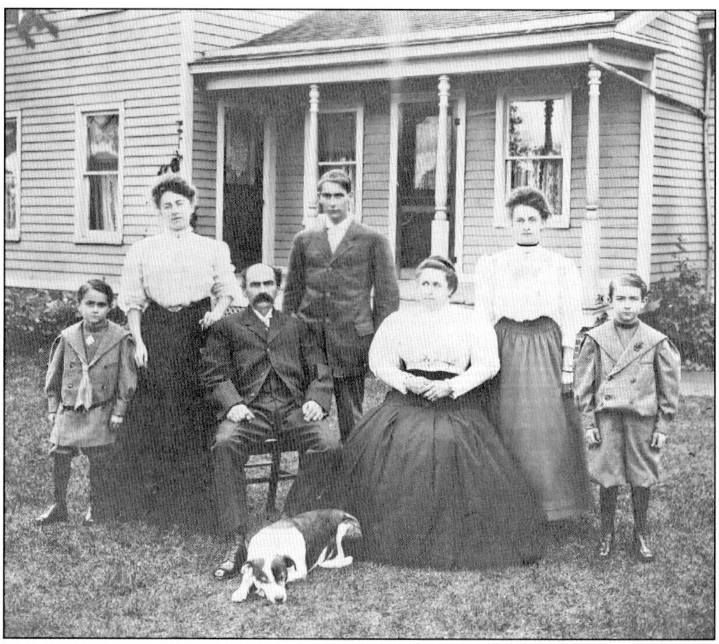

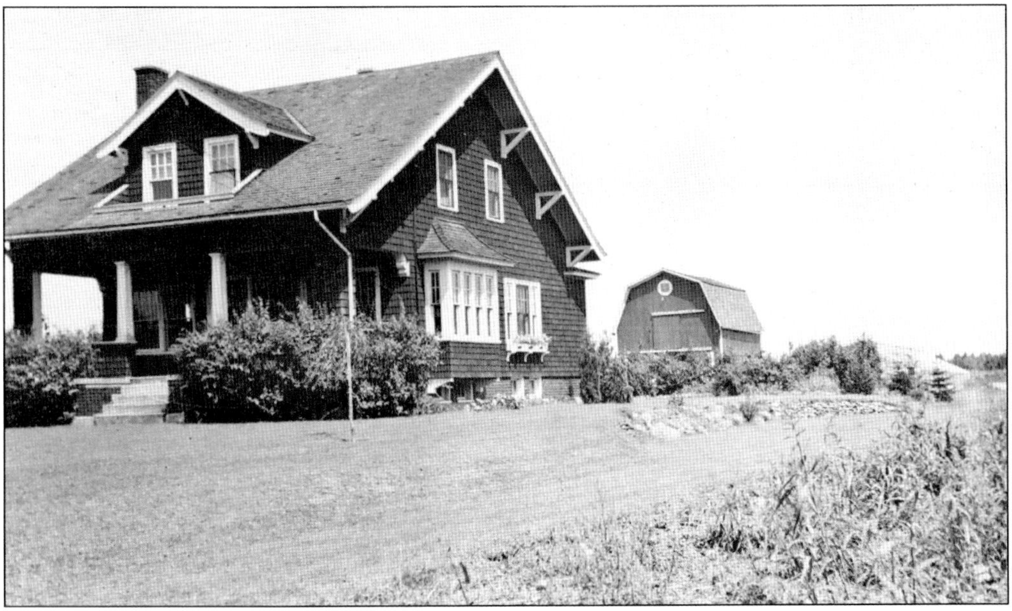

Harvey Mayer built 710 Five Mile Line Road, a brown cedar shingled bungalow in the arts and crafts style, for his wife as a gift. She died before it was completed during the flu epidemic after World War I. The house was eventually sold to the Metcalfe family in 1924. Ward Metcalfe was responsible for bringing electricity to the area, his house and farm being the first to have it installed. The Metcalfe farm produced Golden Jubilee and Fischer peaches, cherries, and pears. They were famous for growing long-stemmed dahlias, shipped in rough Webster-made coffin boxes, to markets in New York City. The picture at right, taken in 1937, shows Ward Jr. and Lois Metcalfe with baskets of peaches. (Courtesy of Lois Metcalfe Bircher.)

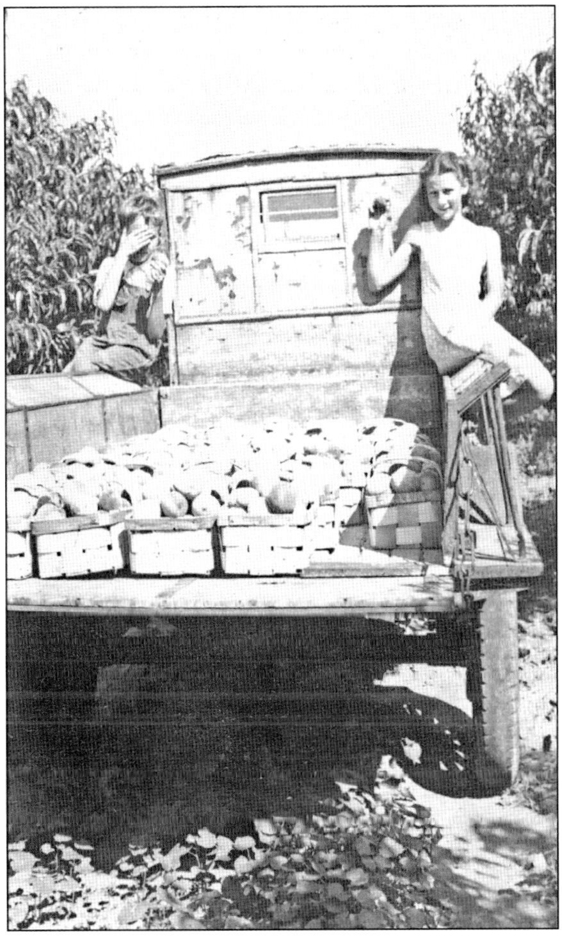

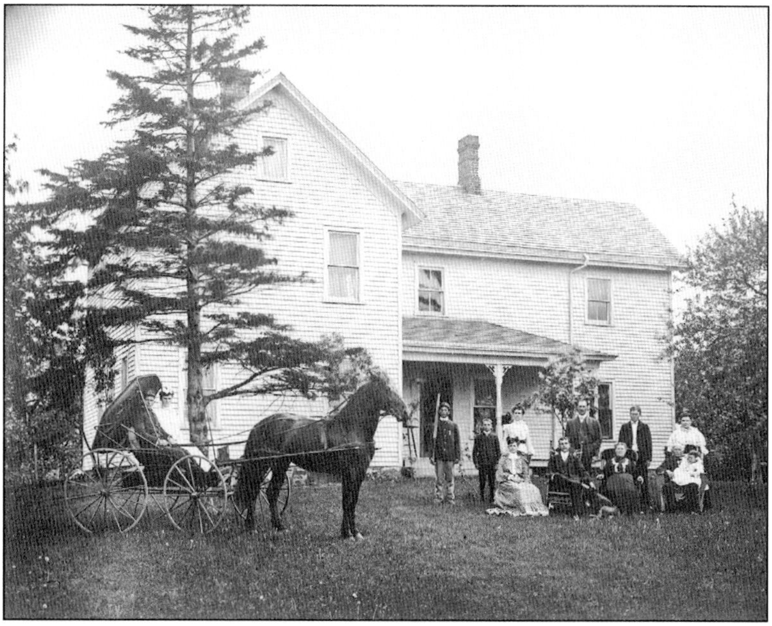

Johann "Georg" Schlegel and his wife, Salome, and six children, emigrated to Webster from Germany around 1852. They are seen seated to the far right in this photograph. The Schlegel Road was named for son John in recognition of his civil war service. (Courtesy of the Schlegel family.)

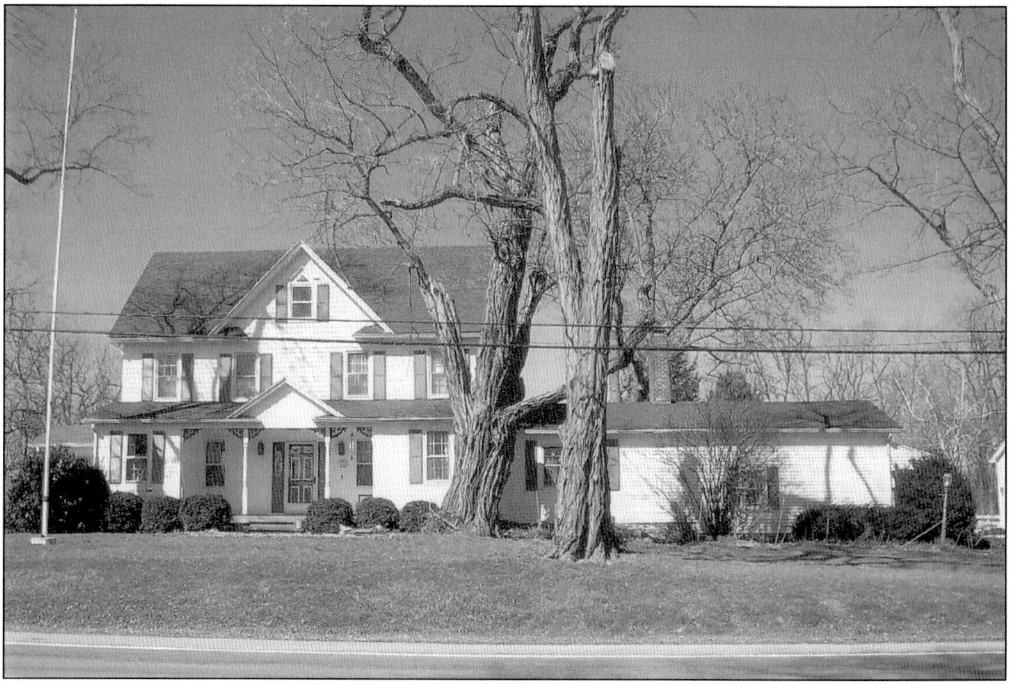

The farmstead at 1826 Lake Road has a Webster connection to the War of 1812. During a naval battle on September 11, 1813, six English ships commanded by Sir James Yeo were attacked by 10 American ships commanded by Commodore Isaac Chauncy. One of the cannonballs fired during the encounter was plowed up by Henry Barnard, the owner of the property in 1927. It was a 32-pound cannonball, the size used by the Americans. This farm was also the first electric test farm in the nation sponsored by Westinghouse Electric Company and Rochester Gas and Electric Company. The farmhouse kitchen, dairy milk house, and barns were mechanized to take the drudgery out of the daily chores of the farm.

Four

HAMLETS OF WEBSTER

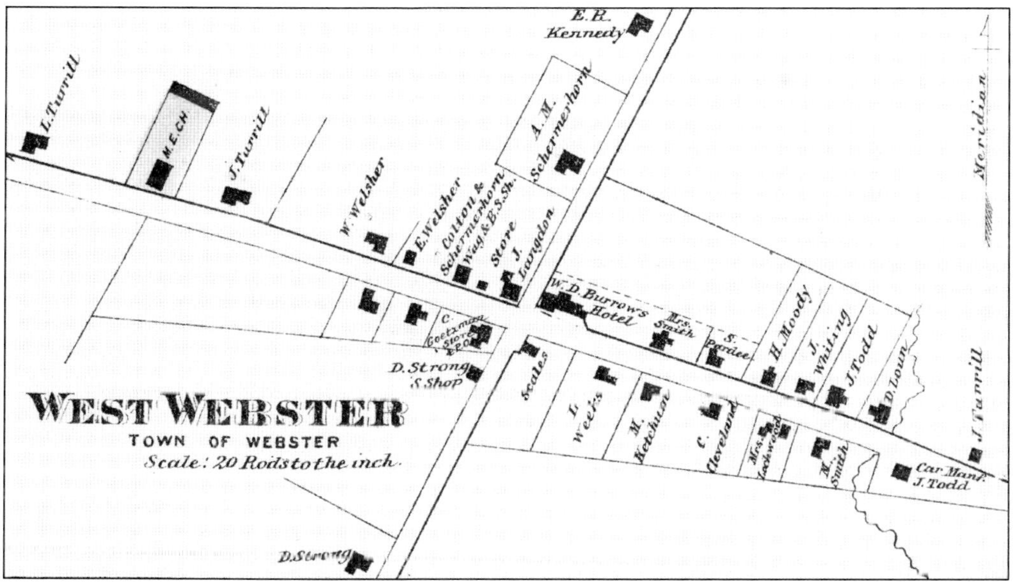

The town of Webster comprises 34 square miles. Several hamlets were settled in the eastern, western, and northern sections of the town. Because of the concentration of people living there, these hamlets had post offices or train stations of their own, which helped to define them as a separate community. This map shows the hamlet of West Webster taken from the 1872 Atlas of Monroe County, New York by F. W. Beers and Company.

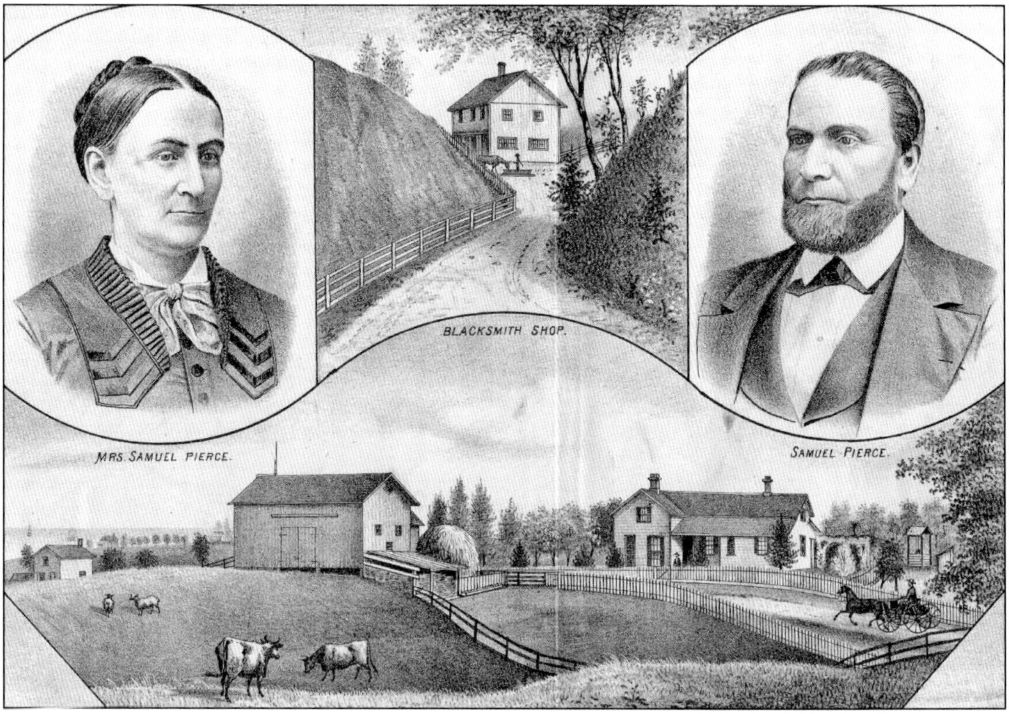

Samuel Pierce and his wife were important Webster residents as shown by these engravings from the Monroe County Atlas of 1877. The Pierce home was built c. 1820 and had 17 rooms at 566 Bay Road. One of Webster's earliest blacksmith shops was owned by Mr. Pierce and located on the corner of Bay Road and Lake Road. They also had a brick-making business.

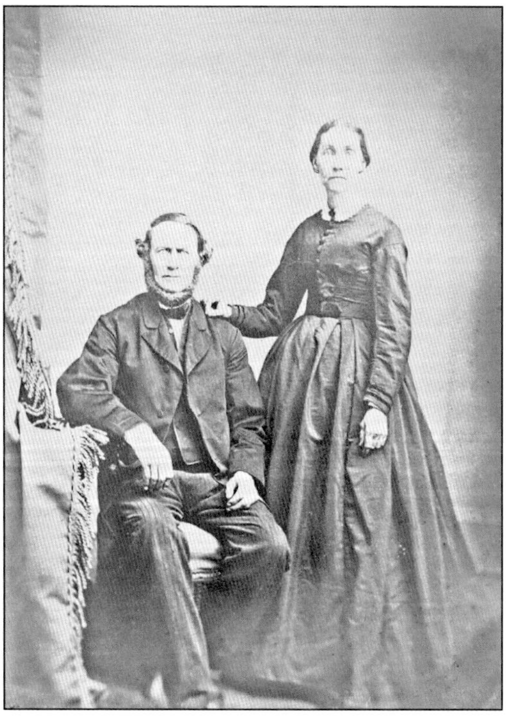

Seba Granger, in 1846, purchased approximately 26 acres of land on the east side of what is now Bay Road, a mile south of Lake Ontario. On February 23, 1847, at age 33, he and Marie Murphy were married. He was a carpenter and built a small home. As his family grew, he constructed a two-story addition. Granger died in 1887, leaving the property to his wife and three surviving daughters. (Courtesy of the Granger Holtz family.)

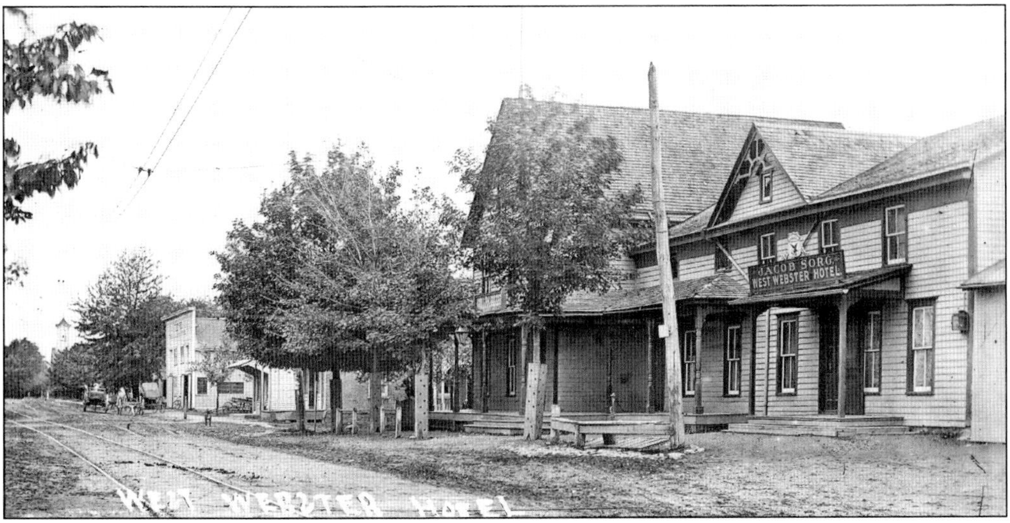

A c. 1828 tavern was erected of cobblestones on the northeast corner of Ridge Road and Gravel Road, the location of the Jade Palace today. The cobblestone tavern burned around 1877, and a Stagecoach Inn was built in 1883, seen in this picture on the right. A short distance to the west is the business of the Todd brothers, a horse shoeing and general repair shop. In the distance is the spire of the original United Methodist Church, built in 1859.

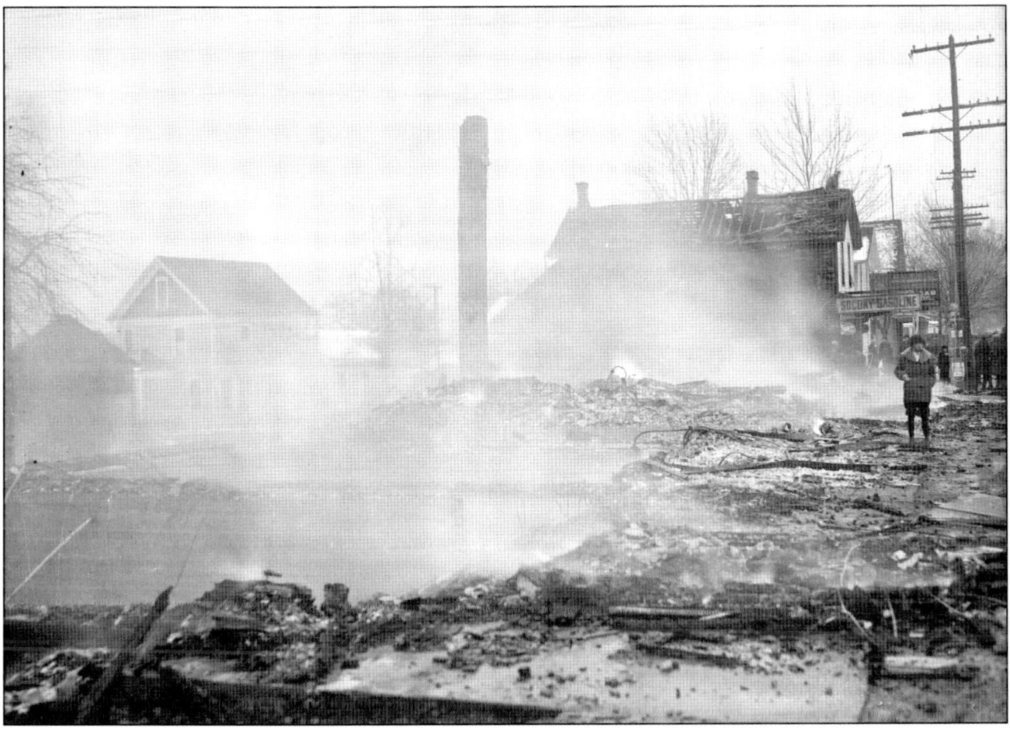

The heart of the business section in West Webster was heavily damaged by a fire on January 15, 1925. They believe it started from an oil stove that exploded in a barbershop. The fire displaced five families and several businesses. Two buildings were destroyed and a third heavily damaged. The blaze was controlled by area fire companies just prior to the cisterns and wells going dry. (Courtesy of the Albert R. Stone Negative collection, Rochester Museum and Science Center.)

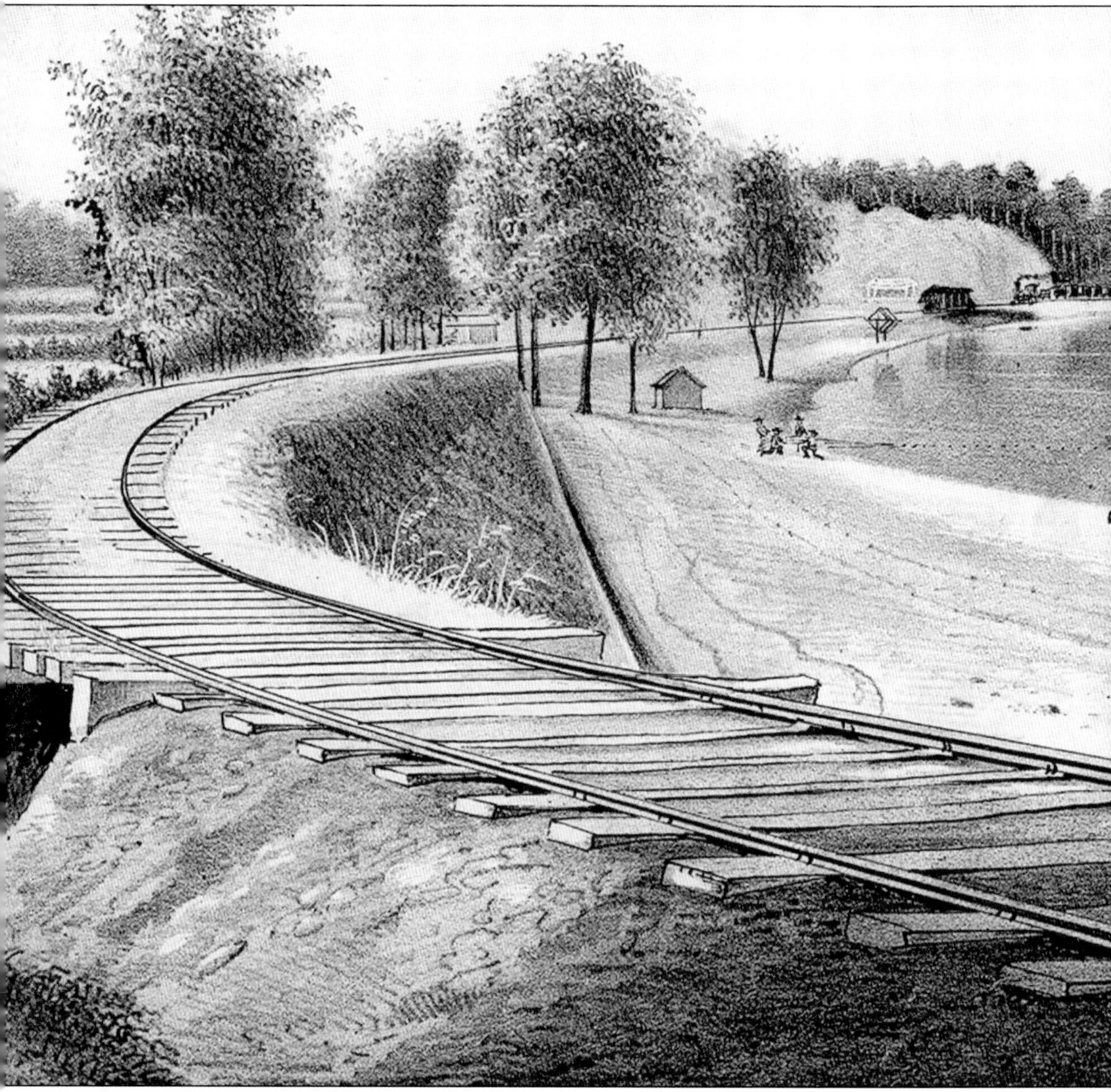

Samuel Pierce donated a land parcel for the railroad right-of-way with the stipulation that a station be erected on the Pierce property and named for the family. The 1877 Monroe County atlas shows a view from Pierce's Station looking west past the underpass to Oklahoma Beach.

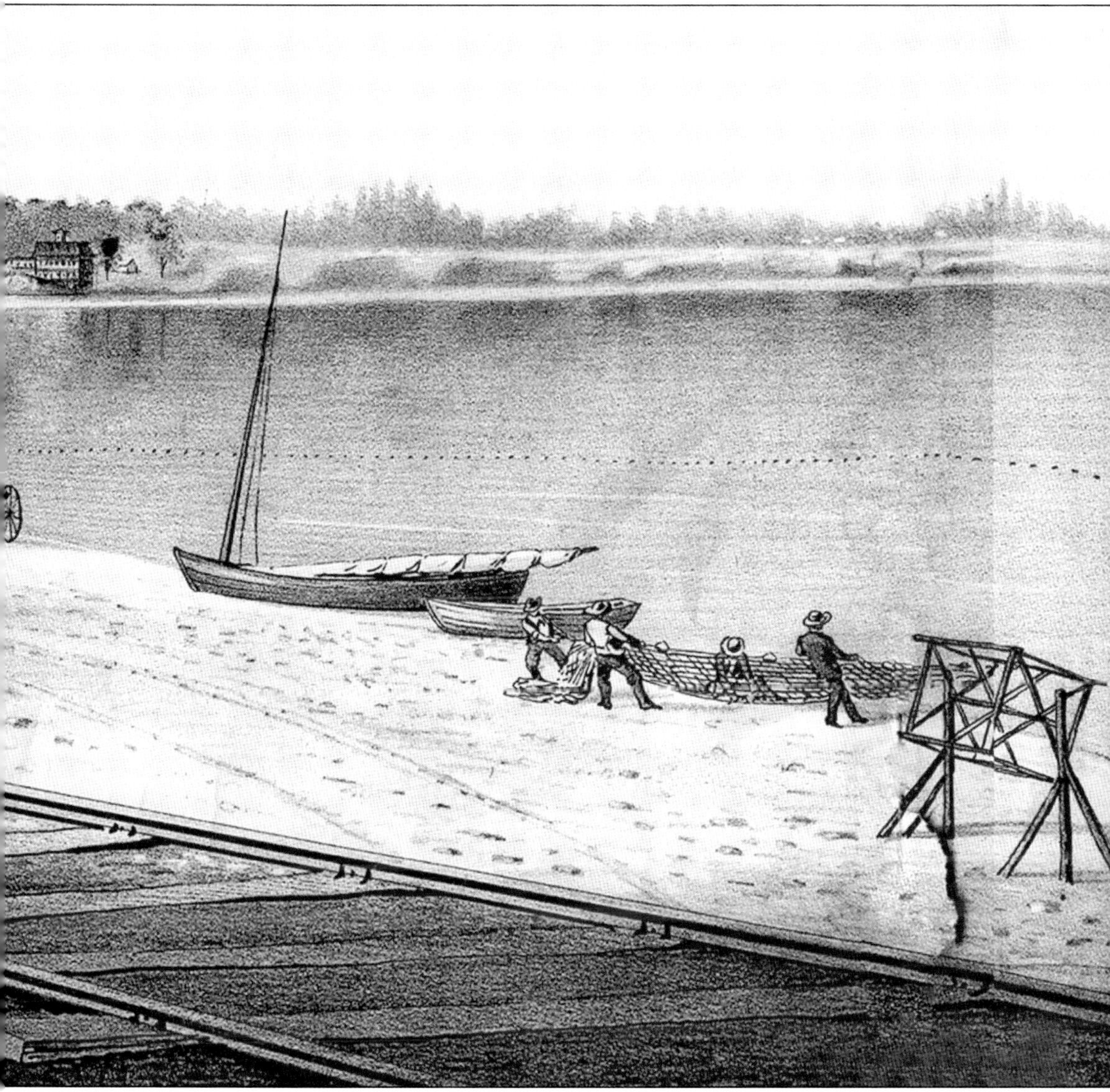

Commercial fishermen are pulling nets in from Lake Ontario. The fishing net winder is shown in the foreground that was used to dry and store the nets. The entrance to Oklahoma Beach is under the railroad trestle, shown far left.

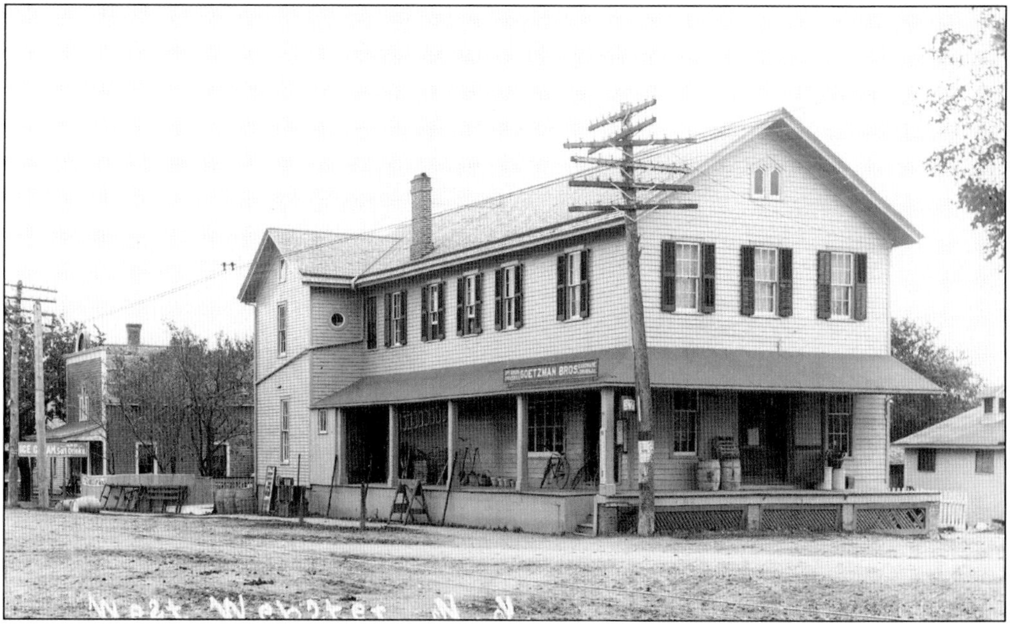

Charles Goetzman constructed this building around 1874. He was appointed postmaster and served for several years while conducting a large mercantile business. He served as Webster supervisor from 1881 to 1884. In 1934, the West Webster Fire Department purchased the building.

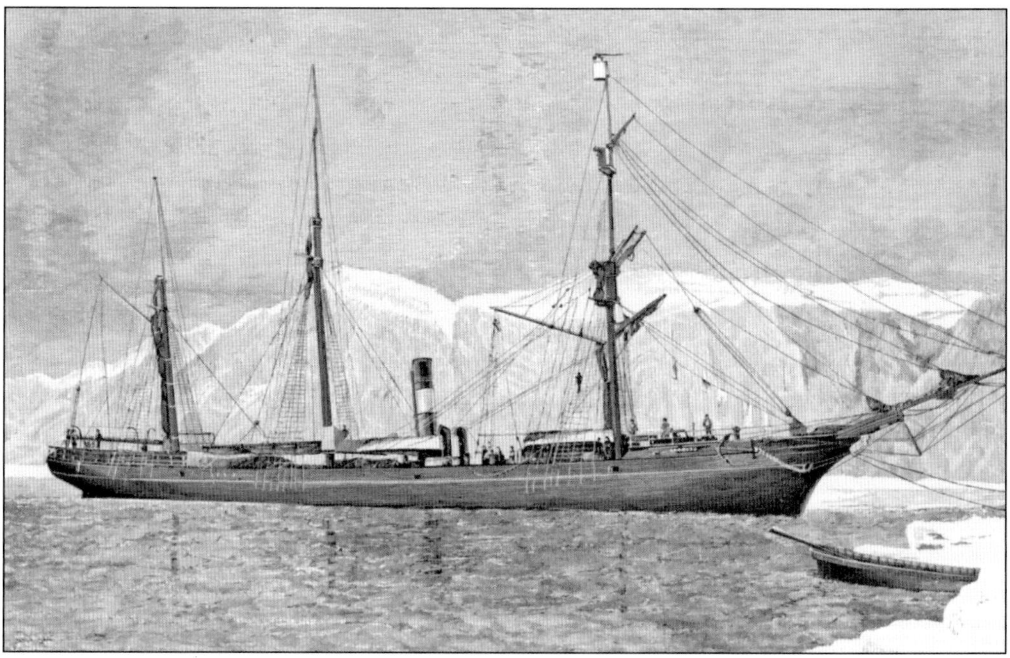

William Cottreall was the Webster resident who coined the name, "Oklahoma," for the Lake Ontario beach where his popular hotel stood. In his early years, he was a U.S. Navy seaman involved with the rescue of the Greely Polar Expedition to Lady Franklin Bay in the Arctic. This important army expedition (1881–1884) set a new record for "Farthest North" and gathered much scientific data. But the men were beset by illness, injury, starvation, and purportedly, cannibalism. This woodcut features their ship, the USS *Proteus*.

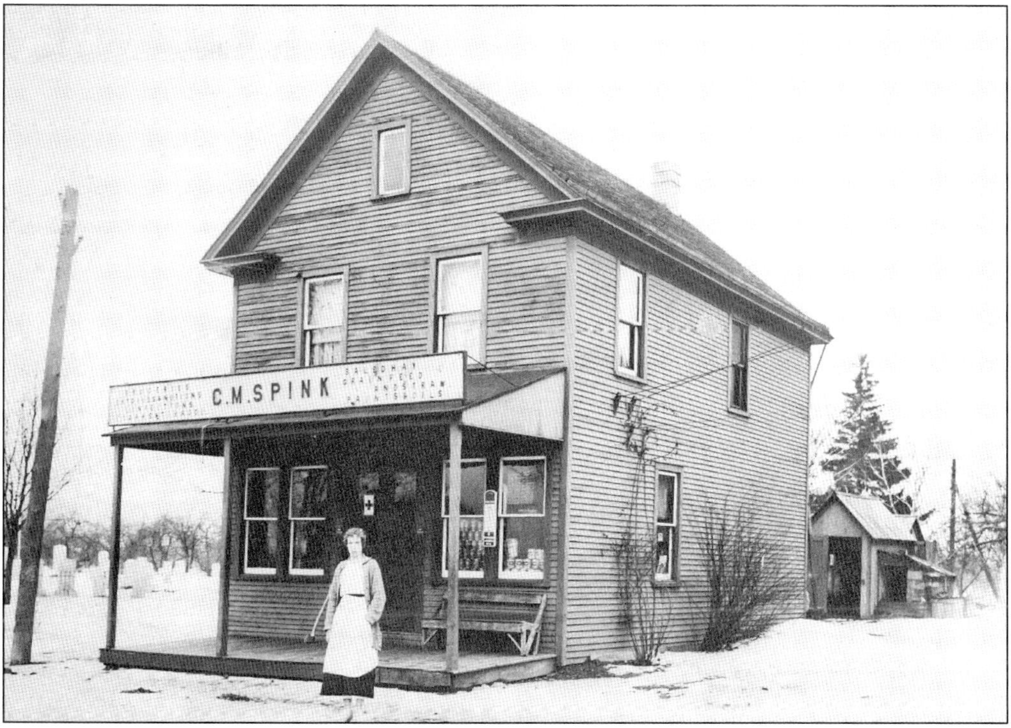

Spink's Store was located on the corner of Ridge Road and Maple Drive in West Webster. Maple Drive was called Cemetery Road at the time. This store was owned by Claude Spink. Ruth Spink is standing in front of the building. The general store carried a variety of items including feed, straw, flour, cigars, dry goods, and groceries, and it also made deliveries. Claude Spink operated a Maxwell Automobile Agency, shown below, in this promotional calendar for 1916. Maxwell was considered one of the top three automobiles in America, along with Buick and Ford. In 1921, Walter R. Chrysler took a controlling interest in Maxwell Motors, and in 1925, the Chrysler Corporation was formed and the Maxwell was retooled into the first Plymouth automobile.

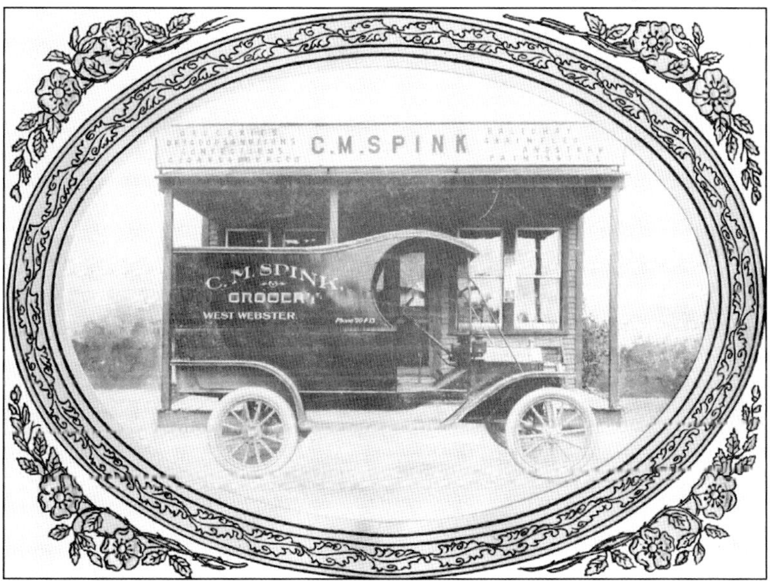

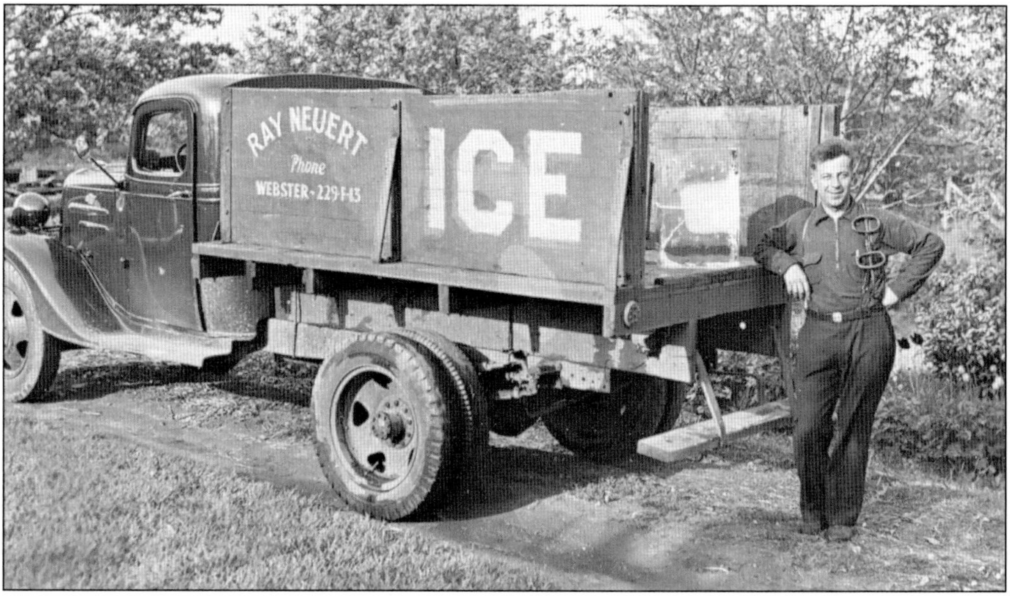

Raymond Neuert operated an ice delivery route in the summer months before mechanical refrigeration was widely used. He had about 250 customers in the neighborhoods of Webster, Penfield, Forest Lawn, West Webster, Nine Mile Point, and Union Hill. The ice was delivered once or twice a week as needed. A card would be placed in the window to alert the iceman that more ice was needed. (Courtesy of the Webster Museum and Historical Society)

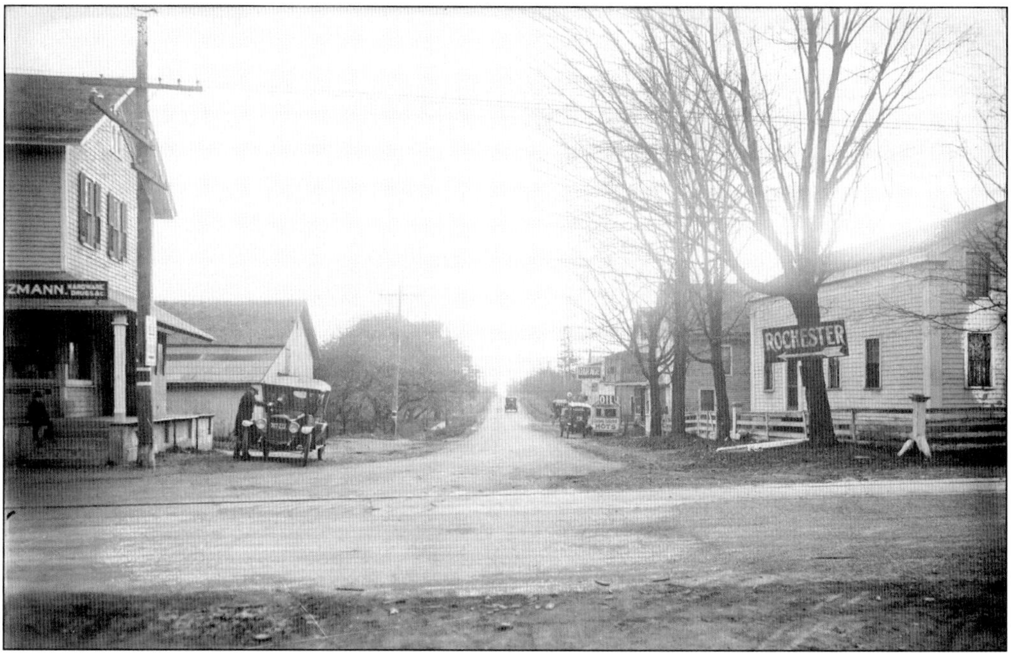

This is a photograph from the early part of the 20th century. It shows the intersection of Ridge Road and Gravel Road looking south through the orchards. The sign on the tree points your way to the float bridge at the southern end of Irondequoit Bay and on to Rochester. The bridge was actually a floating bridge attached by chains to the shoreline. (Courtesy of the Albert R. Stone Negative Collection, Rochester Museum and Science Center.)

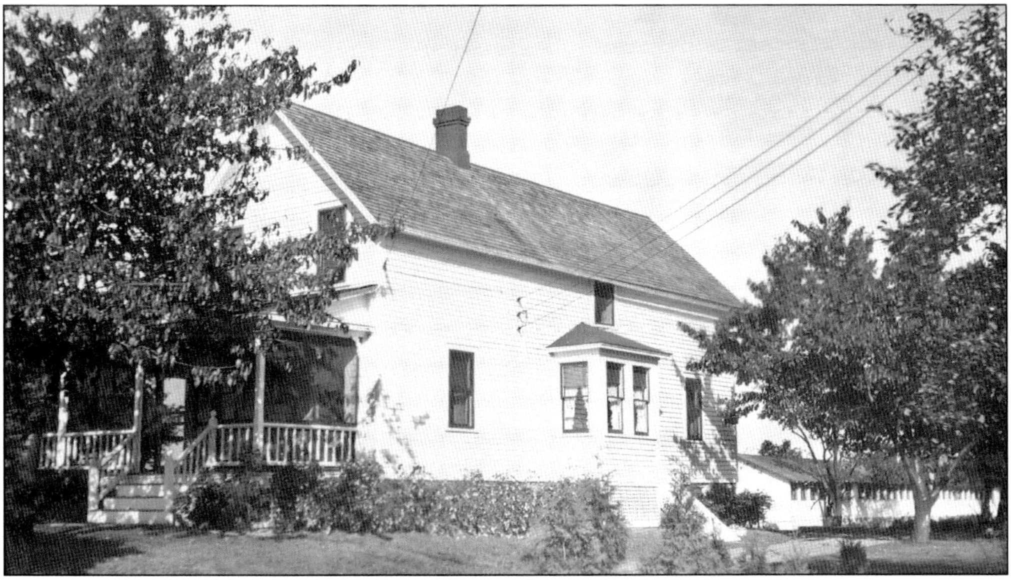

The Reiber brothers, Edwin and Oscar, created a unique bird reserve on their property at Bay Road in West Webster. The picture above, taken in 1923, shows the long, low workshop in the back of the house, which still stands today. (Courtesy of the Reiber family.)

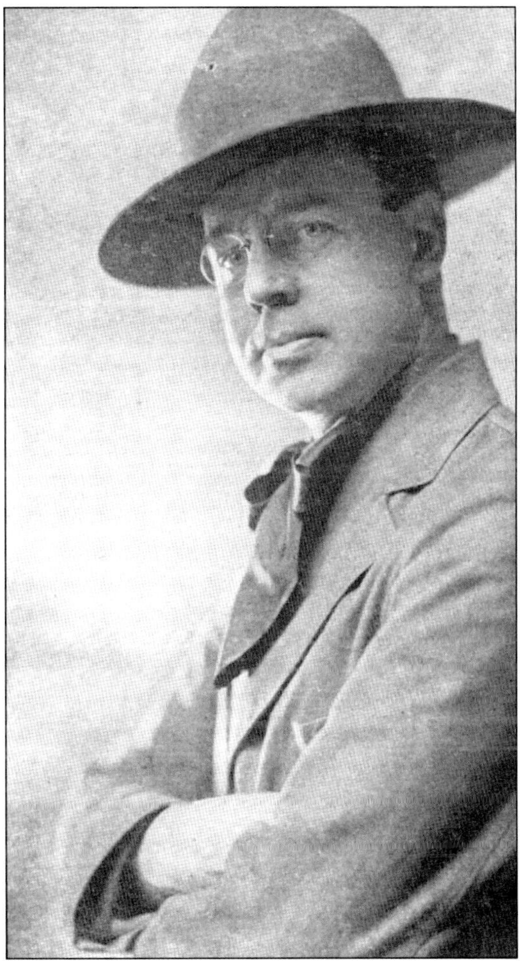

Edwin "the Birdman" Reiber, an ornithologist and taxidermist of note, spent the greatest part of his life studying birds, their habits, and the natural conditions under which they thrive. The Reiber brothers developed an extensive array of birdhouses specific to blue birds, owls, tree swallows, chickadees, wrens, and purple martins. The aim was to artificially reproduce the conditions where wild birds would nest and raise their young. (Courtesy of the Reiber family.)

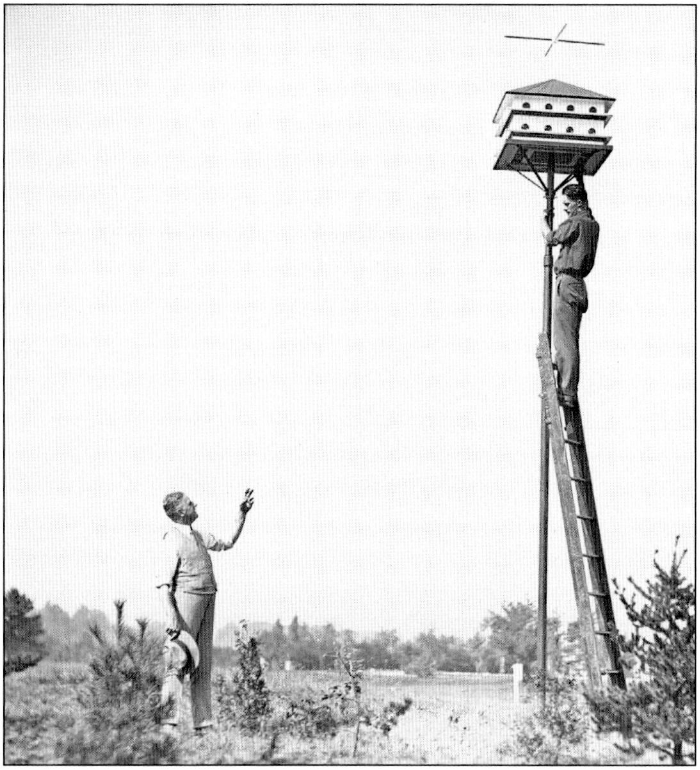

Because birds are excellent at controlling insects, birdhouses were installed on estates, at country clubs, cemeteries, parks, and private homes throughout the United States and Canada. The Reiber family remembers the brothers being paid for their work on the Ford estate in Michigan with a new Ford car. Oscar Reiber—business partner and brother of Edwin—and Ralph—son of Oscar—pictured at left installing a purple martin birdhouse. (Courtesy of the Reiber family.)

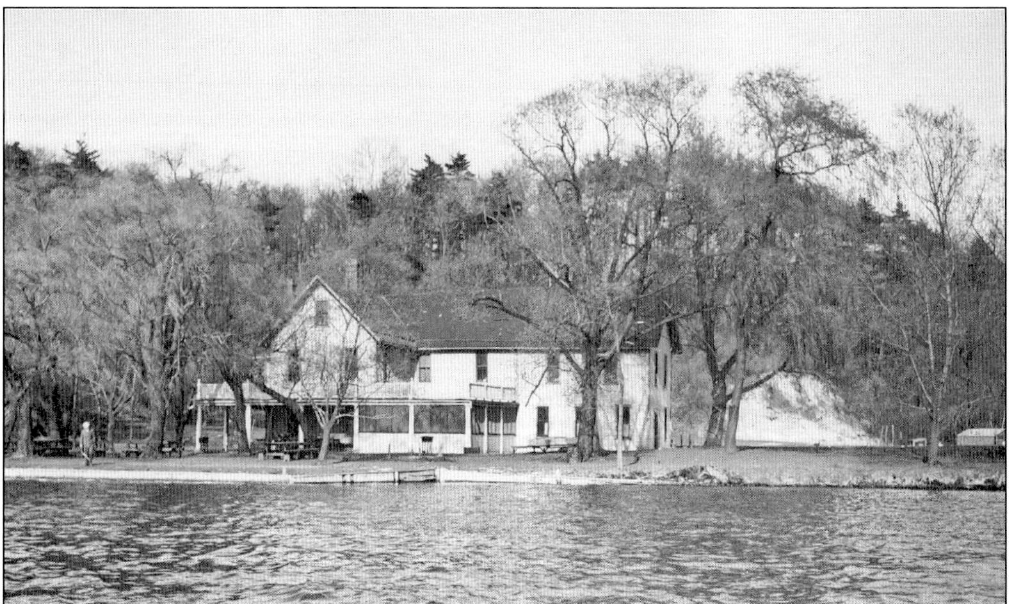

In 1846, John Drake bought the Calvin Cleavland farm. It was located west of the Bay Road and included shoreline on Irondequoit Bay. He built a large hotel, which boasted a ballroom and a long veranda situated so boats could be rowed right up to the front porch. The name was changed to Glen Edith and purchased in 1926 by the Anthony Orlen family. (Courtesy of the Orlen family.)

This plate map from 1902 was produced by J. M. Lathrop and Roger H. Pidgeon and shows the hamlet of Union Hill, the most eastern settlement in the town of Webster. Union Hill got its name in 1865 when residents living in the area wanted to have its own post office. The name Union Hill reflects the unique character of this Hamlet. The name seemed fitting because it was located on a hill that joined both Monroe and Wayne Counties.

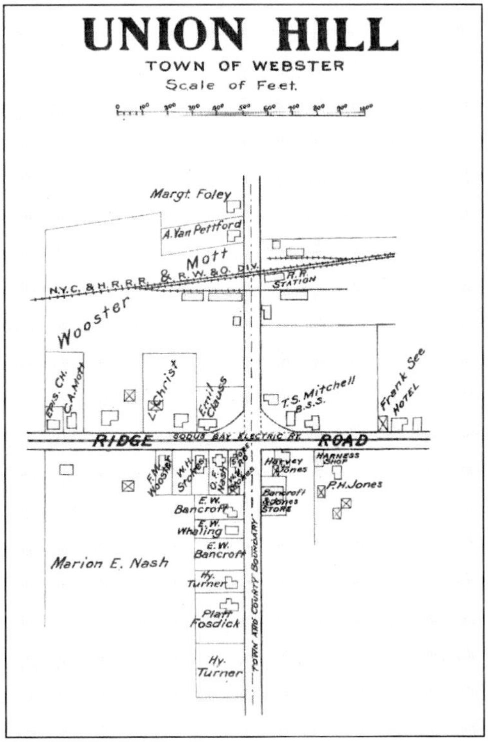

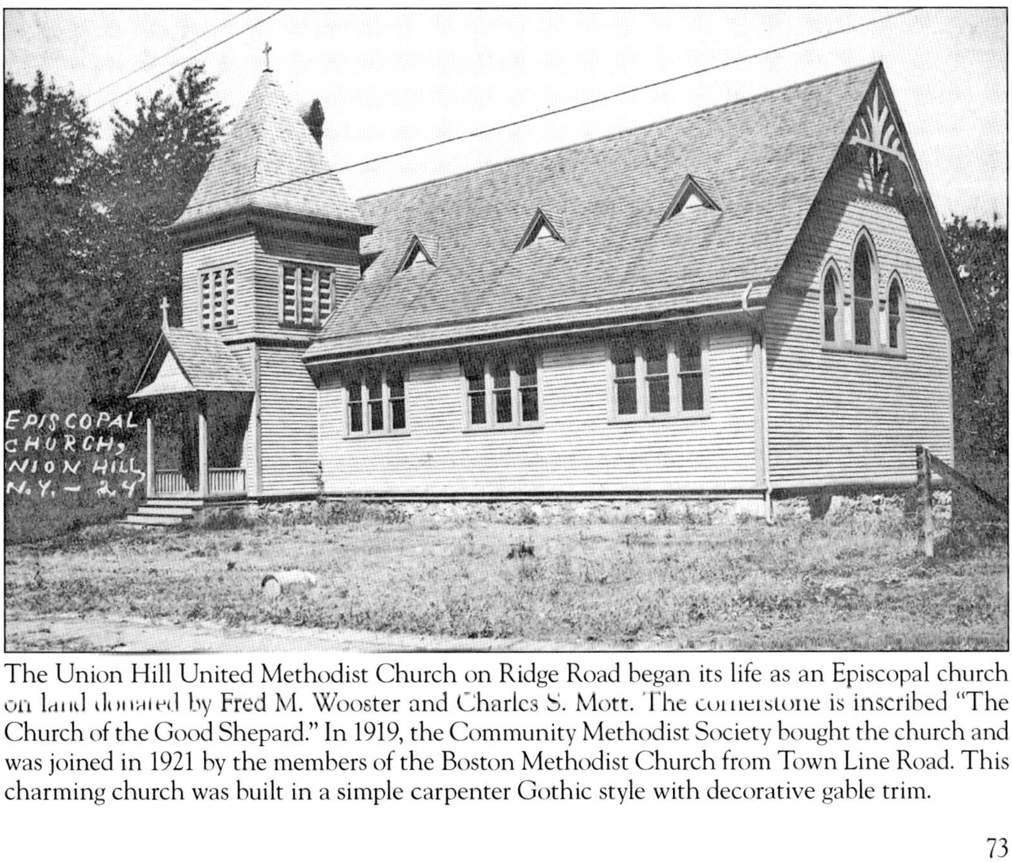

The Union Hill United Methodist Church on Ridge Road began its life as an Episcopal church on land donated by Fred M. Wooster and Charles S. Mott. The cornerstone is inscribed "The Church of the Good Shepard." In 1919, the Community Methodist Society bought the church and was joined in 1921 by the members of the Boston Methodist Church from Town Line Road. This charming church was built in a simple carpenter Gothic style with decorative gable trim.

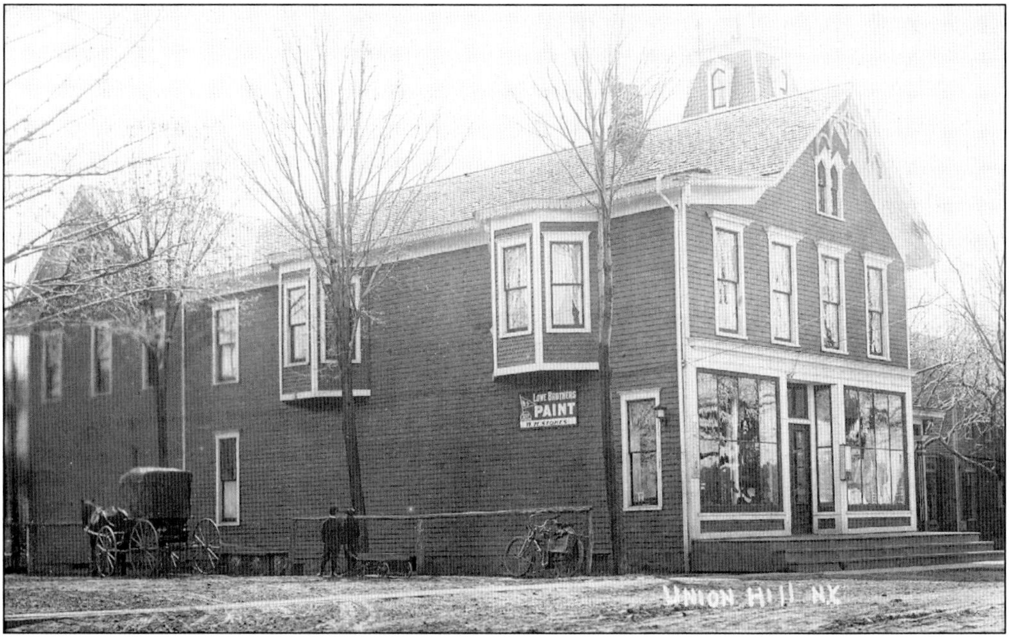

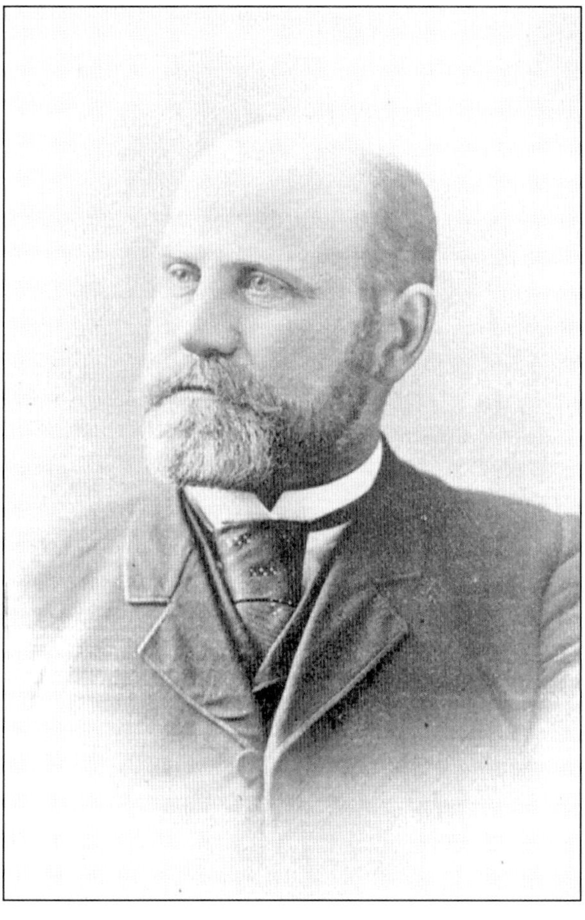

This is the store that was built by Frank M. Jones *c.* 1874. He operated it until 1886 when he sold it to William Stokes. Today it is the very popular Union Hill Country Store where you can get a few groceries or stay for a great meal. It's located on the southwest corner of County Line Road and Ridge Road.

The Honorable Frank M. Jones was born in Union Hill on November 18, 1842. He was a successful business owner and postmaster of Union Hill for 10 years. His general store in Webster Village was considered one of the best in Monroe County. In 1890, while supervisor of the Town of Webster, he was elected to the New York State Assembly. He introduced the bill to build a bridge over the headwater of the St. Lawrence River.

Carl Wooster and his wife, Stella Mae Wooster, are pictured in the family home on the south side of Ridge Road near the County Line Road in Union Hill. Carl Wooster was president of Wooster Fruit Farms, a group of seven area farmers, and also a respected dairyman known for his breeding of Holstein-Freisian cattle. During World War II, he served in Washington D.C. as a marketing chief of the War Food Administration. (Courtesy of John VanAlstyne.)

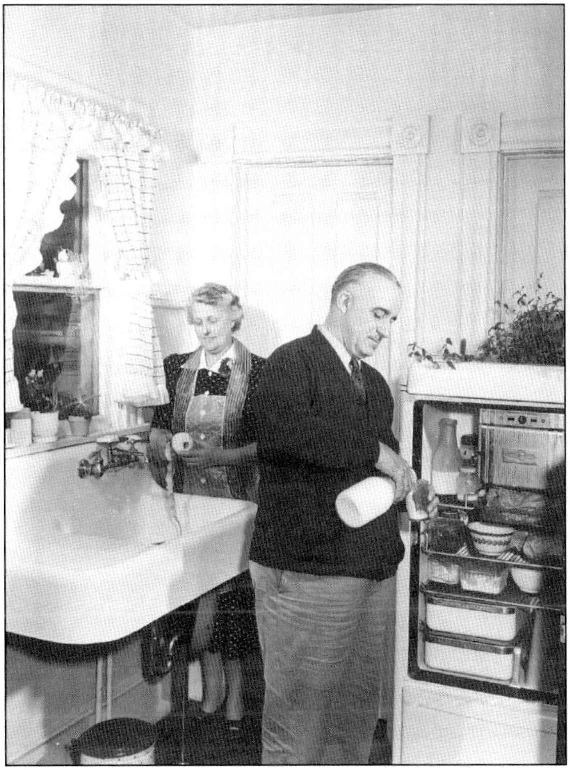

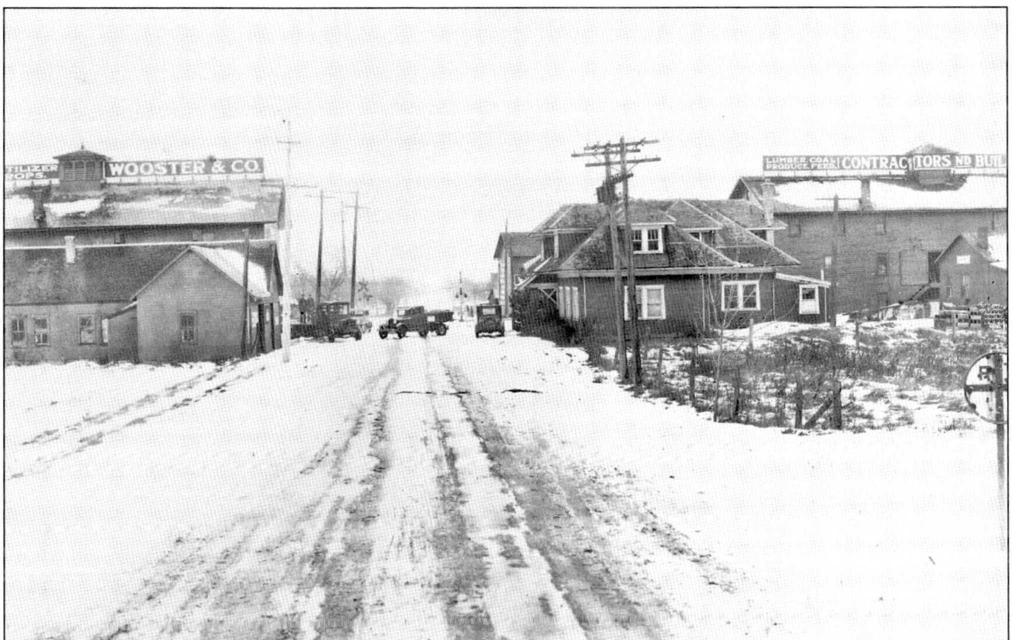

This photograph shows County Line Road, looking north toward Lake Ontario on a snowy day around 1920. The Wooster and Company warehouses are on both sides of the road and were involved with many aspects of agricultural business, selling produce, fertilizer, and building supplies. (Courtesy of John VanAlstyne.)

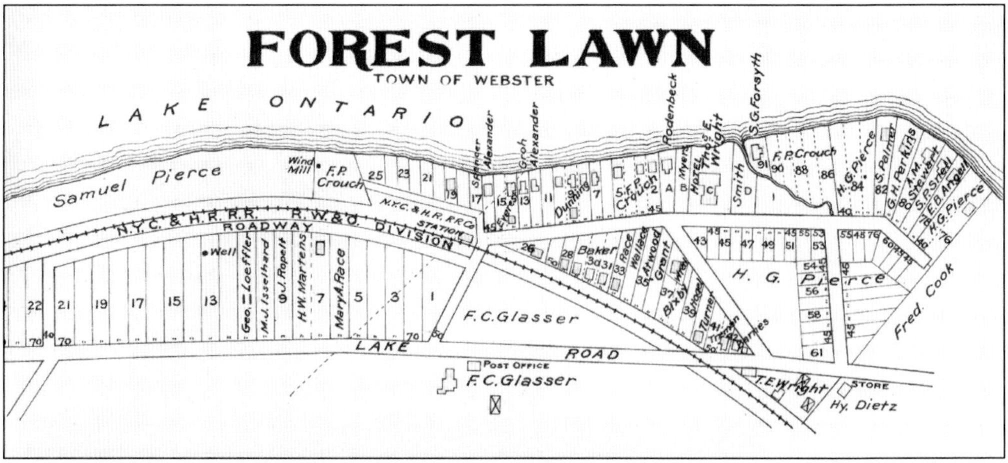

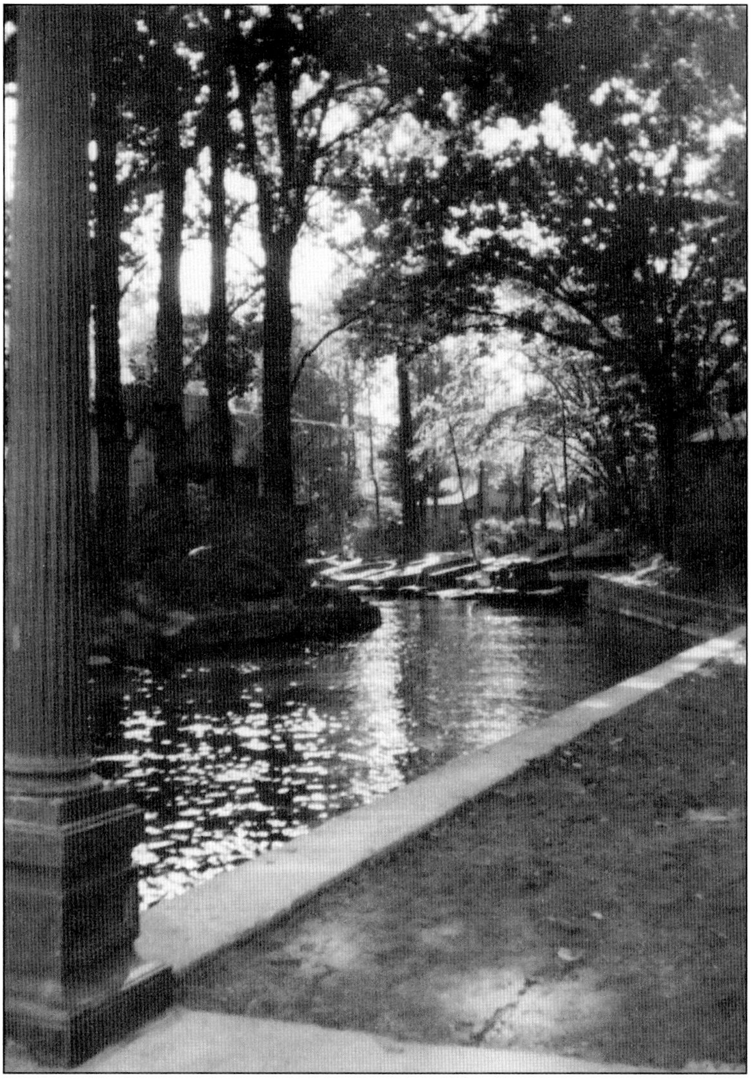

This plate map from 1902 was produced by J. M. Lathrop and Roger H. Pidgeon. One of the most picturesque communities in the town of Webster is the lakeside hamlet of Forest Lawn. Attorneys Horace Pierce, son of Samuel Pierce, with his friend George Forsyth developed the land into a summer vacation community in 1888. The Rome, Watertown, and Ogdensburg Railroad already had a station nearby. The land at the mouth of the Shipbuilders Creek, seen below, was level to the lake, making it a perfect location for a vacation development.

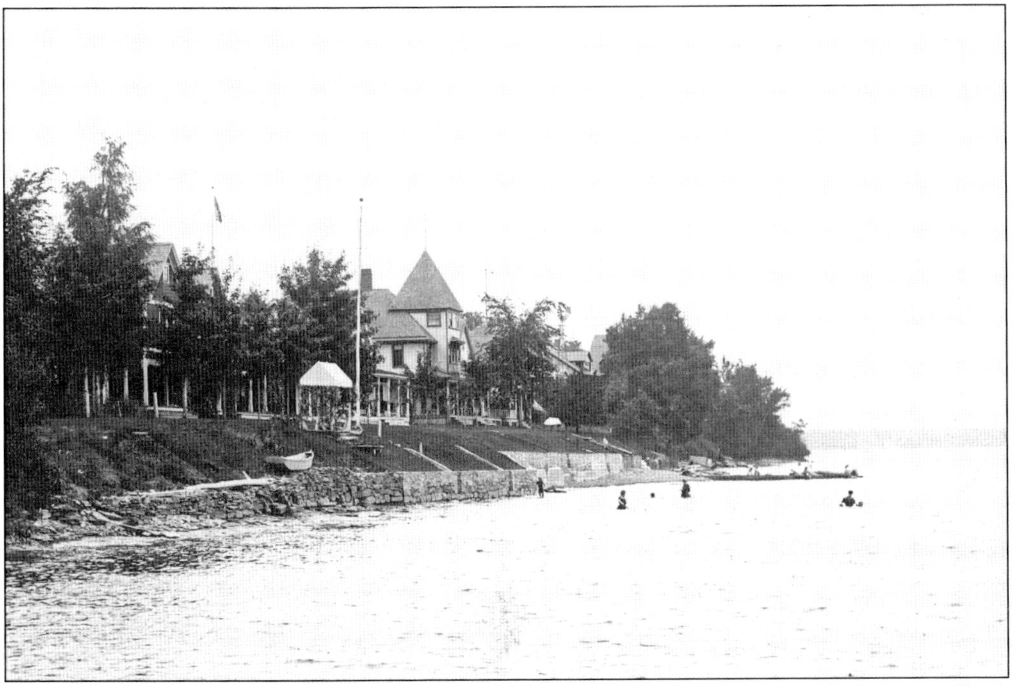

This postcard view shows swimmers in Lake Ontario. The home of Mark and Theresa Pollock Aldridge, which has a square observation tower, is pictured. Built around 1890, the family has owned the house for several generations. (Courtesy of the Robert Holtz family.)

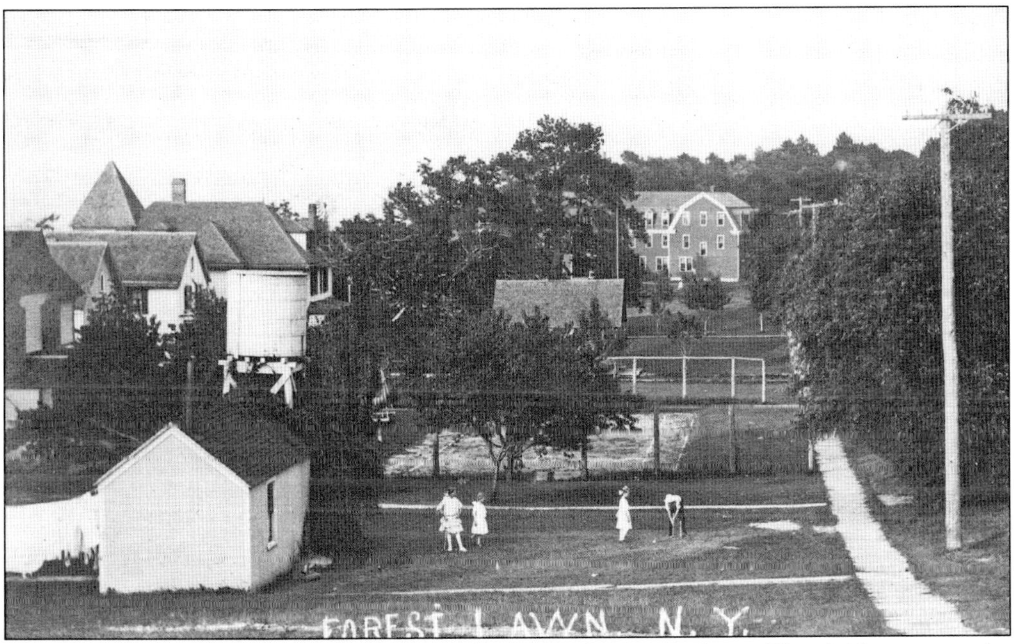

This Forest Lawn postcard shows children playing on the croquet lawn. The clubhouse is in the background, and the white water tank, which provided gravity-fed drinking water, is shown on the left. (Courtesy of the Robert Holtz family.)

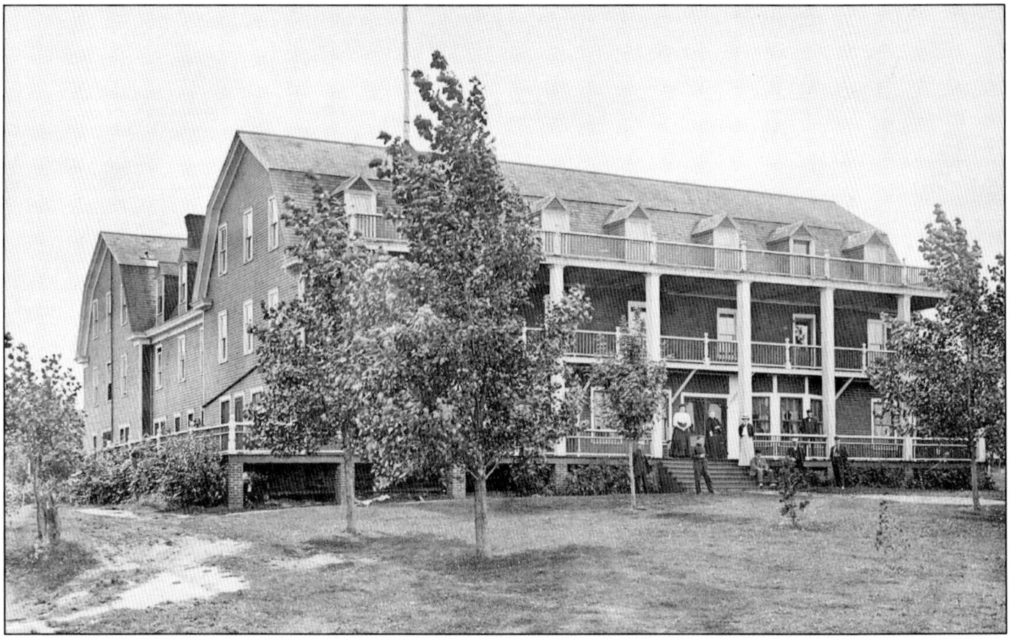

The focal point of Forest Lawn was the clubhouse where members and cottagers could come for meals, weekly dances, and parties. This postcard shows the second clubhouse built, containing 40 rooms. The building was one of the largest structures on the lakeshore and anywhere in the area. The clubhouse was completely destroyed by a raging nighttime fire in 1908 and not rebuilt. (Courtesy of the Robert Holtz family.)

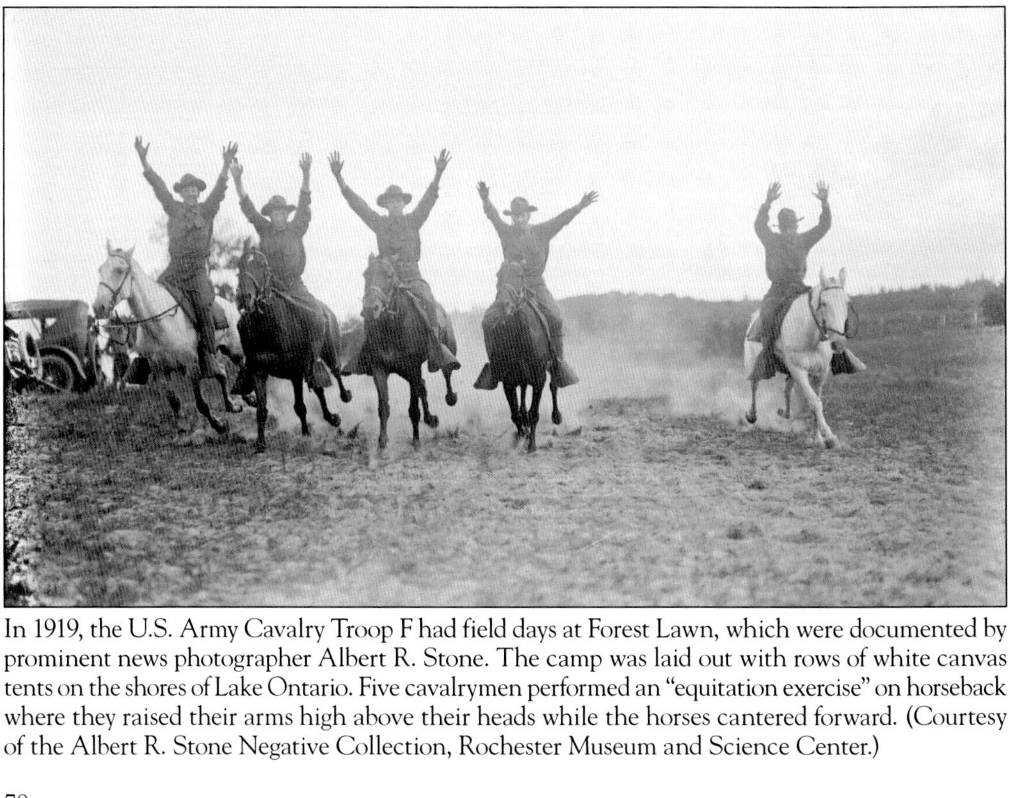

In 1919, the U.S. Army Cavalry Troop F had field days at Forest Lawn, which were documented by prominent news photographer Albert R. Stone. The camp was laid out with rows of white canvas tents on the shores of Lake Ontario. Five cavalrymen performed an "equitation exercise" on horseback where they raised their arms high above their heads while the horses cantered forward. (Courtesy of the Albert R. Stone Negative Collection, Rochester Museum and Science Center.)

Five

TRANSPORTATION

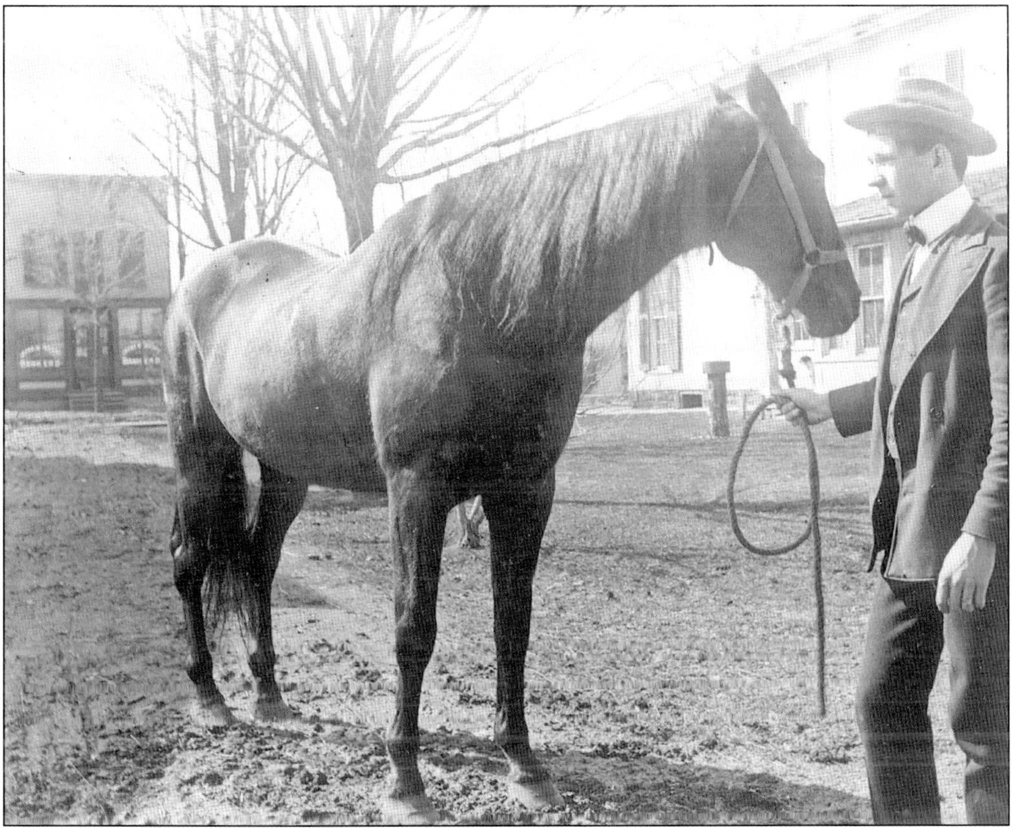

Horses were the most common means of travel in the early years of Webster. They were used to pull wagons and carriages or they were ridden. Nearly every home had a horse. This photograph was taken in the side yard of the Hawley home on South Avenue around 1903, currently the parking lot of the Willard Scott Funeral Home. Notice the first Jayne and Mason Bank, which was across the street.

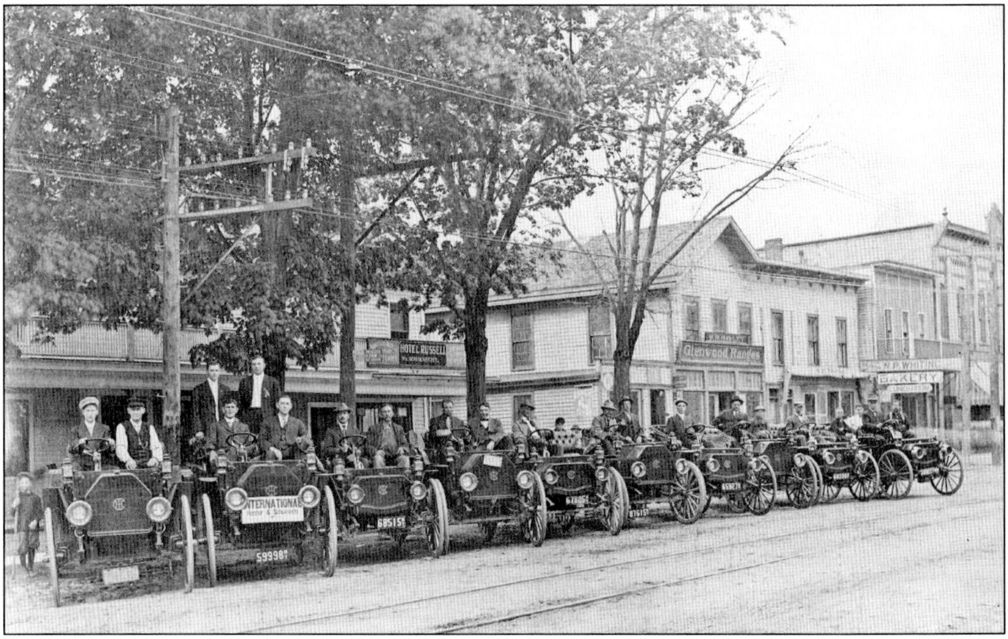

This photograph, taken on West Main Street in front of Hotel Russell, was managed or owned by William Schuknecht in the early 1900s. It shows a variety of models of the International vehicles parked out front. The sign hung on the grill of the second vehicle from left reads, Henner and Schuknecht Agents. (Courtesy of the Reiber family.)

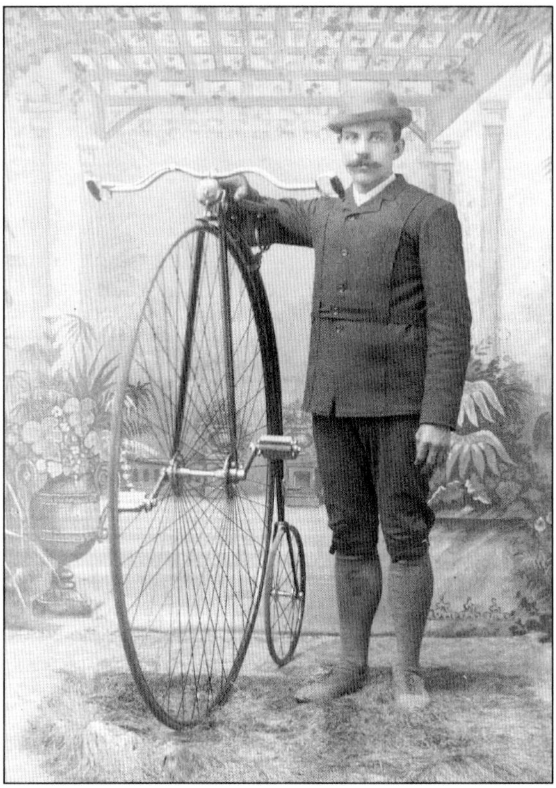

This is a picture of Jacob Neuert posing with his bicycle. The bicycle, a Columbia dating back to 1876, was purchased for the price of $49.50. It was later donated to the Webster Museum and Historical Society where it can be seen today. Relatives of Neuert continue to ride the bicycle for museum events. (Courtesy of the Webster Museum and Historical Society.)

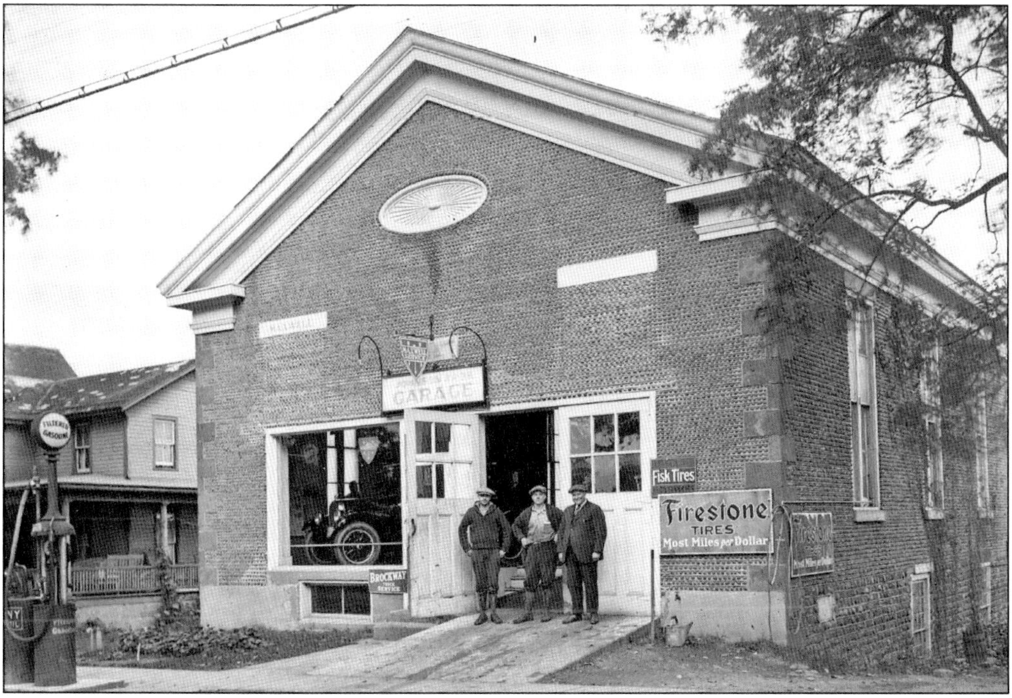

Elmer and Raymond Johnson purchased the former Universalist Church, a cobblestone building, around 1925 and converted it to a garage and car dealership. They sold the Maxwell and Chalmers automobiles, later the Plymouth and Chrysler automobiles. The upstairs was used as a showroom, and the mechanical work was done in the basement. Today the building houses Webster Automotive.

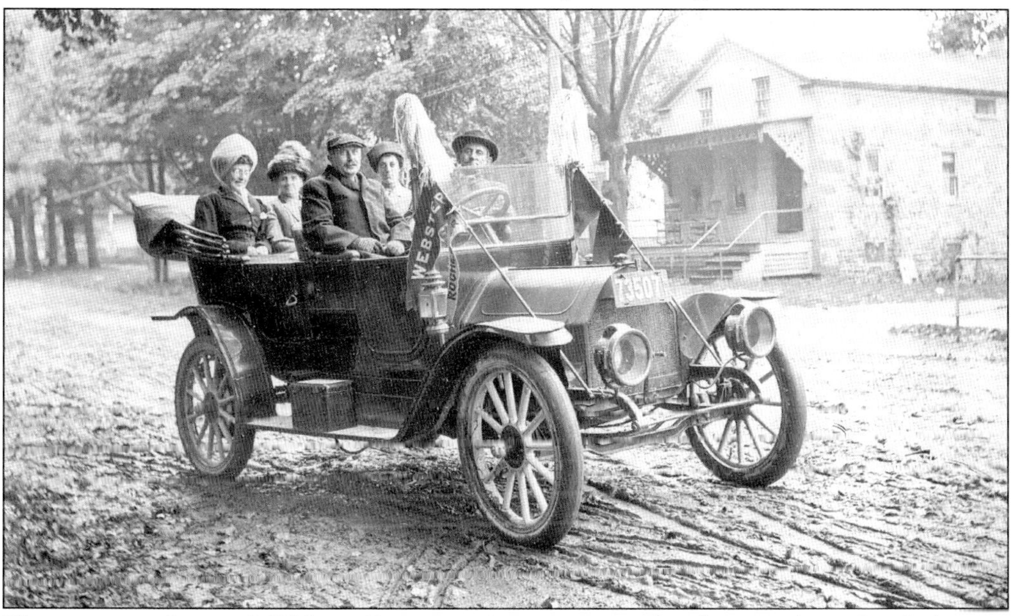

This car, complete with Webster Banner and pom-poms, is heading north on South Avenue near the four corners around 1910. The car was owned by Ansel Wright. Note the early 1830s cobblestone house in the background, which is still standing today. This photograph was taken by George Wall.

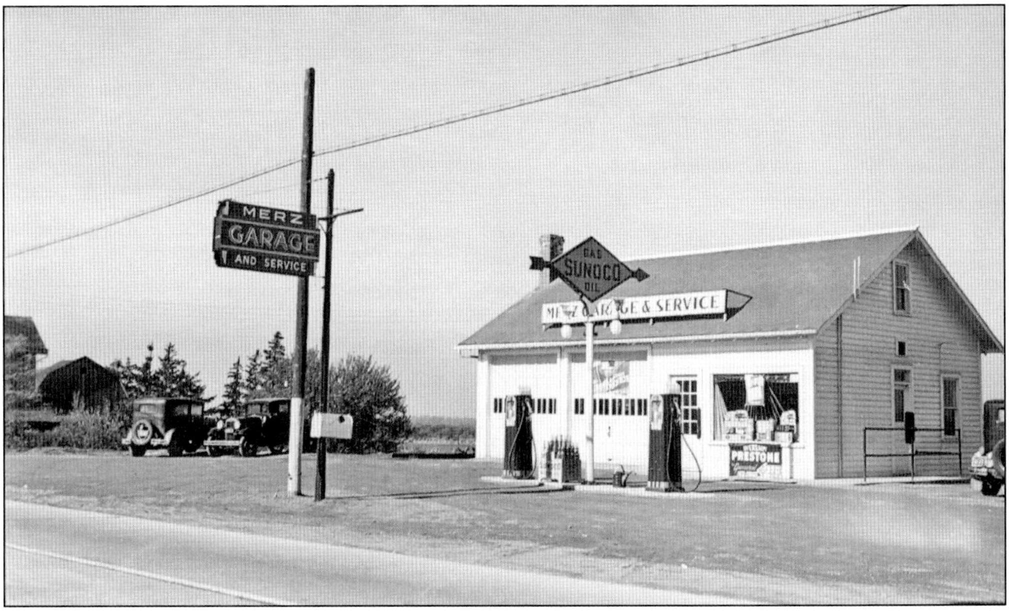

Elmer Merz opened a garage in West Webster on Ridge Road just west of Gravel Road about 1928. In 1936, he built a new garage seen here at 1186 Ridge Road. In the 1940s, his sons Gerry and Robert worked for him. In 1950, Elmer added two bays to the west, and in 1960, his son Robert (Mort) bought the business from him. (Courtesy of the Merz family.)

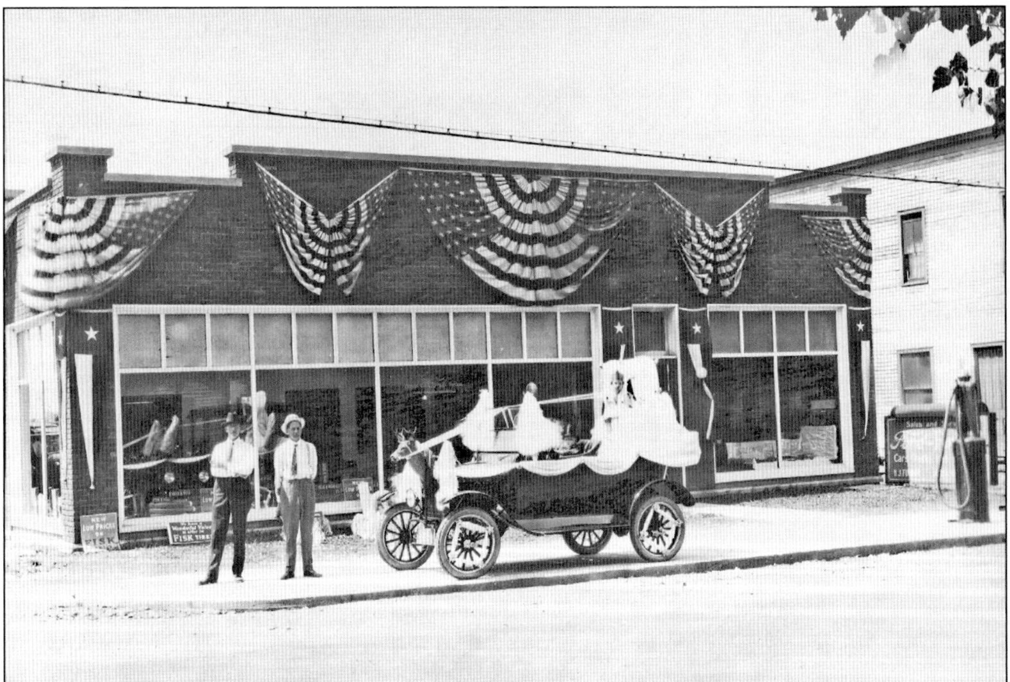

Furber's Ford Agency, located on North Avenue, was built by Herbert J. Furber Sr. of Ontario. Herbert secured the franchise for the Ford cars and trucks in 1915 and opened up shop on Ridge Road in Ontario center. About 1920, he built a branch showroom, service station, and sales office in Webster. Furber is second from the left in this c. 1923 photograph.

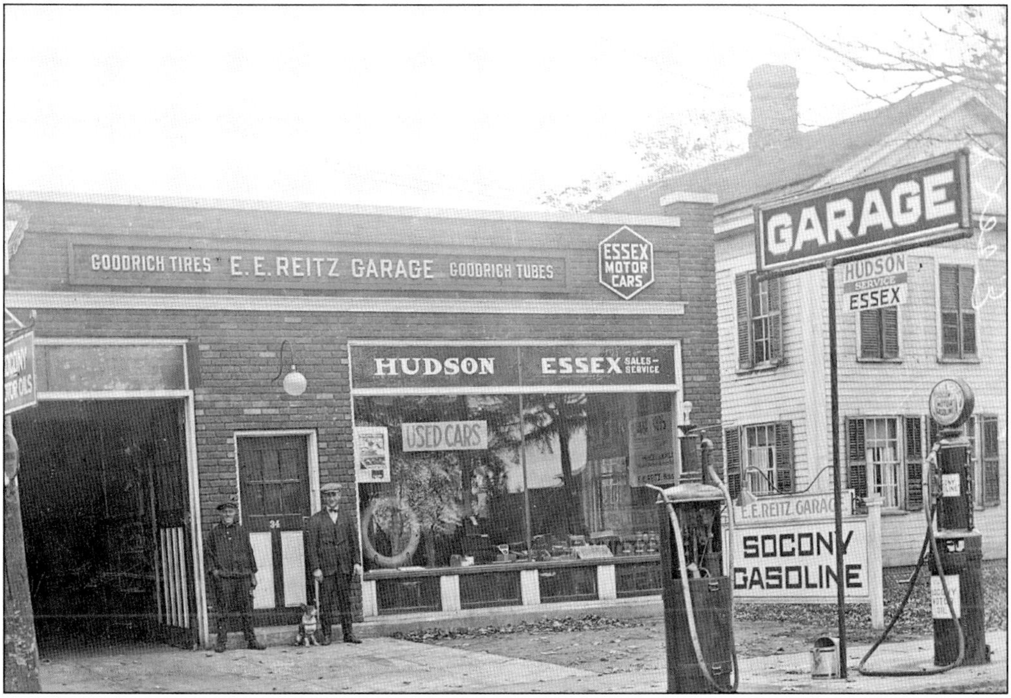

Emil E. Reitz operated an auto-repair shop, which he built around 1915, at 32 West Main Street. He became a Hudson Automobile dealer at the same location, until 1942, when World War II curtailed the automobile business. The postcard above shows the building as it looked before the second-story addition. The photograph below, taken on October 26, 1926, shows the upstairs back office with Emil's wife, Dora, doing some book work with help from the family dog. Today the building houses a bookstore, Yesterday's Muse. (Courtesy of Carol Reitz.)

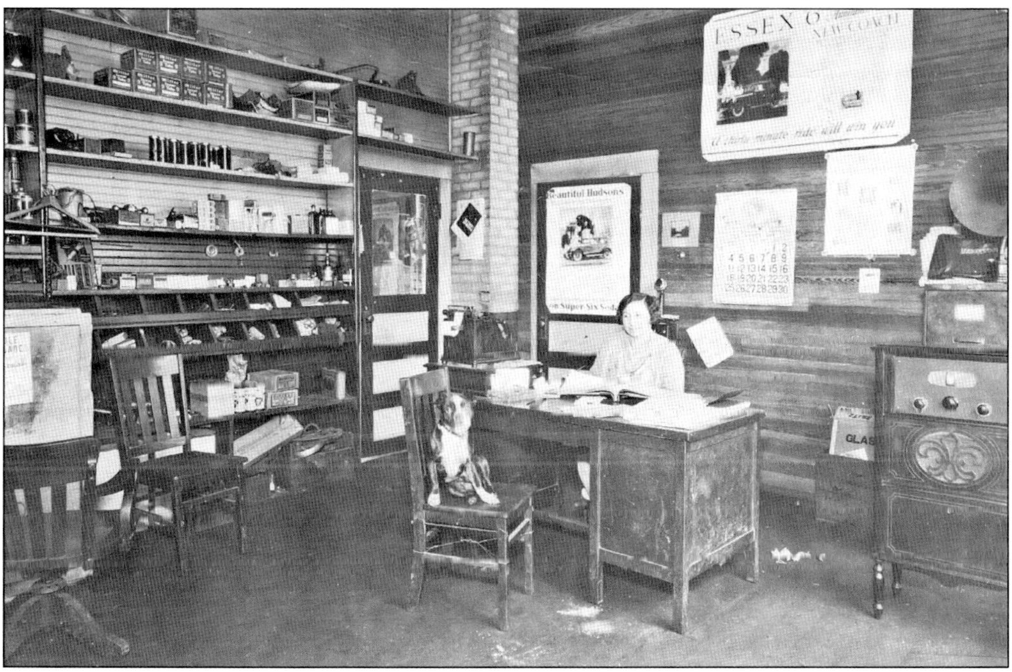

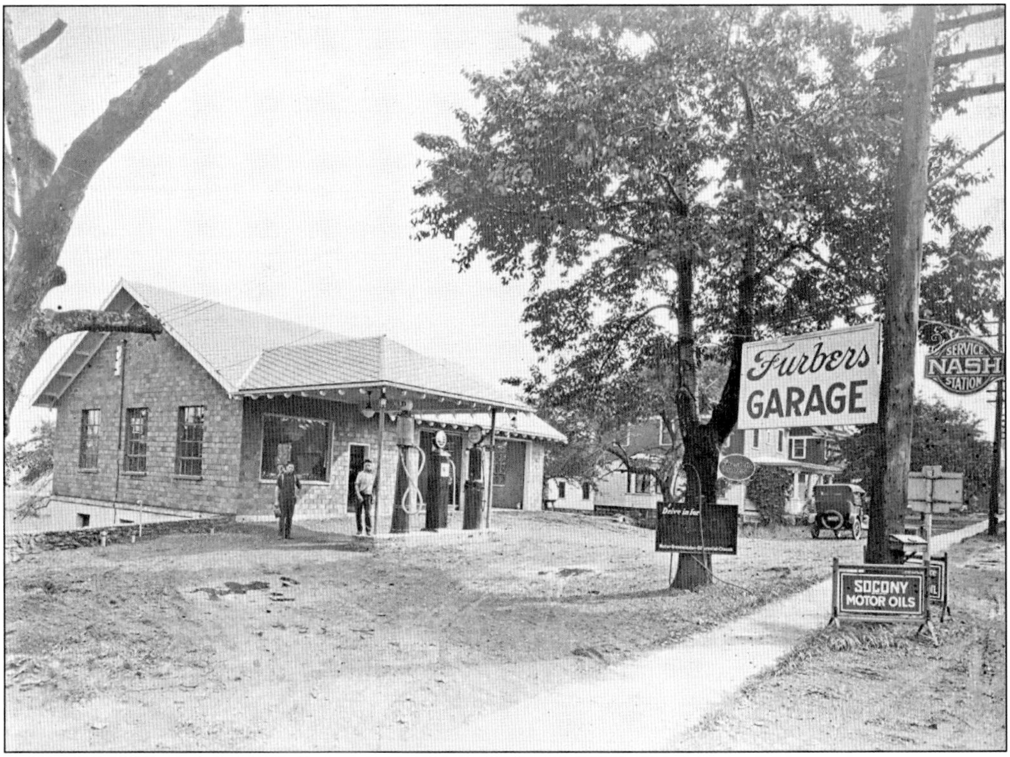

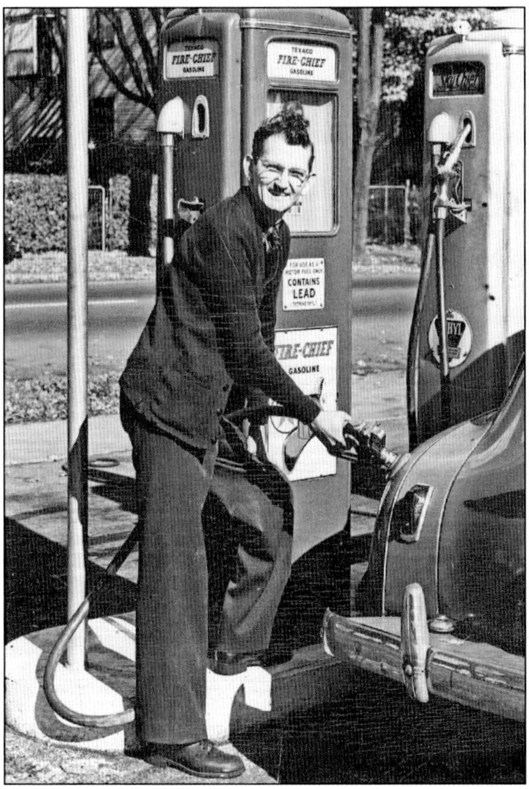

Before Everette Furber was old enough to drive, he started working for his uncle at Furber's Ford on North Avenue. He soon became a skilled mechanic, and when he was only 21 years old, he built and opened his own garage on Ridge Road in 1926. John Furber, his father, worked with him for three years before returning to farming. Everette and his wife, Wilhelmina "Billy," lived next door and ran the business for many years.

Finns Garage, on East Main Street, was started by George (pictured at left) and Wilfred Finn in 1939. They did general repair, sold gasoline, and serviced the Webster school buses. In the mid-1960s, Tim Finn joined the business and operated it when his dad and uncle retired. In the mid-1970s, Texaco left the upstate area and the Finns bought the property. Today Tim's son Kevin and five employees are continuing the tradition. (Courtesy of the Finn family.)

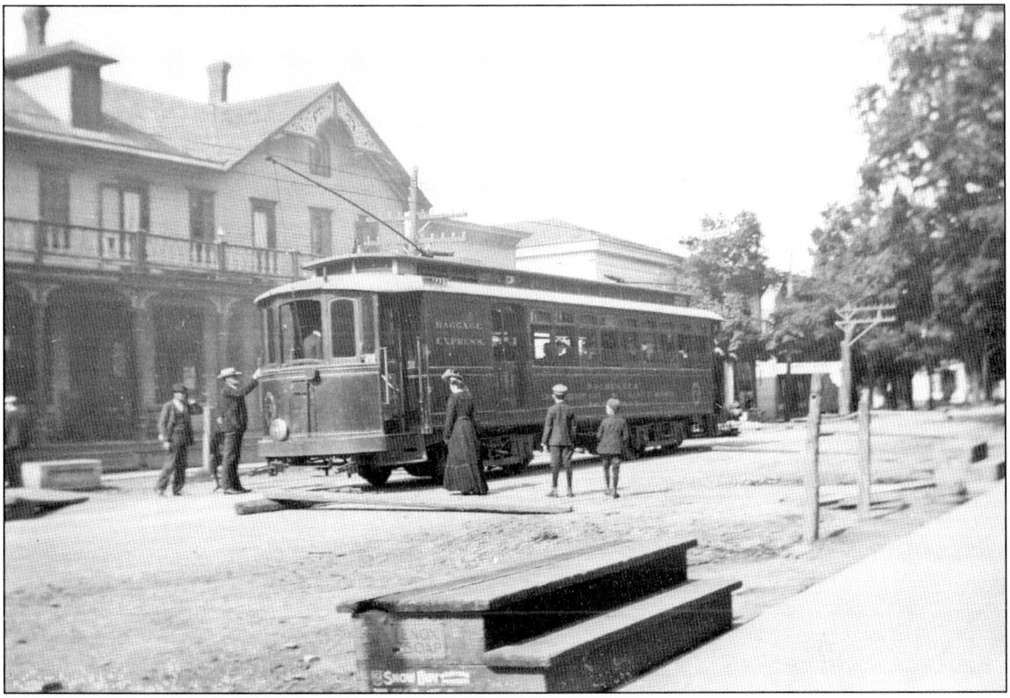

The Rochester and Sodus Bay Railway was completed in 1900. The trolley ran between 6 a.m. and 9 p.m. The time of the run between Rochester and Sodus Bay was two hours and 19 minutes. The *c.* 1910 photograph above shows the afternoon trolley at the Webster Hotel. During the apple blossom season each May, tickets were issued for weekend trips to Sodus Point.

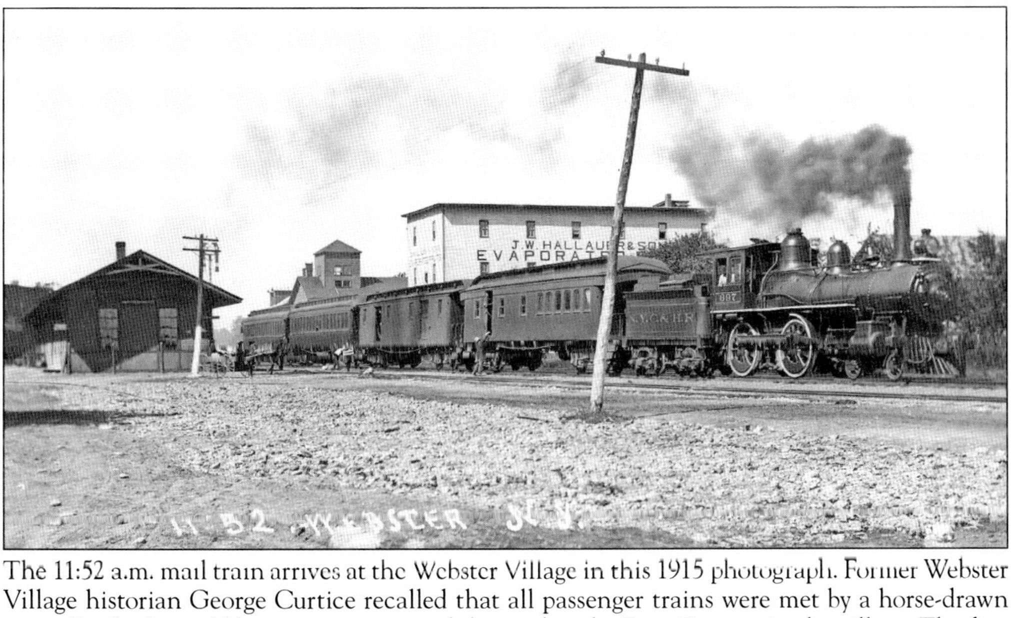

The 11:52 a.m. mail train arrives at the Webster Village in this 1915 photograph. Former Webster Village historian George Curtice recalled that all passenger trains were met by a horse-drawn carryall, which would bring passengers and the mail to the Four Corners in the village. The first telephone in the village connected the rail station, pictured above, to the post office.

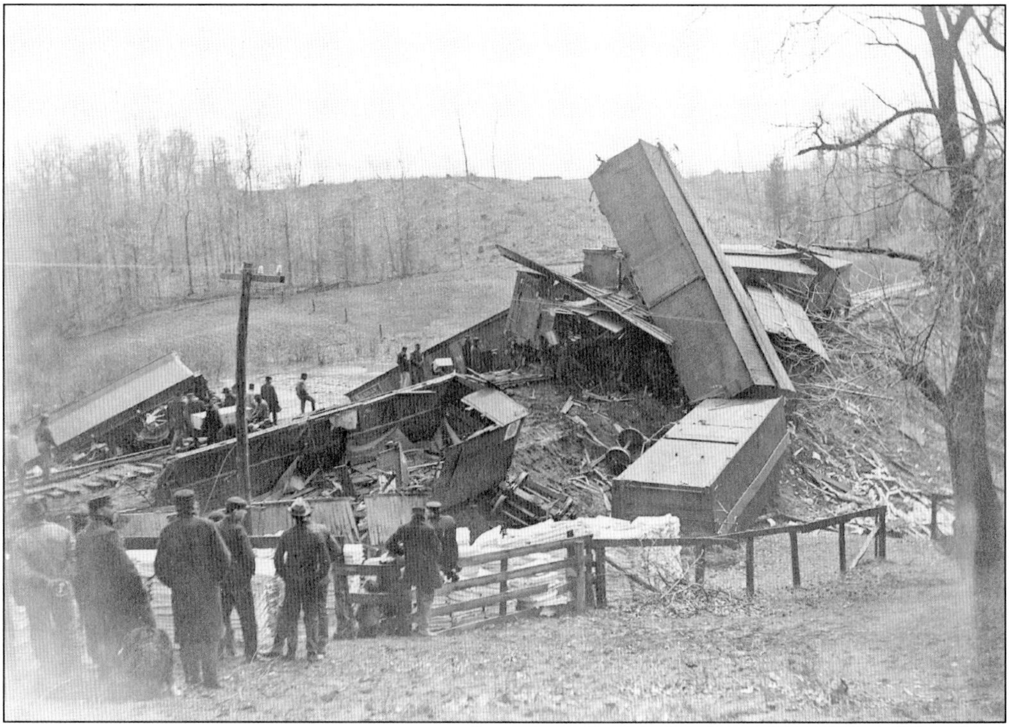

Nelson I. Smith, a professional photographer in Webster, captured this image of a train wreck on Vosburg Road, near what was the Cripps Farm. A culvert under the tracks washed out and caused 19 cars to derail on the freight train heading east from the Charlotte Station in Rochester, New York. Fortunately lives were spared when a westbound train, carrying 900 passengers, was flagged to stop near Webster Village.

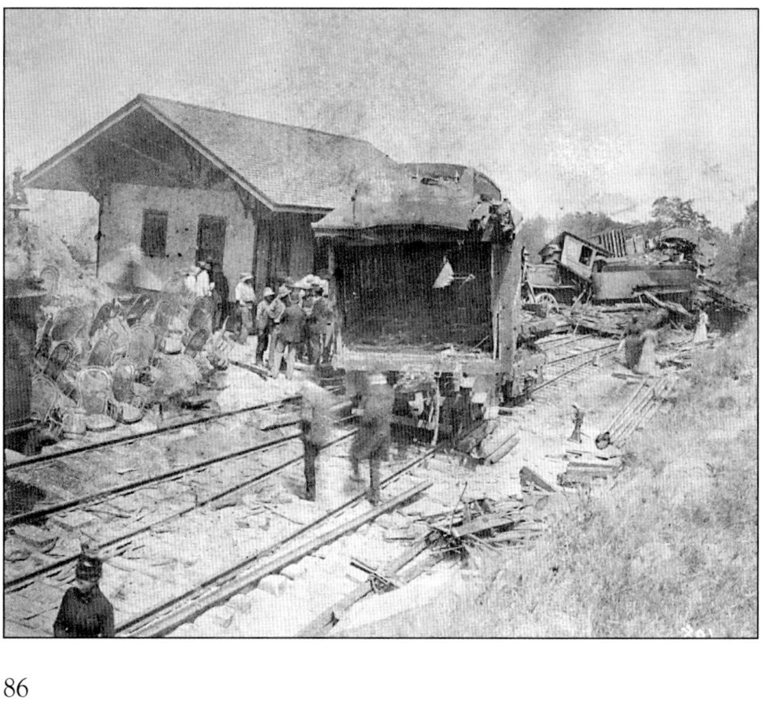

A fatal train crash at the Forest Lawn Station occurred August 10, 1889. A stub train from Windsor Beach backed down to the station with four cars when, from the east, an express train running late, and speeding, crashed into the stub train. The last two cars of the stub train were destroyed on impact.

Six

Vacations and Pastimes

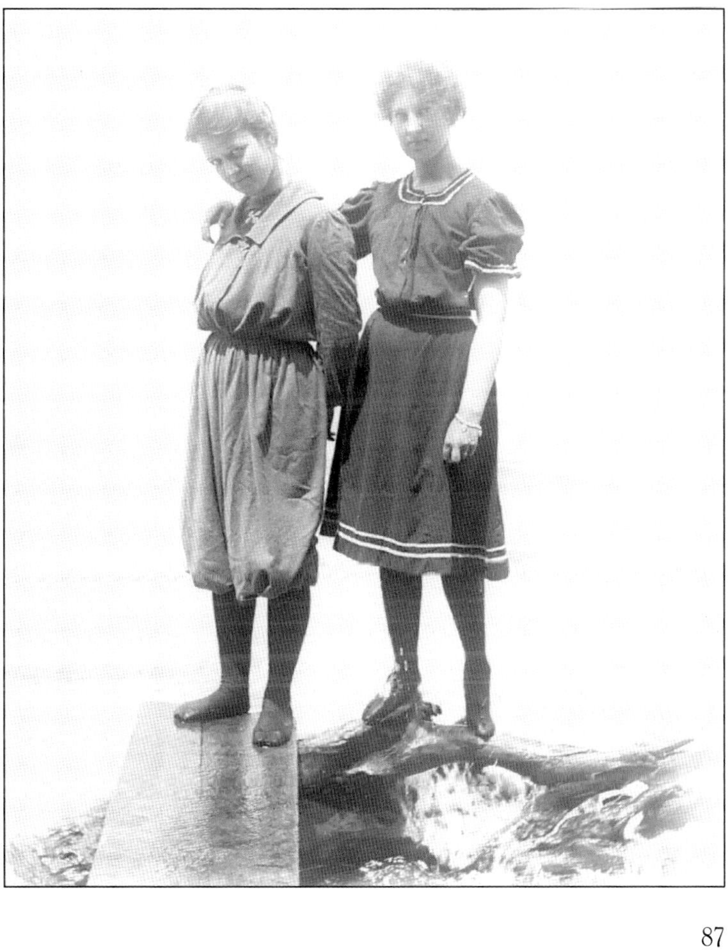

In the hot, humid days of summer, many Webster residents went to Lake Ontario to cool off. These young women were taking advantage of the brisk waters at Nine Mile Point.

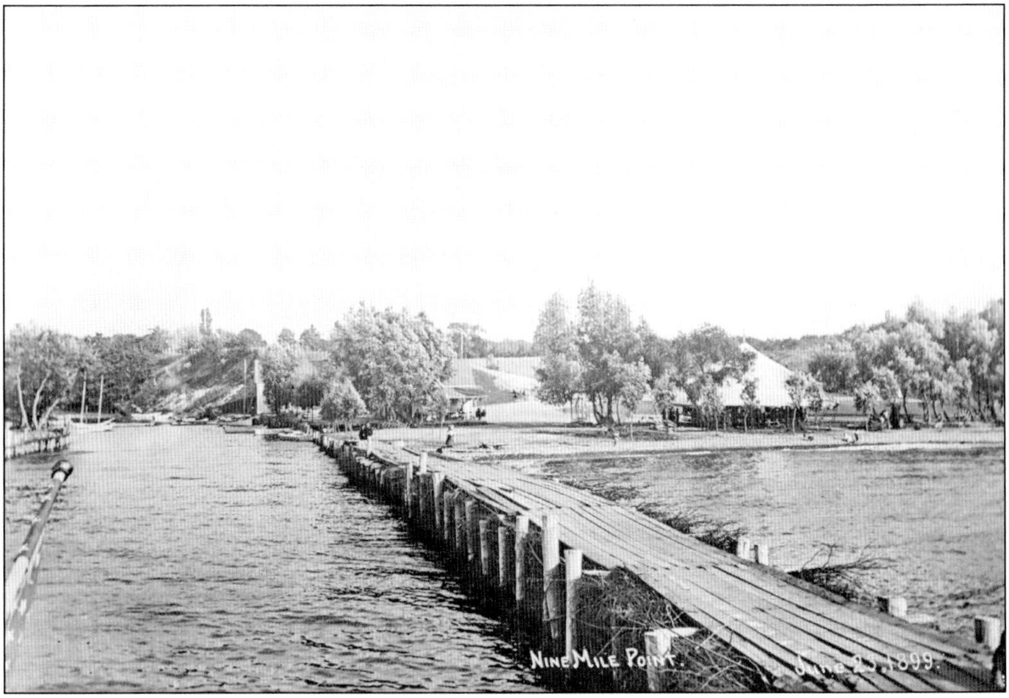

The "brush pier" at Nine Mile Point, seen in this *c.* 1890 photograph, was a chore to maintain. Farmers would collect the trimmings from their fruit trees and haul them to the shore on Hiram and May Wright's property. Each year, the trimmings were used to construct the temporary pier.

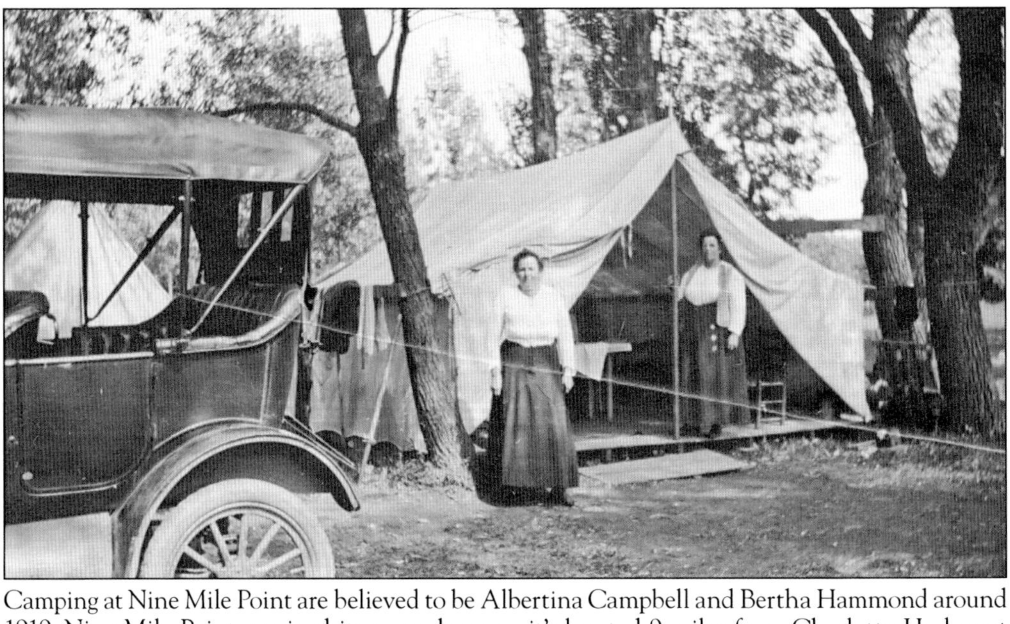

Camping at Nine Mile Point are believed to be Albertina Campbell and Bertha Hammond around 1919. Nine Mile Point received its name because it's located 9 miles from Charlotte Harbor at the mouth of the Genesee River.

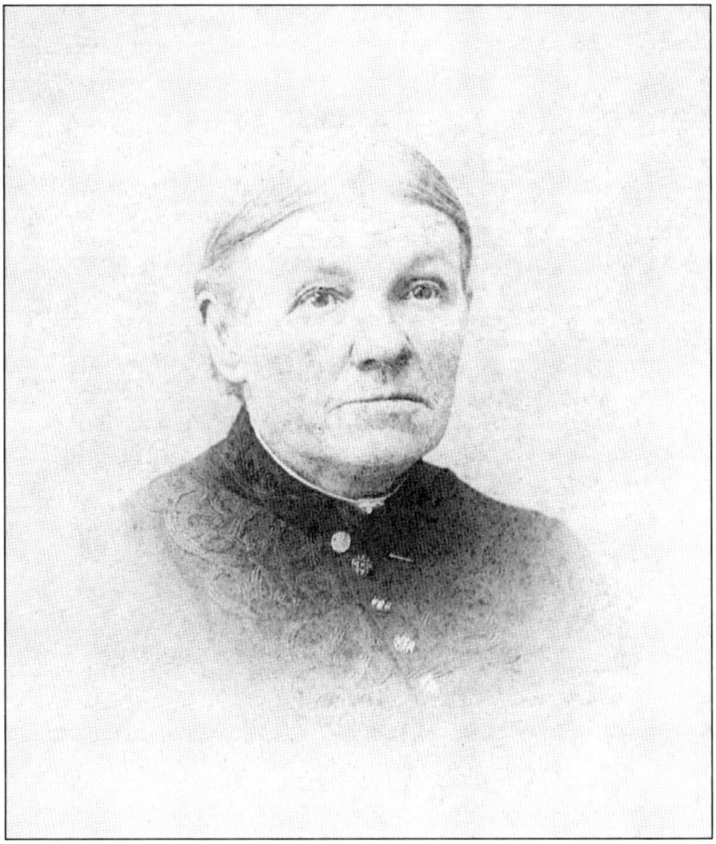

Minerva Foster Strowger, in the 1880s, started a boardinghouse at Nine Mile Point by providing rooms and meals to fishermen. The business evolved into the Nine Mile Point Hotel, the location of Hedges Restaurant today. (Courtesy of the Webster Museum and Historical Society.)

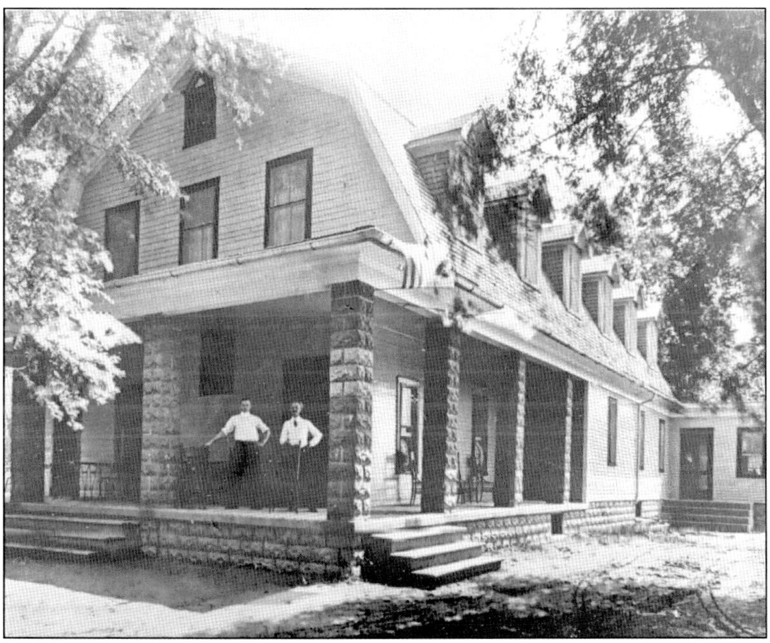

The hotel business increased substantially as the years went by, and a larger hotel replaced the first smaller one. The new one had 12 bedrooms on the second floor, a large dining room area, a bar, a kitchen on the main floor, and a large dining porch. Townspeople entertained the notable politician William Jennings Bryan in the 1920s at the Nine Mile Point Hotel.

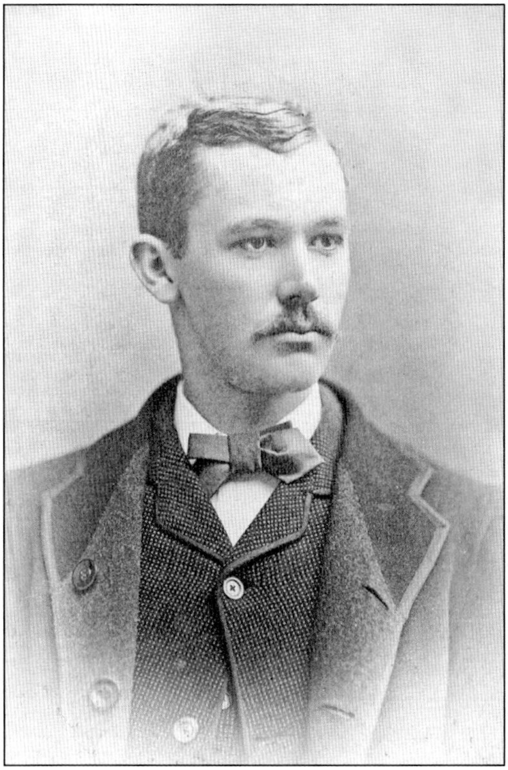

Hiram W. Wright is seen at left at age 21 in 1886. Hiram married May Foster Strowger in 1888, and together they developed an interest in rearing and training horses. They enlarged their lakefront farm into a summer resort, later known as Nine Mile Point Park and Wright-on-the-Lake Camp. (Courtesy of the Webster Museum and Historical Society.)

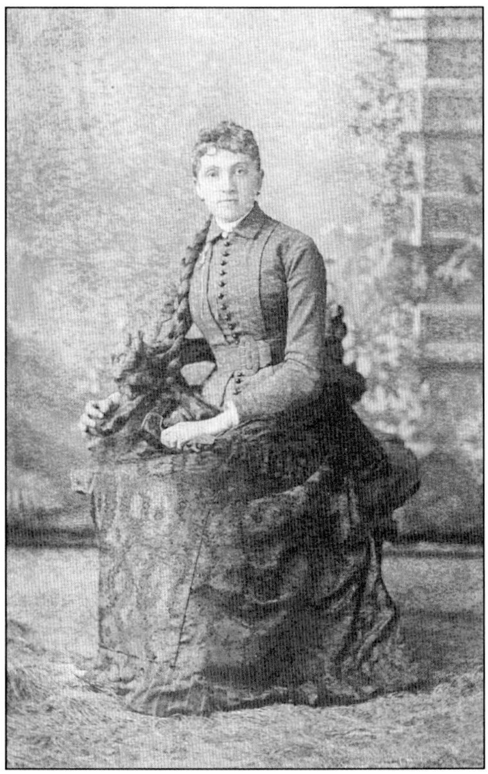

May Foster Strowger Wright is shown here at age 18 in 1885. May was the great granddaughter of Abram Foster, one of the first settlers in Webster. Hiram and May were parents of Earl D. Wright and Erva Wright Smith. (Courtesy of the Webster Museum and Historical Society.)

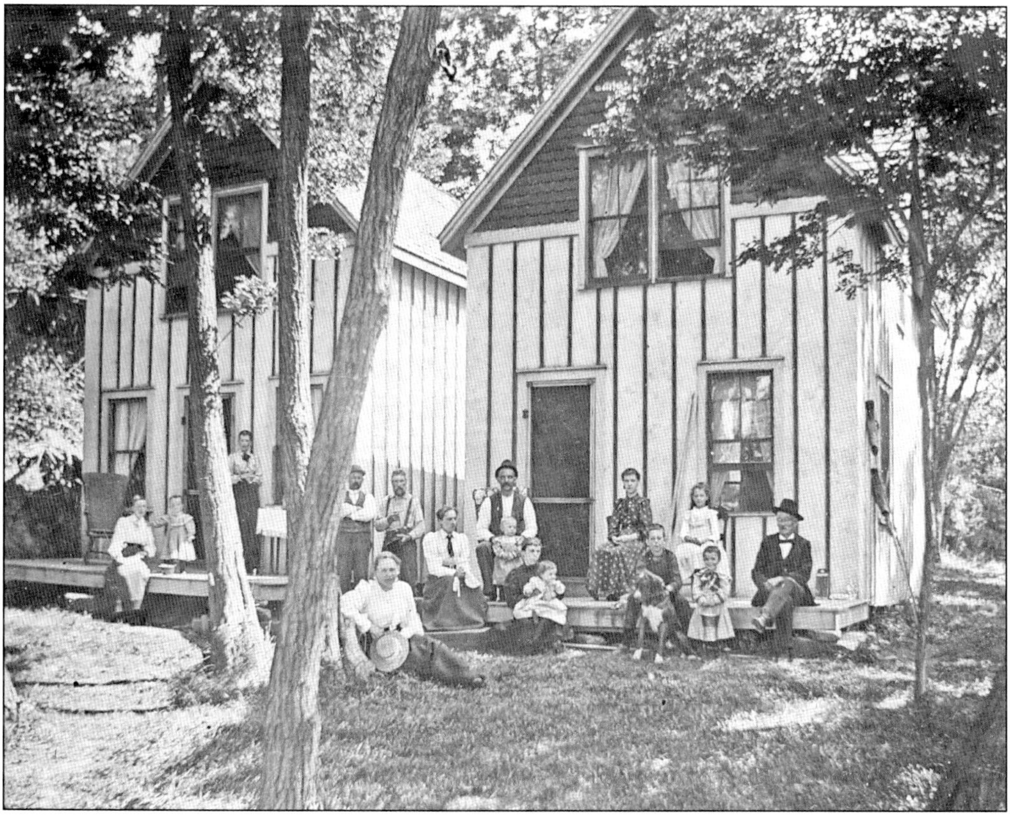

An attractive summer resort, Locust Glen, was located about a half mile west of Nine Mile Point on the shore of Lake Ontario. The property, with easy access to the water, was located on the Burnett farm and managed by George N. Hawley and Mrs. Hugh McKay. It had a well-kept lawn, swimming facility, harbor for small boats, and a tennis court shaded by locust trees. There were three cottages available to rent at a weekly rate.

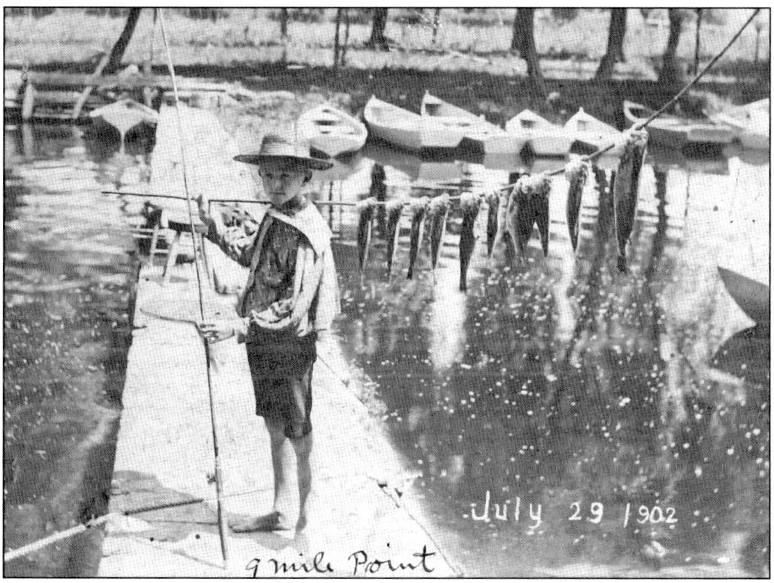

A young Earl D. Wright is seen in this picture fishing in the channel at Nine Mile Point. It appears that he was very successful.

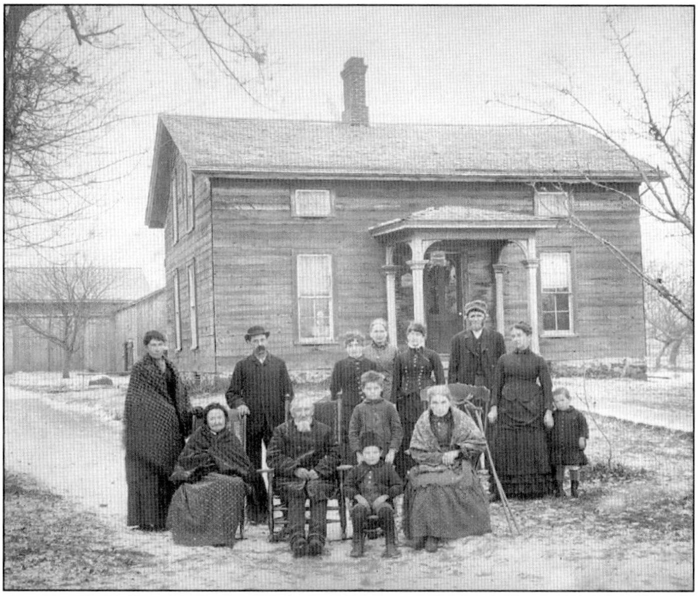

The Chapman house, located at the northwest corner of Webster Road and Klem Road, is seen in this c. 1885 photograph. The following are, from left to right: (seated) Susan Wright Ruggs, Noah Chapman, Claude Wright (seated in front of Tom Wright), Ellen Hughes Chapman (second wife of Noah); (standing) Abby Chapman, Walter Wright, Susan Wright, Melissa Chapman Mack, Asa Mack, Lodisa Chapman Wright, and Dick Wright. (Courtesy of Ed and Lorrie Wright Jones.)

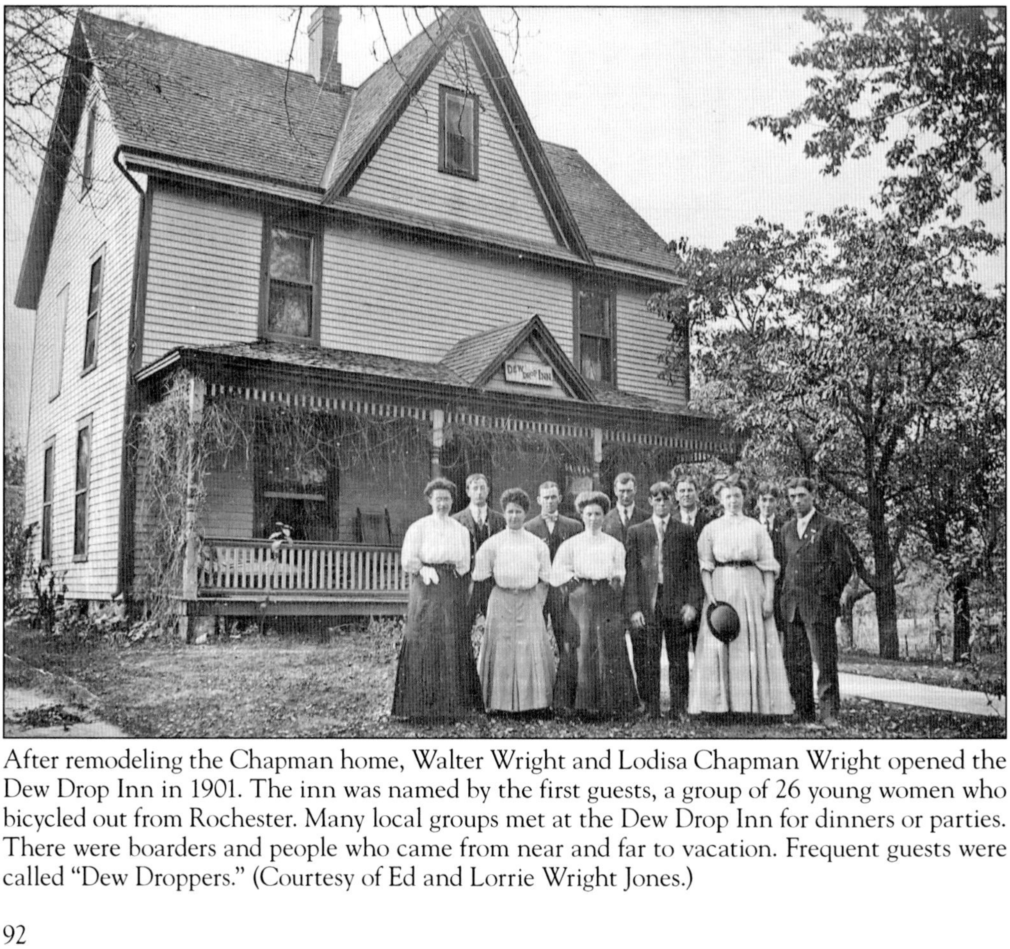

After remodeling the Chapman home, Walter Wright and Lodisa Chapman Wright opened the Dew Drop Inn in 1901. The inn was named by the first guests, a group of 26 young women who bicycled out from Rochester. Many local groups met at the Dew Drop Inn for dinners or parties. There were boarders and people who came from near and far to vacation. Frequent guests were called "Dew Droppers." (Courtesy of Ed and Lorrie Wright Jones.)

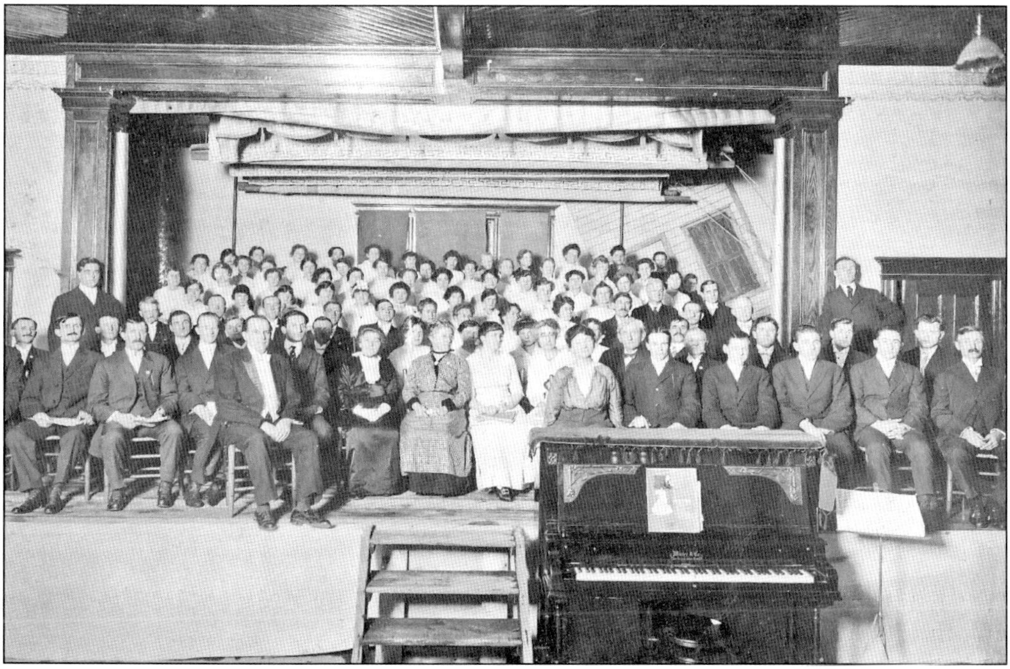

This chorus was organized in November 1914 and sang and practiced at the Webster Grange through the winter months. In the spring, around April, they joined with similar singing groups, which Mr. Barnhardt was leading, in a grand songfest held at Edgerton Park, Rochester. Over 1,000 voices participated, and the chorus from Webster made the trip out and back by chartered car on the Rochester and Sodus Bay Railroad.

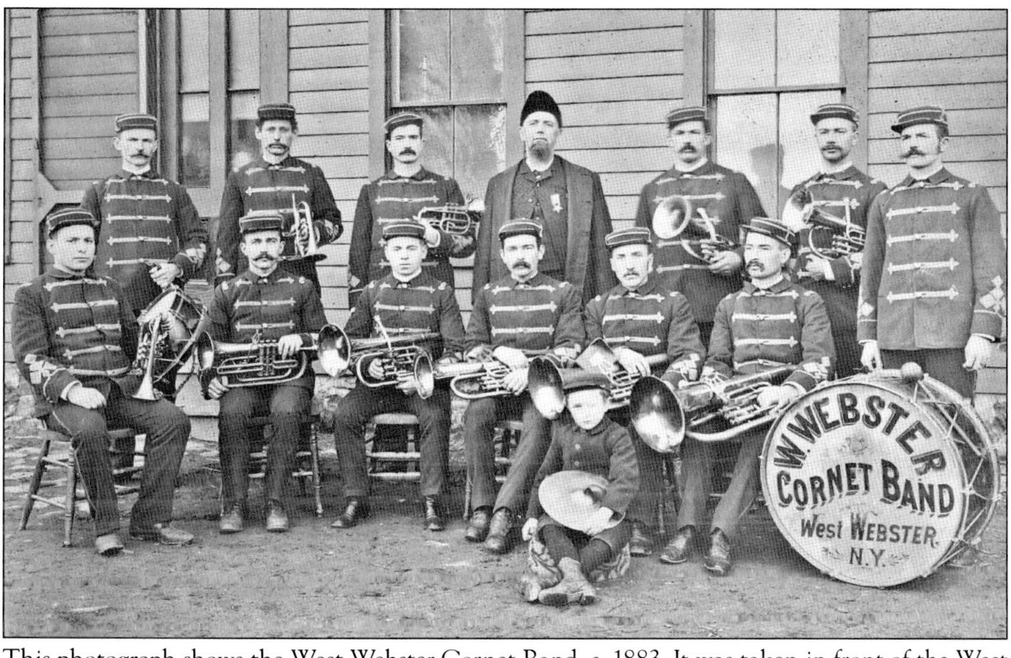

This photograph shows the West Webster Cornet Band, c. 1883. It was taken in front of the West Webster Hotel located at the corner of Ridge Road and Gravel Road. Thought to be in this group are the following: W. Bancroft, Billy Saller Jr., Billy Saller Sr., Mat Shrader, and Charles Goetzman.

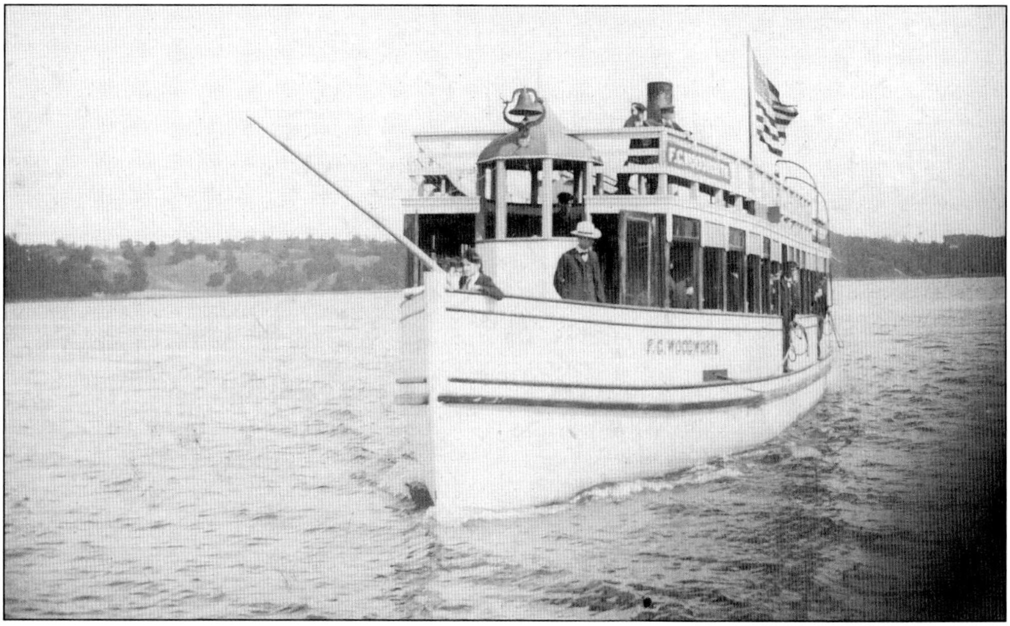

In 1885, Orlo Walzer built this steamboat, the *Woodworth*, at Drakes Landing on the Irondequoit Bay. It was owned and operated by Capt. Fred C. Woodworth. This propeller-driven, double-decker boat could carry 200 passengers. A 25¢ ticket covered a trolley ride to Glen Edith (Drake's Landing), the steamboat to Seabreeze on the lake and a second boat to Charlotte Beach. (Courtesy of Pat Wayne.)

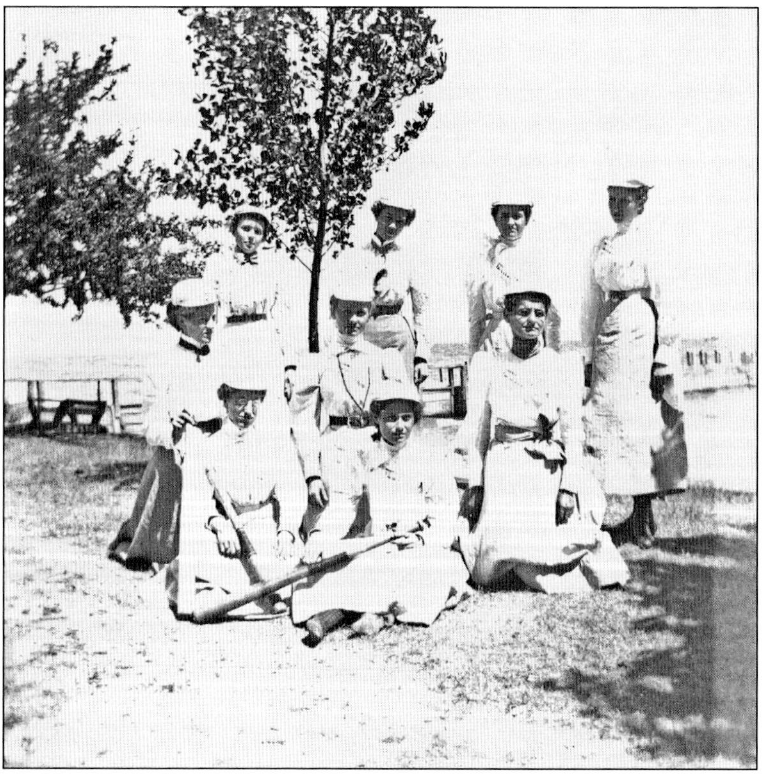

This photograph shows the "Webster All Wrights" baseball team. It was taken at the game against the Hilton Breezes at Manitou Beach, Hilton, on August 15, 1899. The players included, from left to right, (first row) Edith Wright and Carrie Ebner; (second row) Libbie Woodhull, Barbara Miller, and Mary Strowger; (third row) Daisy Foster, Mae Hadden, Grace Greene, and Anna Keller.

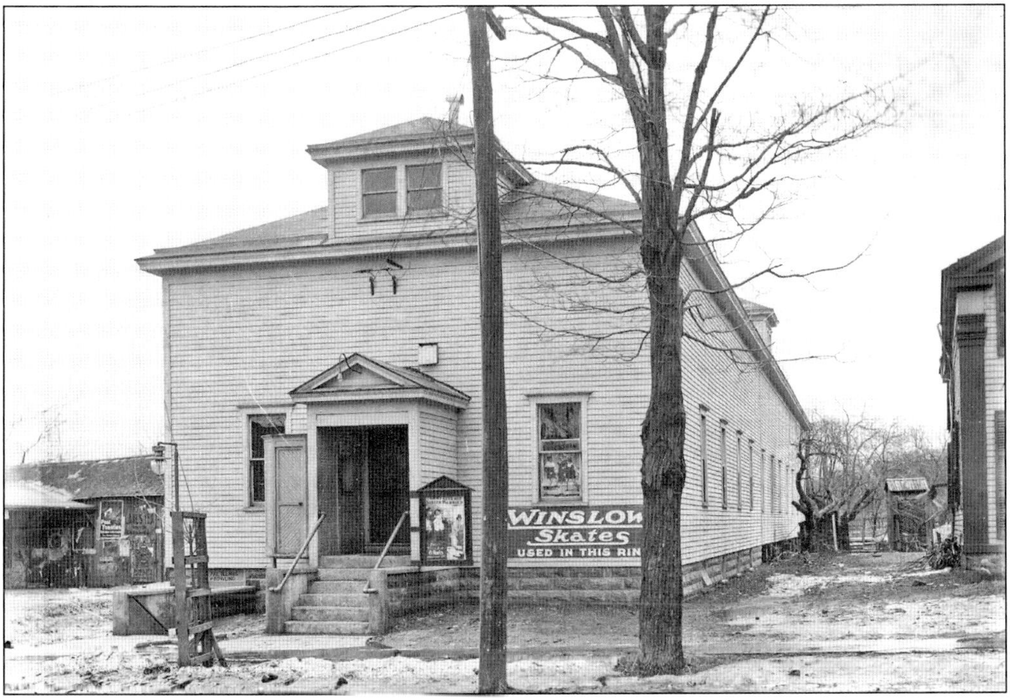

Sawyers Hall was located on North Avenue, where the Webster Cleaners building is located today. Sawyers Hall offered a variety of entertainments. It served as the Webster High School basketball court for games until the new high school was built in 1925. At one time, it had the largest roller-skating floor outside of Buffalo, along with a bowling alley and silent movies. It operated from 1909 until 1921. The building burned in the 1950s.

This is an early picture from Inspiration Point, located south of the Bay Bridge. It was part of a large farm owned by Carl and Otto Drew. It had spectacular views of Irondequoit Bay and Lake Ontario since it was located high above the shore. The Drew brothers wanted to share its scenic beauty, so they made improvements to the area and opened it for visitors. There were campsites, picnic tables, and benches.

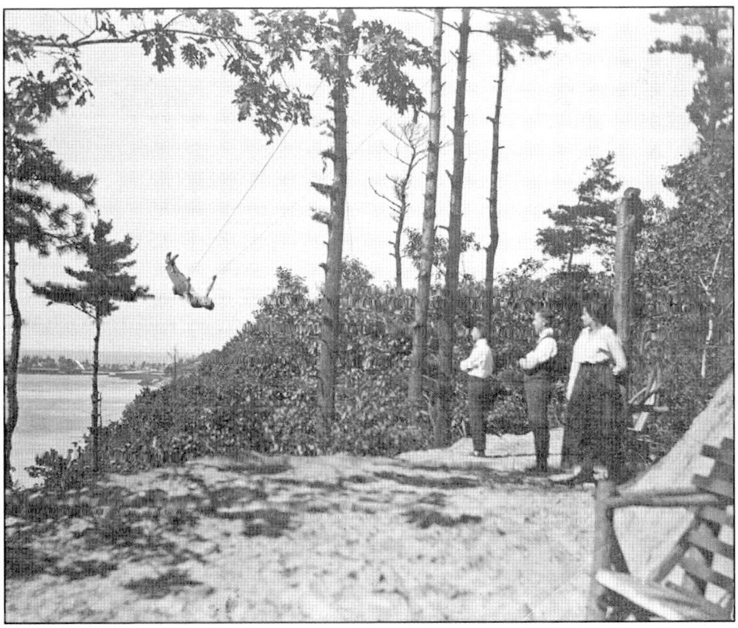

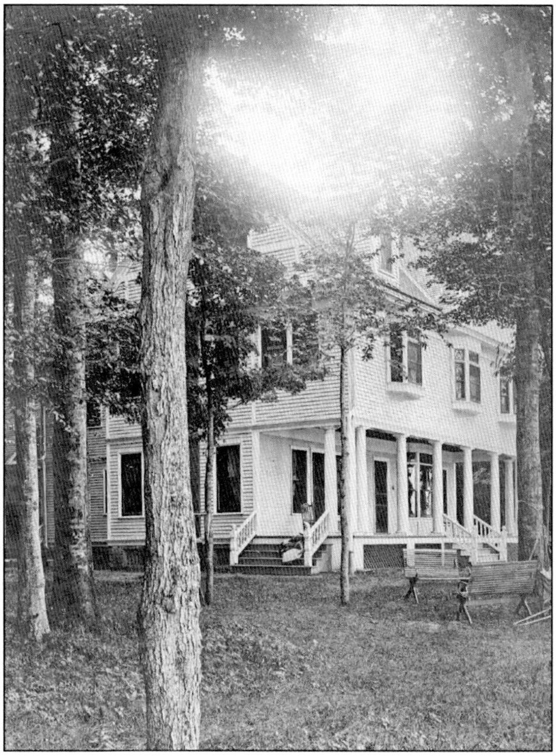

In the late 19th century, several distinguished Rochester families built summer homes along Lake Road. The William B. Hale family, who resided on Prince Street in the city, built a beautifully designed natural clapboard home. The wooded coastal property contained noteworthy gardens designed by the famous landscape architect Fletcher Steele. Kate Louise Hale Trahey, one of William B. Hale's three daughters, lived in the house until her death in 2000. (Courtesy of the Thomas Gosnell family.)

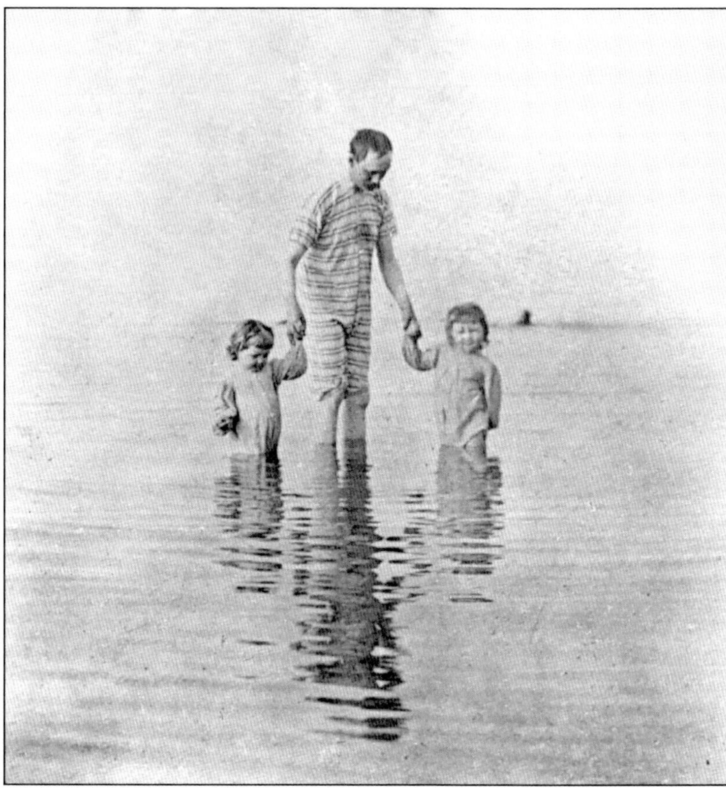

This c. 1890 photograph shows William B. Hale and his daughters Esther and Annette bathing in the waters of Lake Ontario by their summer home. Hale was an officer in the Lawyers Cooperative Publishing Company and the owner of Forest Farms on Whiting Road, which raised prize Brown Swiss cows, geese, and White Holland turkeys. (Courtesy of the Thomas Gosnell family.)

The Hale family relaxes on the veranda of their Lake Road summer home in this elegant photograph. Clara Hale, William Hale's wife, is sitting on the porch with friends, and her daughter Esther Hale Saunders is sitting on the steps, on the left, and her daughter-in-law Josephine Booth Hale is on the right. (Courtesy of the Thomas Gosnell family.)

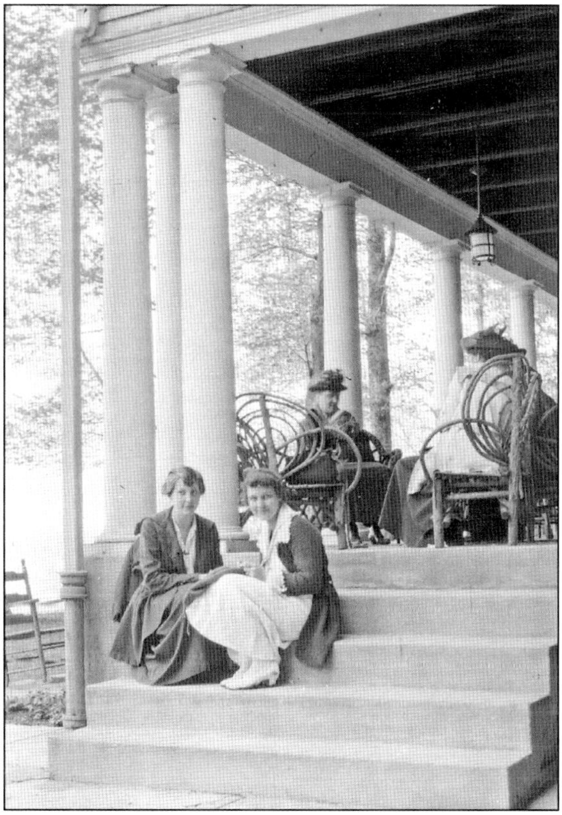

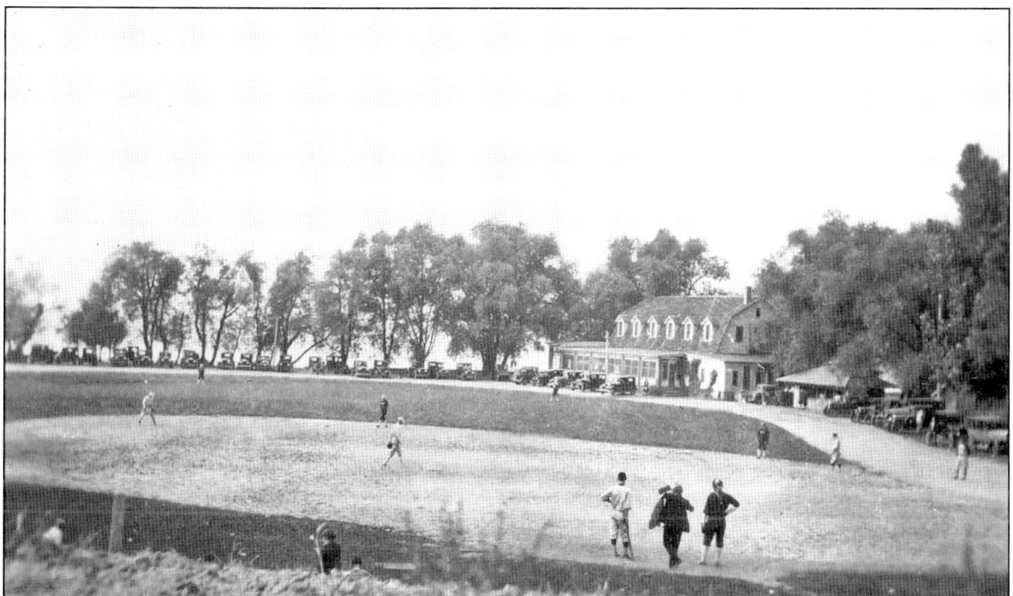

The photograph above shows the Nine Mile Point Hotel with additions that were made for more dining and kitchen space. Hiram and May Wright dynamited the hill and filled in the swampy area to the west of the hotel along the shore. It became a popular place for local amateur baseball games.

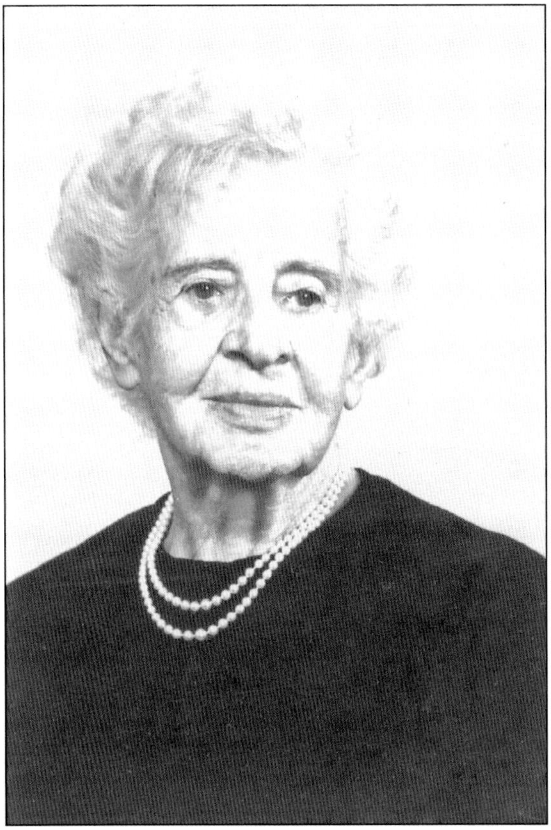

Eleanor Gleason was the daughter of William and Ellen Gleason. The family founded Gleason Works, an important machine tooling company. Eleanor owned the cottage at 1124 Lake Road. This Arts and Crafts–style summer home, featuring a stucco finish and commanding views of Lake Ontario, was built around 1920. It is now owned by Monroe County. Eleanor attended the University of Rochester, which was the first year the women were admitted. Eleanor's sister Kate was a pioneering mechanical engineer and a well-known feminist. The photograph at left was taken in 1960. (Courtesy of the Gleason family.)

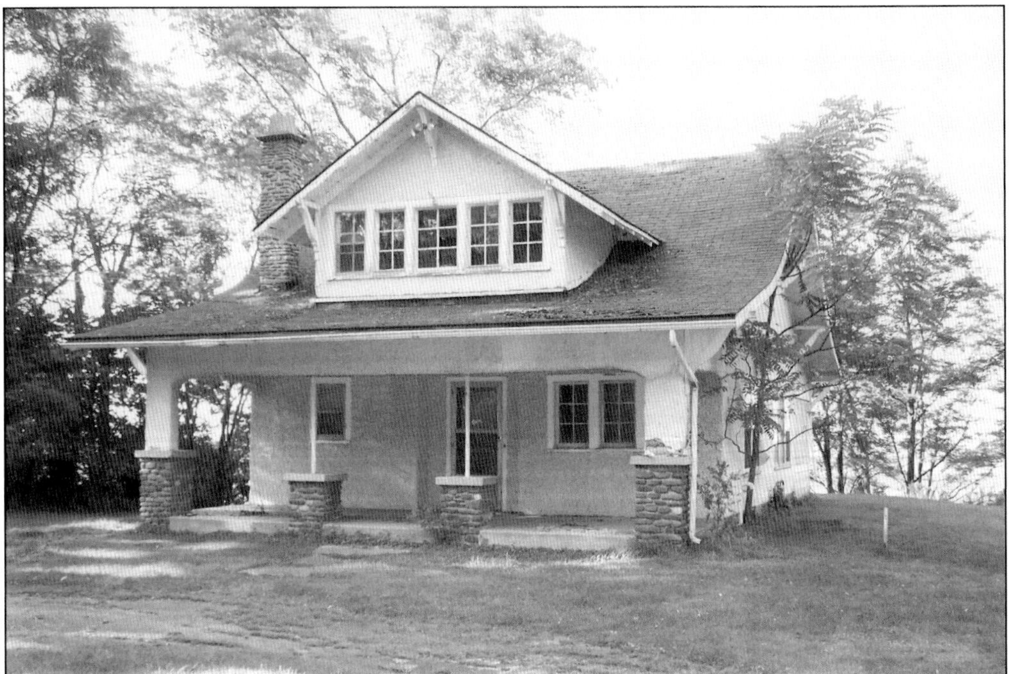

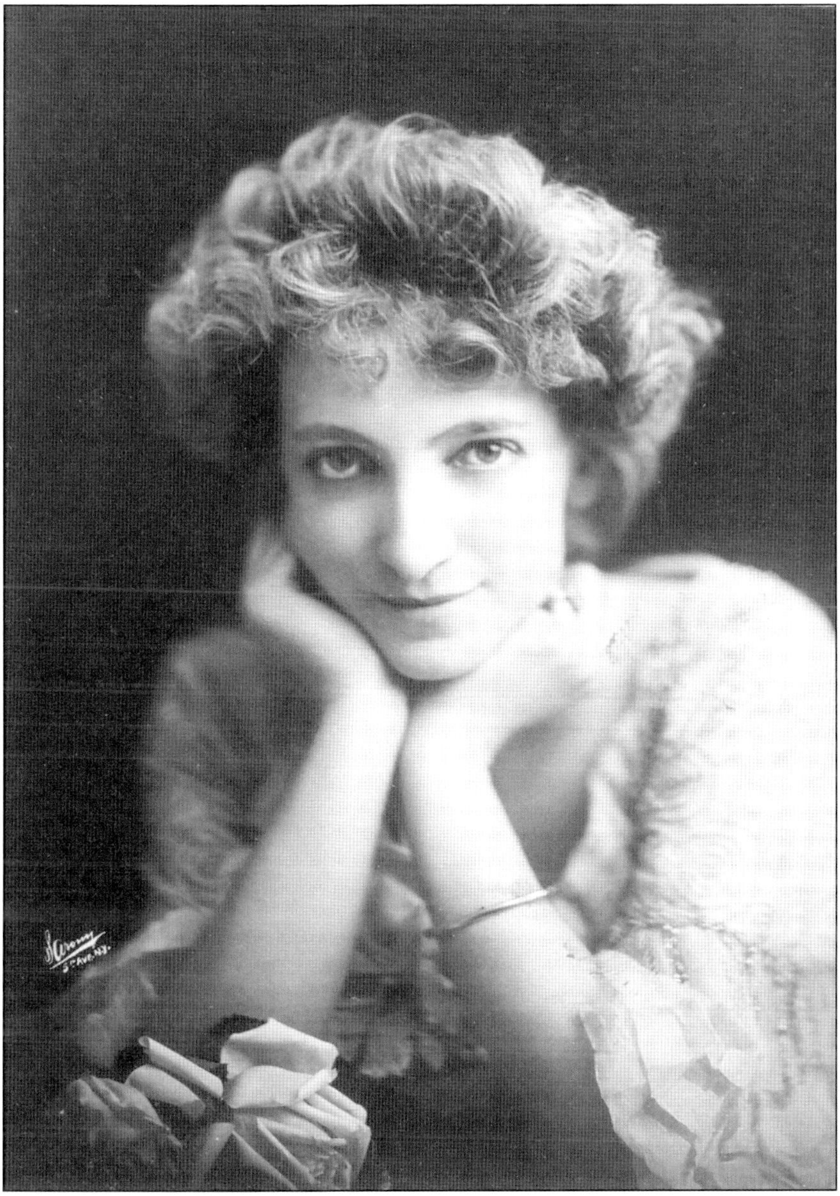

Jessie Bonstelle was one of America's pioneering female stage producers and directors. She was also a talented actress and acting coach. "Jessie" was her stage name, but she was originally named Laura Justine Bonestelle. She was born in 1871 and spent her childhood and teen years at the family farmhouse at 614 Hard Road. She sang and performed in many local productions and attended high school at the Nazareth Academy. She appeared in many productions at the Schubert Theatre on Broadway in New York City. Her obituary credits her with coaching actors William Powell, the *Thin Man*, and Frank Morgan, the *Wizard of Oz*. In 1922, Bonstelle bought the Temple Beth El in Detroit, Michigan, for $500,000 and had it converted into a theater. It was purchased in 1956 by Wayne State University and renamed in her honor as the Bonstelle Theatre. This building is on the National Register of Historic Places. Bonstelle died in 1932 and is buried at Mount Hope Cemetery next to her husband, fellow actor Alexander Hamilton Stuart. (Courtesy of the New York Public Library.)

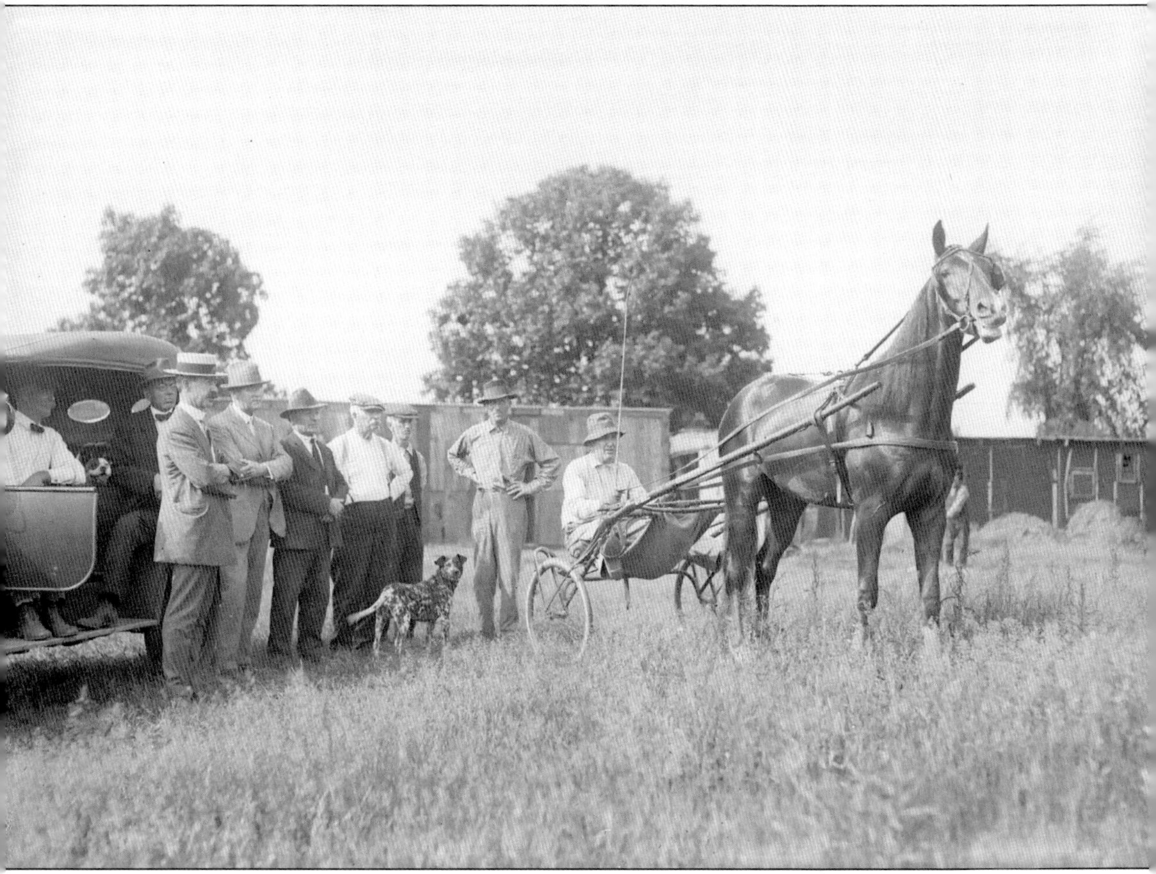

In 1917, Webster's racetrack was opened to the public. It was a half-mile track on land leased from William Kittelberger. It was north of the Immanuel Evangelical Lutheran Church on West Main Street. Sheds were built for the horses, and a small grandstand and a judge's stand were erected on the grounds. Many people came from all over the county to enjoy the races in Webster. It remained a fun destination for about 10 years. Pictured in the photograph above, taken in 1922, are members of the Webster Driving Park Association. The following are, from left to right, unidentified (man in car), William F. Kittelberger (president of the Webster Driving Park Association), Dr. Frank Collins, George Mason, Charles Sallabin (marble and granite dealer in Webster), Dr. James E. Smith (veterinary surgeon), and two unidentified men. Trainer George B. Morgan sits in the sulky. (Courtesy of the Albert R. Stone Negative Collection, Rochester Museum and Science Center.)

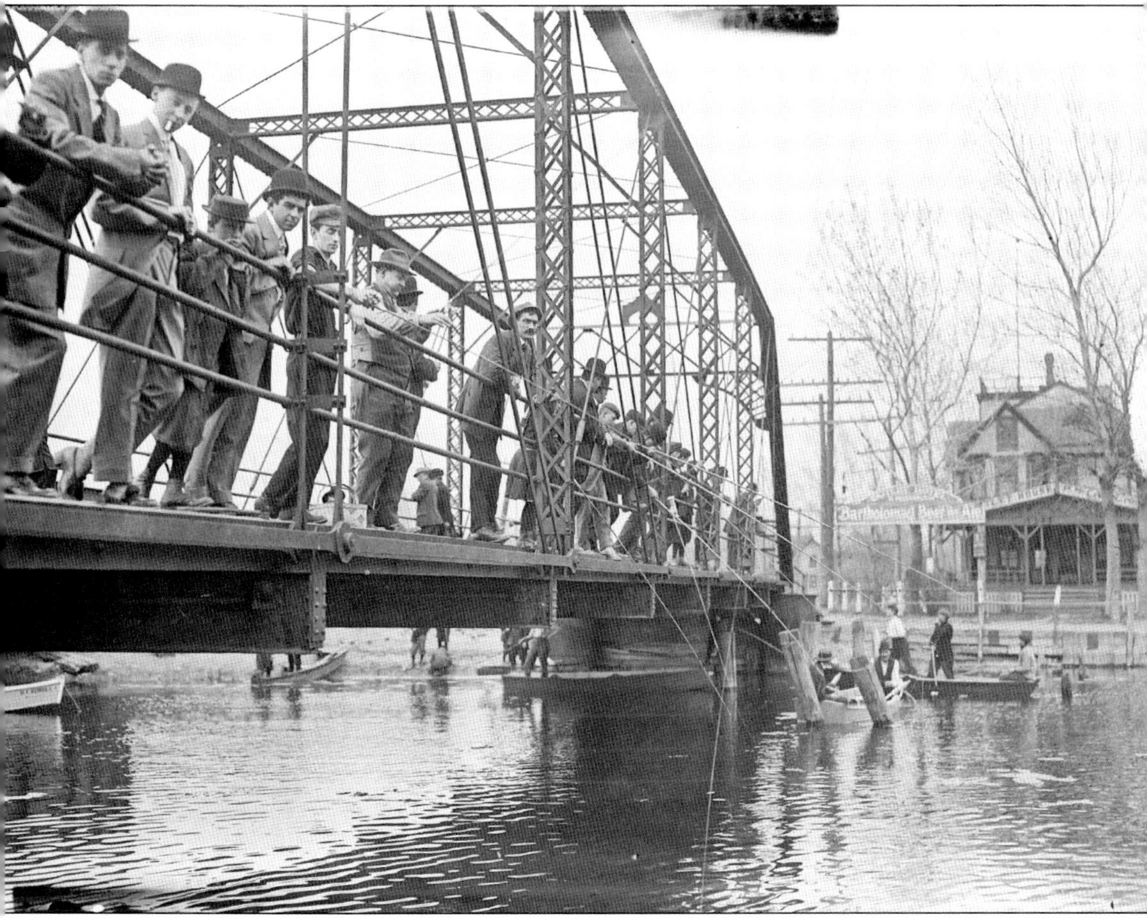

This photograph, taken by Albert R. Stone for the *Rochester Herald* in 1911, shows men fishing from the deck of the bridge over the Irondequoit Bay outlet. In the background is the Outlet House complete with a large advertisement for Bartholomay Brewing Company in Rochester, New York. Today this building houses the Mayer Marina. (Courtesy of the Albert R. Stone Negative Collection, Rochester Museum and Science Center.)

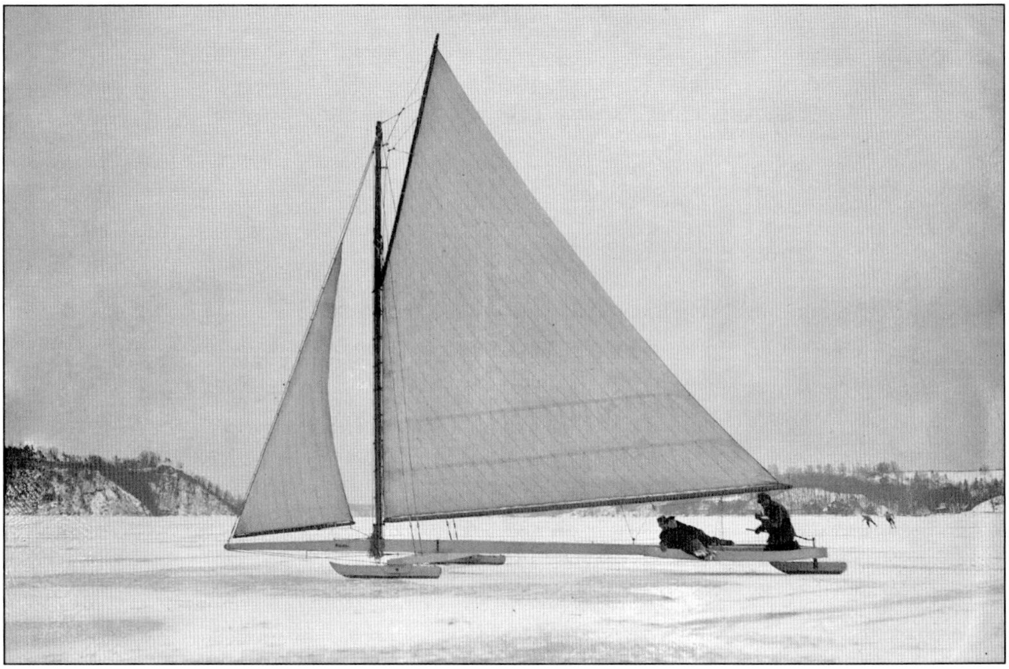

Recreation on Irondequoit Bay in the winter months included iceboating, as seen in this early *c.* 1917 photograph. The *Whistler*, as this boat was called, was the speed champion of Irondequoit Bay in 1917. (Courtesy of the Albert R. Stone Negative Collection, Rochester Museum and Science Center.)

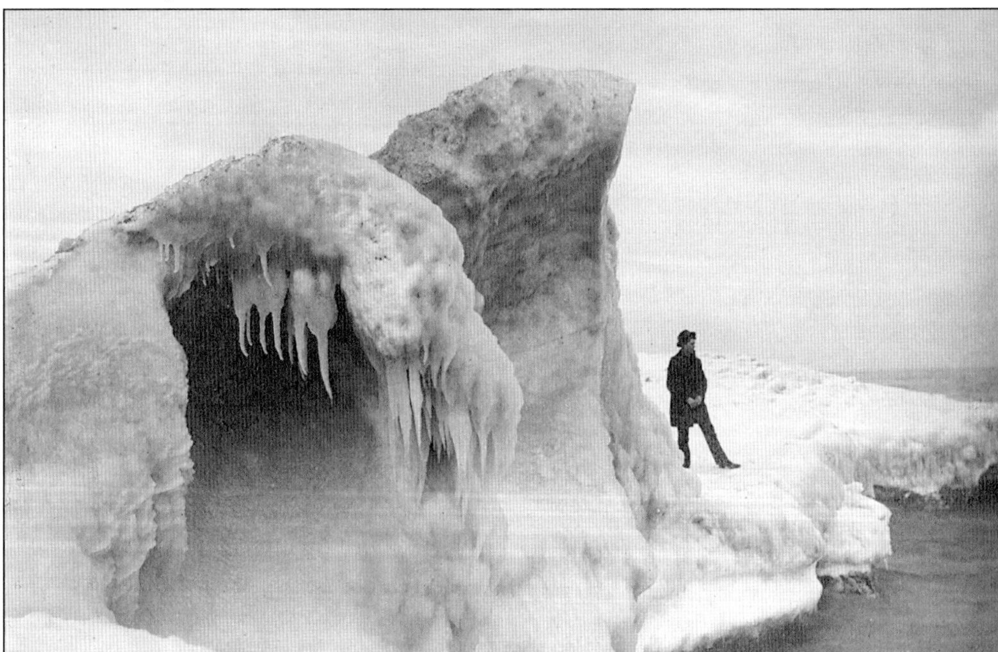

Throughout the years, many photographs have been taken along the lakeshore during the winter months. The ice formations can be very unusual, this is a picture taken around 1900 near Nine Mile Point.

Seven

Our Old Homes

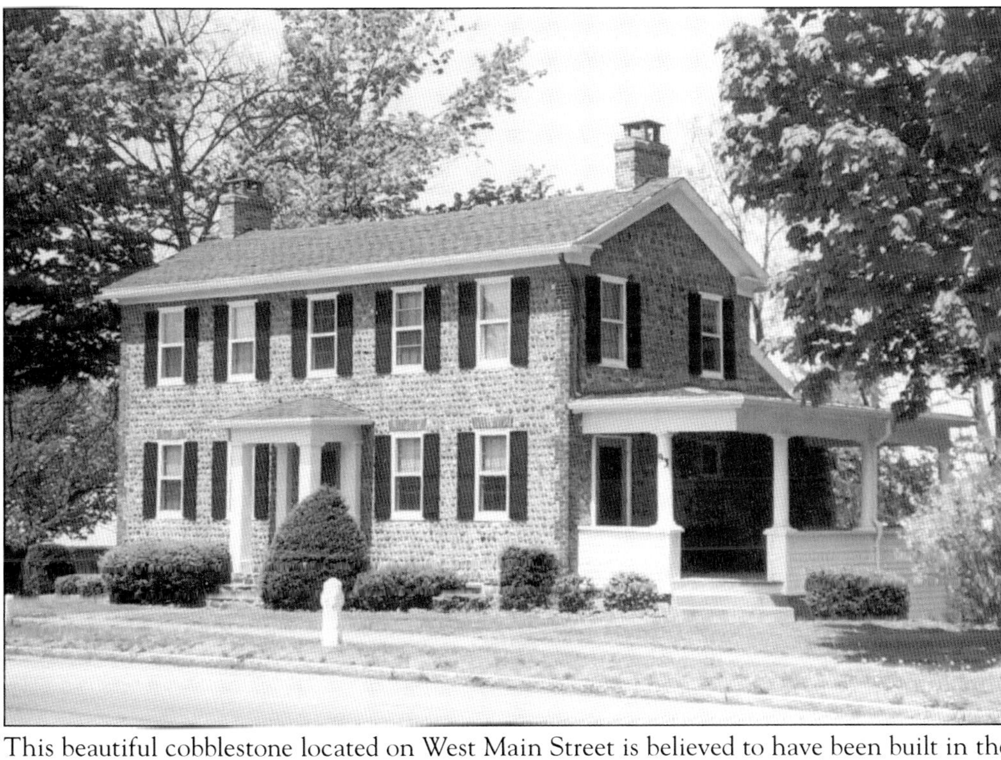

This beautiful cobblestone located on West Main Street is believed to have been built in the mid-1840s. In 1868, Fawnl A. Swift deeded the property to Ednah and Eugene Dean; it remained in the Dean family for over 70 years. Cobblestone buildings are a type of construction found most frequently in New York State. Most in this area are found along the southern shore of Lake Ontario.

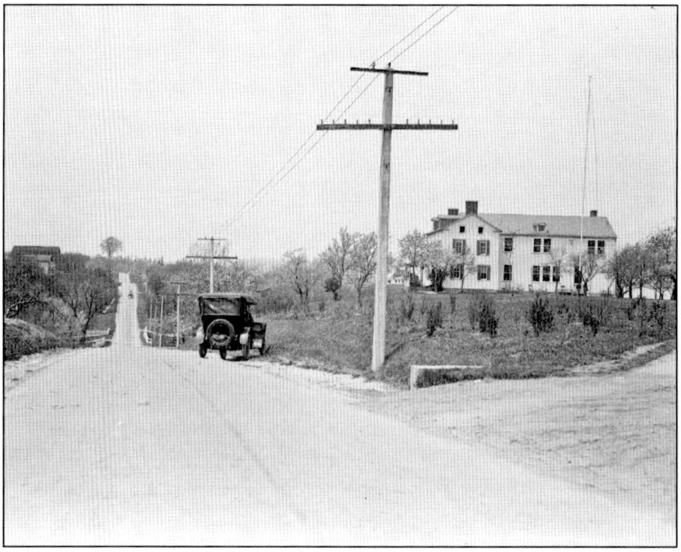

John Whiting built this beautiful home overlooking Lake Ontario around 1835. The house and land remained in the family until about 1866, when it was sold to Jacob Bonenblust. In 1904, the property was purchased by New York State to be a state psychiatric hospital. In 1937, the state transferred the property to Monroe County. (Courtesy of the Albert R. Stone Negative Collection, Rochester Museum and Science Center.)

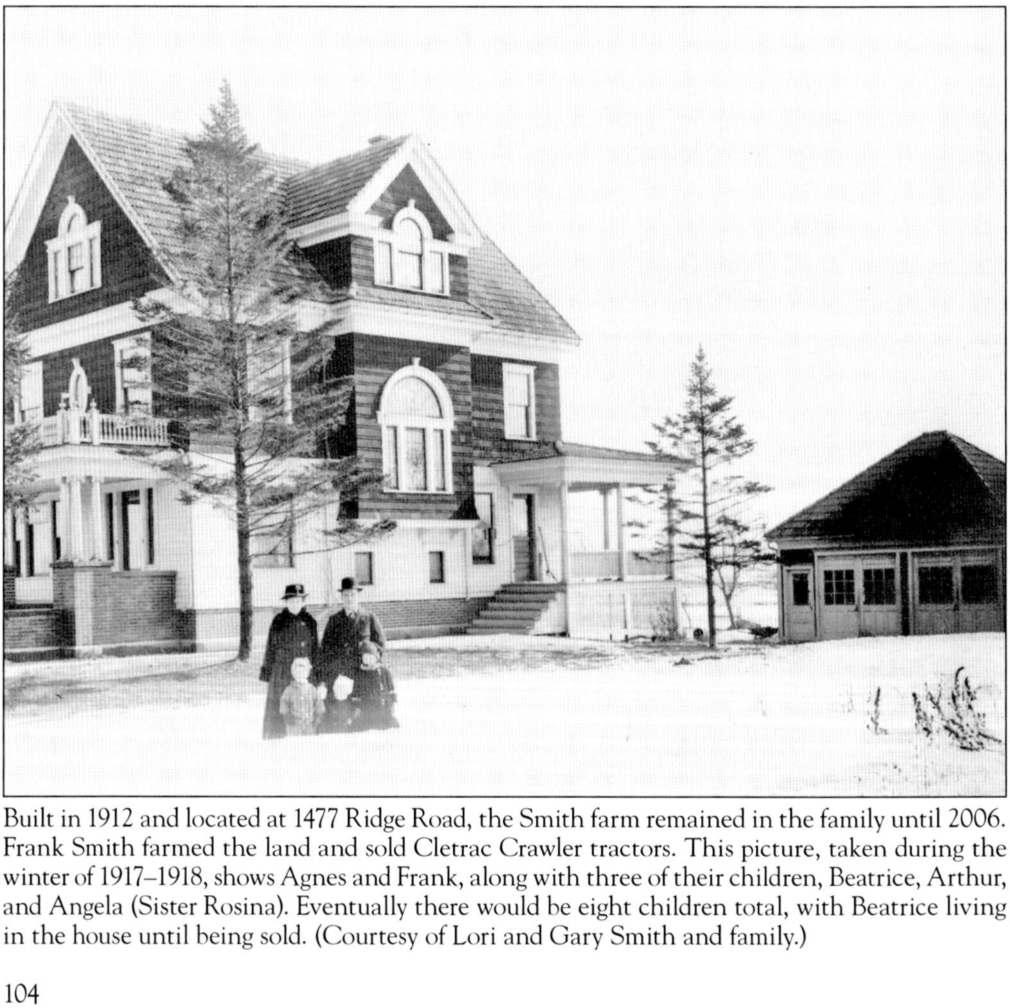

Built in 1912 and located at 1477 Ridge Road, the Smith farm remained in the family until 2006. Frank Smith farmed the land and sold Cletrac Crawler tractors. This picture, taken during the winter of 1917–1918, shows Agnes and Frank, along with three of their children, Beatrice, Arthur, and Angela (Sister Rosina). Eventually there would be eight children total, with Beatrice living in the house until being sold. (Courtesy of Lori and Gary Smith and family.)

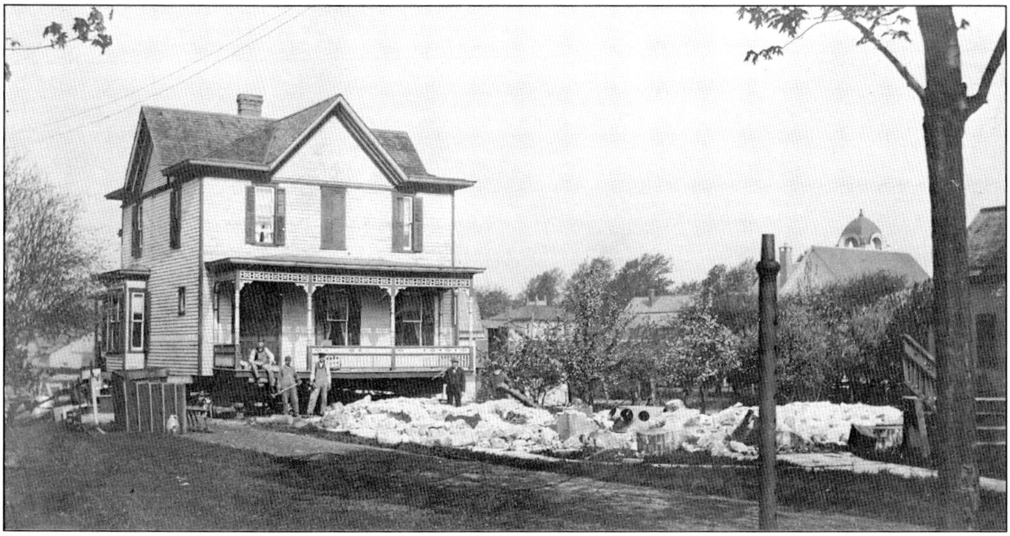

The photograph above shows the home of George G. and Marietta Mason, built c. 1891, on Dunning Avenue. The Masons decided to build a larger home in 1908 and moved their home and barn back, turning them to face Elm Street. They had their new home constructed in the Colonial Revival and Queen Anne style. The exterior of the home has brick on the bottom and a clay tile roof. The interior contains beautiful quarter-sawn white oak trim and an original full-body shower in the master bathroom. The home was completed in 1909. George was a partner in the Jayne and Mason Bank on East Main Street in the village. The home is listed on the National Register of Historic Places.

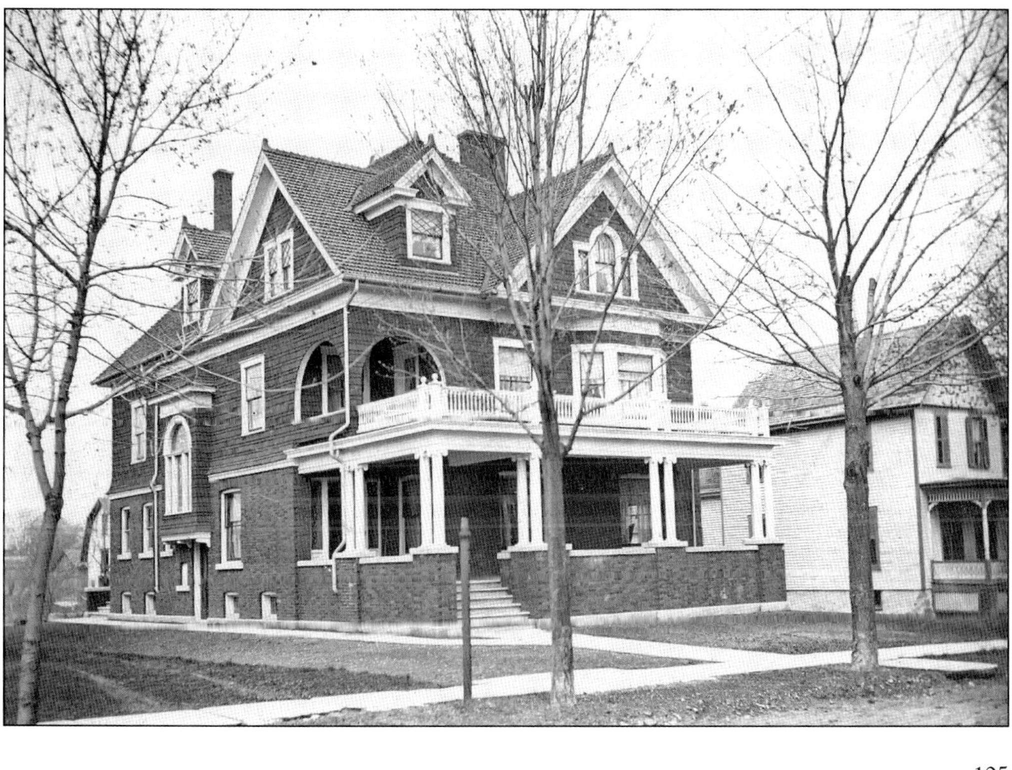

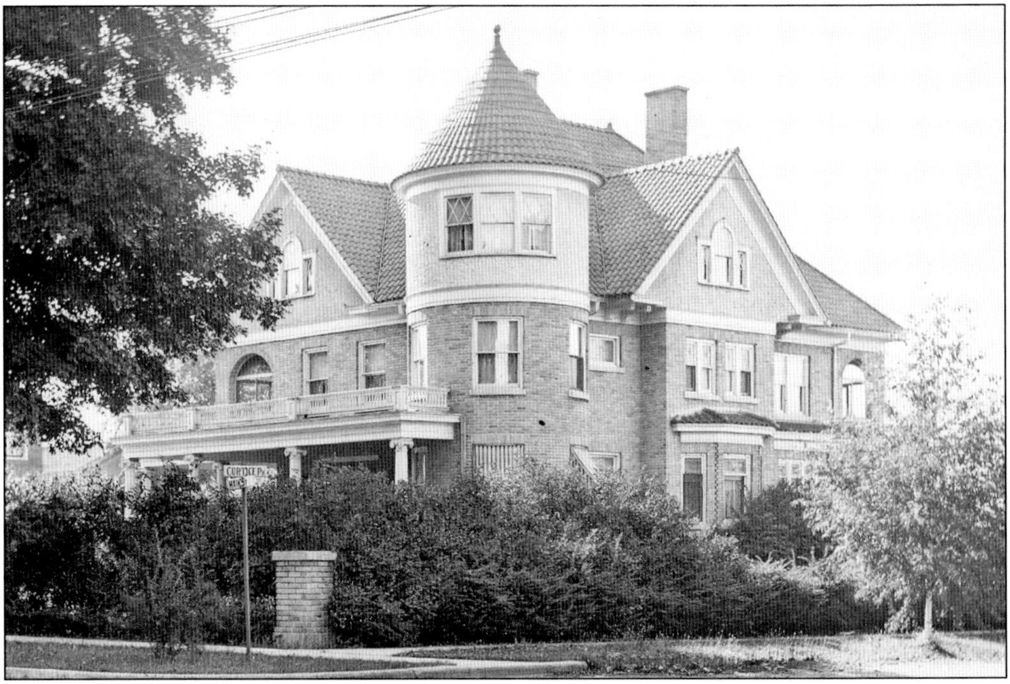

William C. Jayne's house on the corner of Curtice Park and East Main Street was built in 1917–1918. Jayne was a partner with George G. Mason in the Jayne and Mason Bank in the village. He was a successful businessman and his home reflected that. It is a beautiful Colonial Revival–style with a large round corner tower popular in the earlier Queen Anne–style architecture. The home is listed on the National Register of Historic Places.

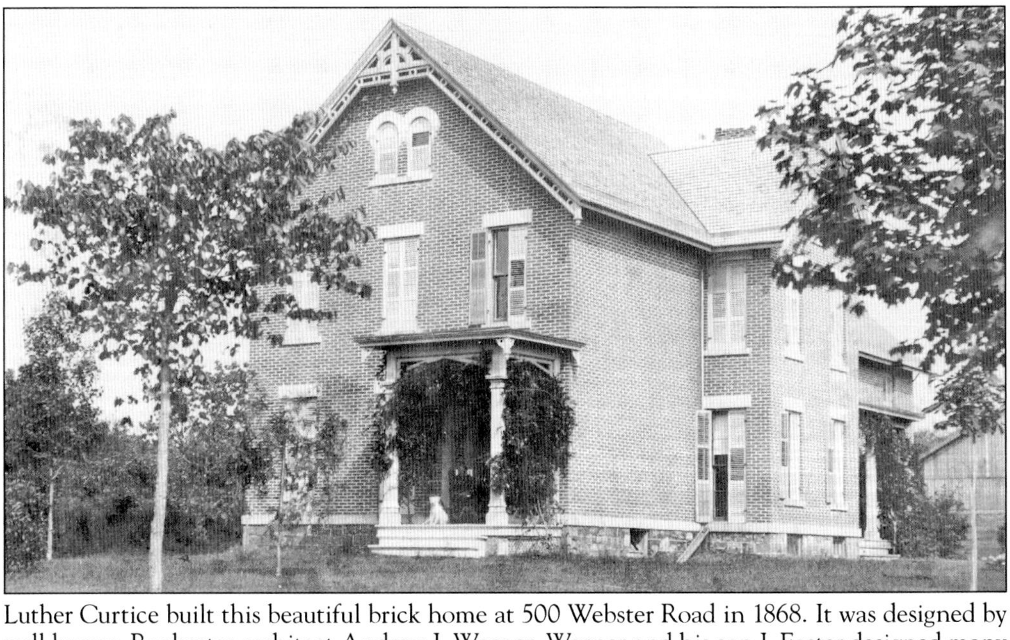

Luther Curtice built this beautiful brick home at 500 Webster Road in 1868. It was designed by well-known Rochester architect Andrew J. Warner. Warner and his son J. Foster designed many buildings in Rochester and the surrounding area. Luther Curtice was the Webster Supervisor from 1862–1863 and a successful farmer and businessman.

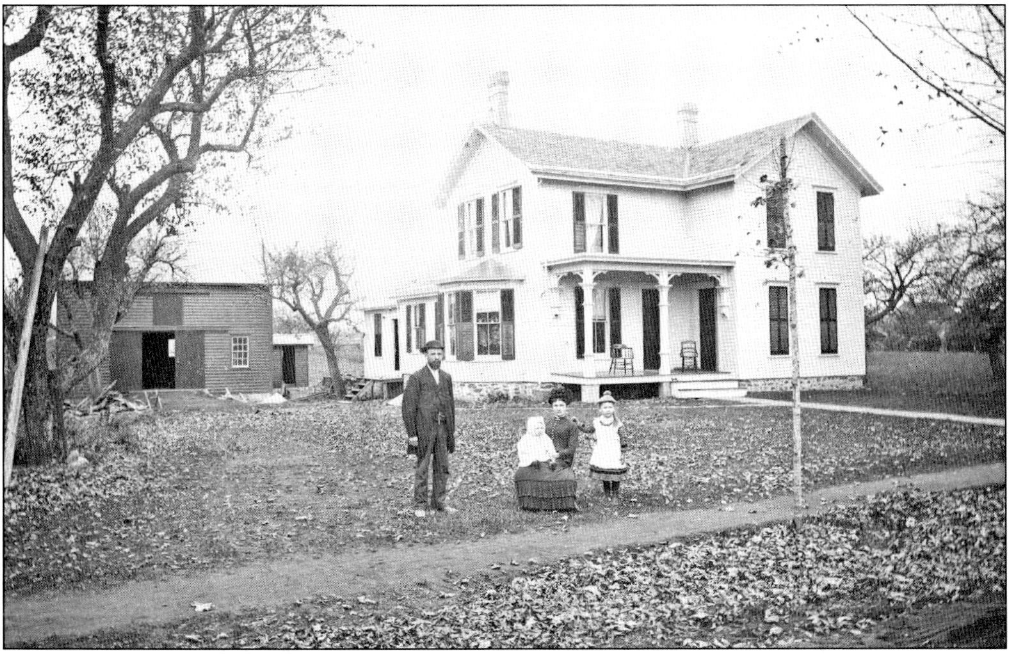

This is the home of John and Cora O'Dell, pictured above with their children baby Anna and Florence. The home was located on East Main Street, just west of the Methodist church. (Courtesy of the Webster Museum and Historical Society.)

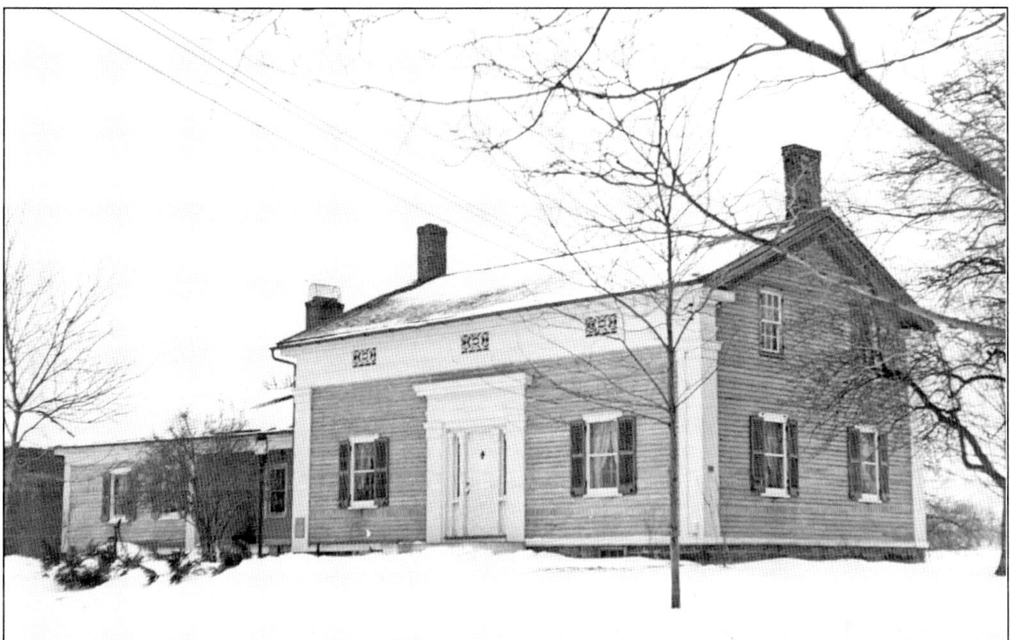

This home, believed to have been built c. 1825, at 920 Salt Road is an excellent example of Greek Revival farm architecture. It is in pristine condition with many of its original features including a large fireplace with a crane and a double Dutch oven, 4 feet deep. Classic architecture from Greece and Rome became fashionable in the early 19th century, because it was seen as a reflection of the ideals of the new nation.

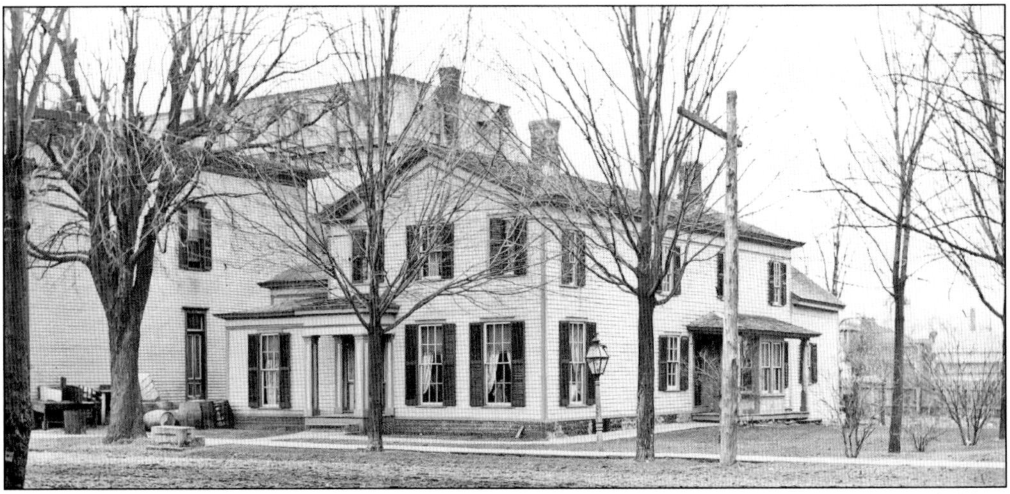

This South Avenue house was built by Timothy B. Corning, who came to North Penfield in 1827 with his brother William J. Corning. They established a mercantile business and a private bank, loaning money and accepting deposits at interest. The home was later owned by George N. Hawley, who operated the store to the north. George Wall later lived there and operated a shop where he was a jeweler, watchmaker, and photographer. He took many of the photographs seen in this book.

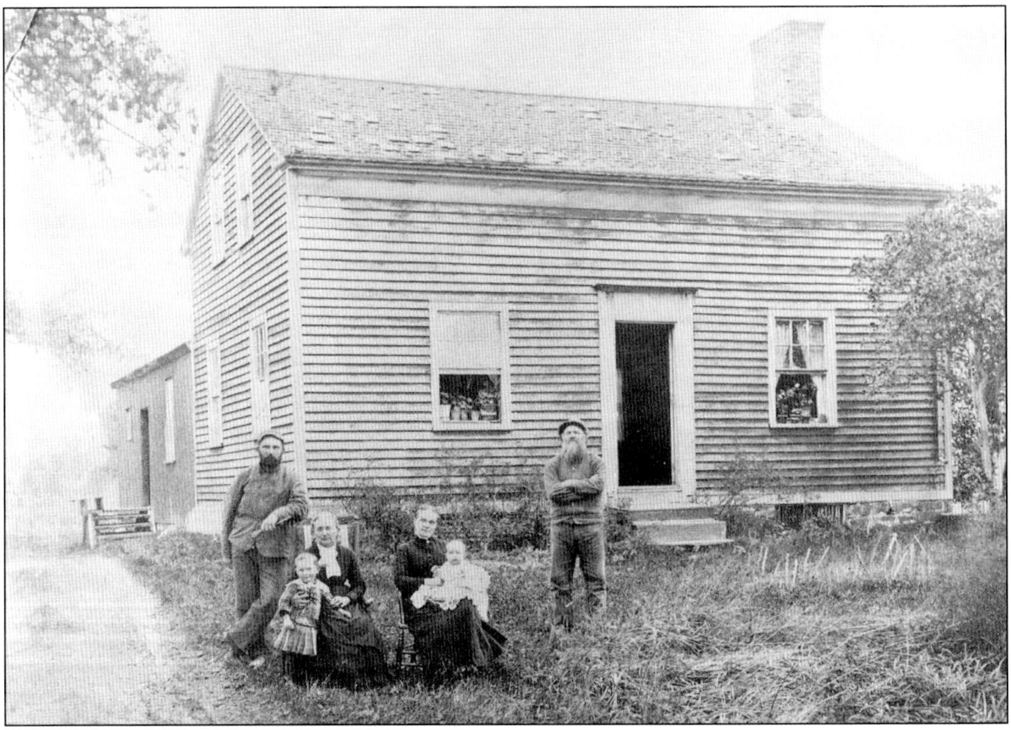

Lyman Wall was born in 1829 to Ebenezer and Hannah Wall, early settlers of Webster. Lyman married Eveline Langdon, the daughter of Fayette and Fannie Langdon of Klem Road in Webster. He soon built a small farmhouse on the northeast corner of Wall Road and Holt Road, seen above. He and his wife raised two boys named Langdon and George. Above are, from left to right, Langdon, Eveline, Clara, and Lyman Wall. The children are unidentified.

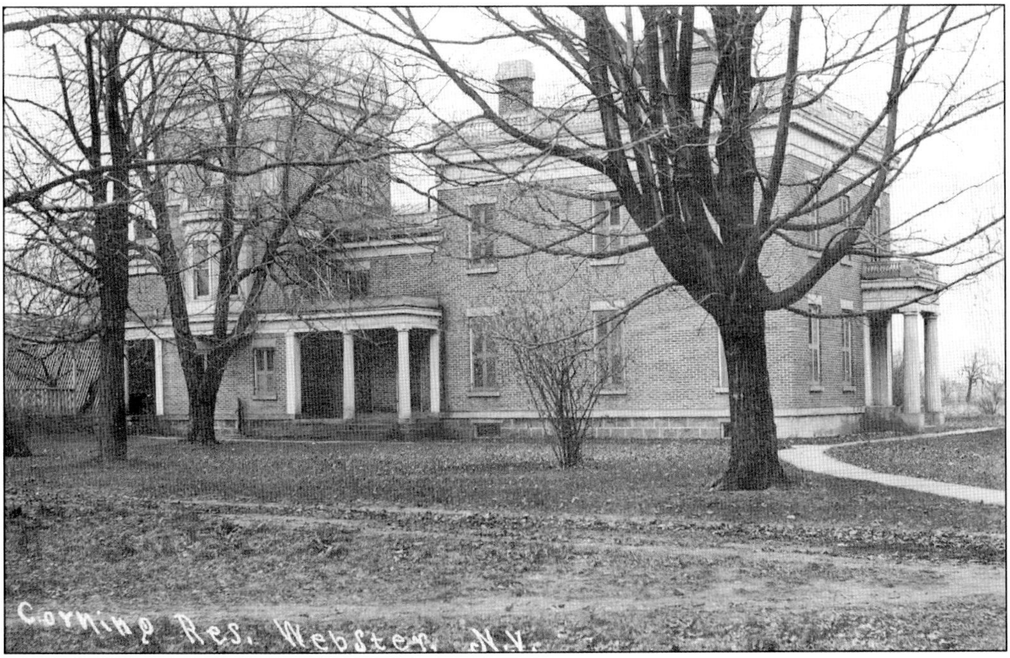

William Corning built this beautiful brick home between 1830 and 1840 on West Main Street. The house contained a built-in pipe organ made of dark mahogany with gold leaf panels. A crystal chandelier containing 5,000 crystals lighted the house for many dances and social gatherings. The pipe organ and crystal chandelier, along with several elegant carriages from the barn, found their way to the Henry Ford museum in Dearborn, Michigan. The house was demolished in 1983. (Courtesy of the Robert Holtz family.)

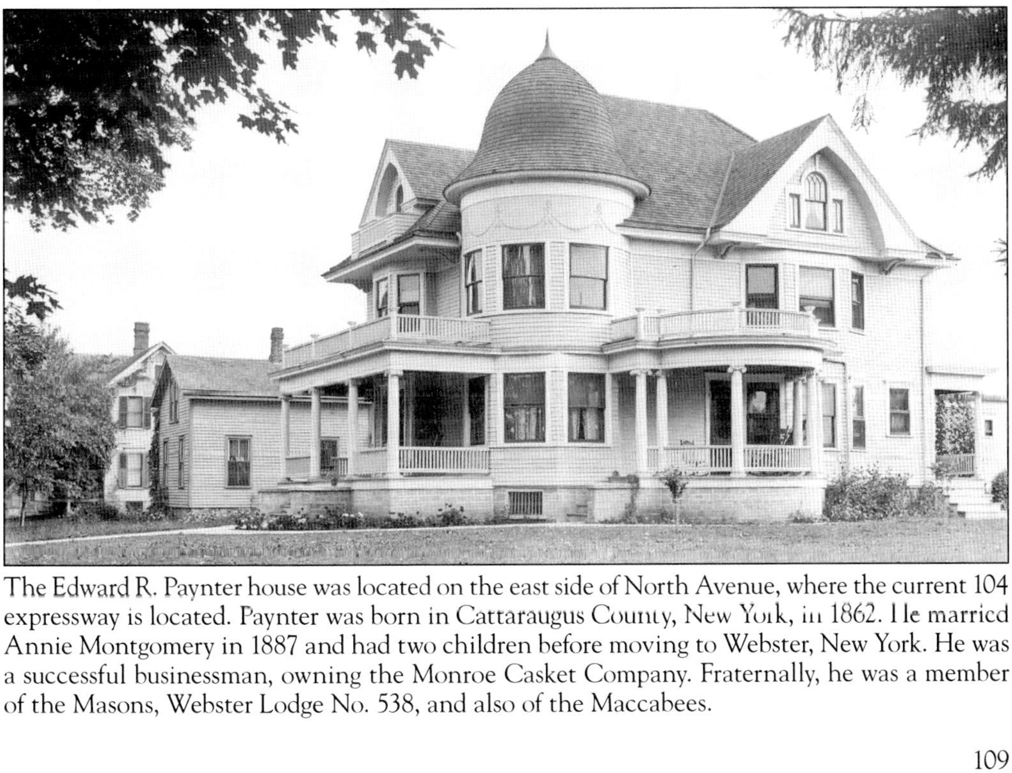

The Edward R. Paynter house was located on the east side of North Avenue, where the current 104 expressway is located. Paynter was born in Cattaraugus County, New York, in 1862. He married Annie Montgomery in 1887 and had two children before moving to Webster, New York. He was a successful businessman, owning the Monroe Casket Company. Fraternally, he was a member of the Masons, Webster Lodge No. 538, and also of the Maccabees.

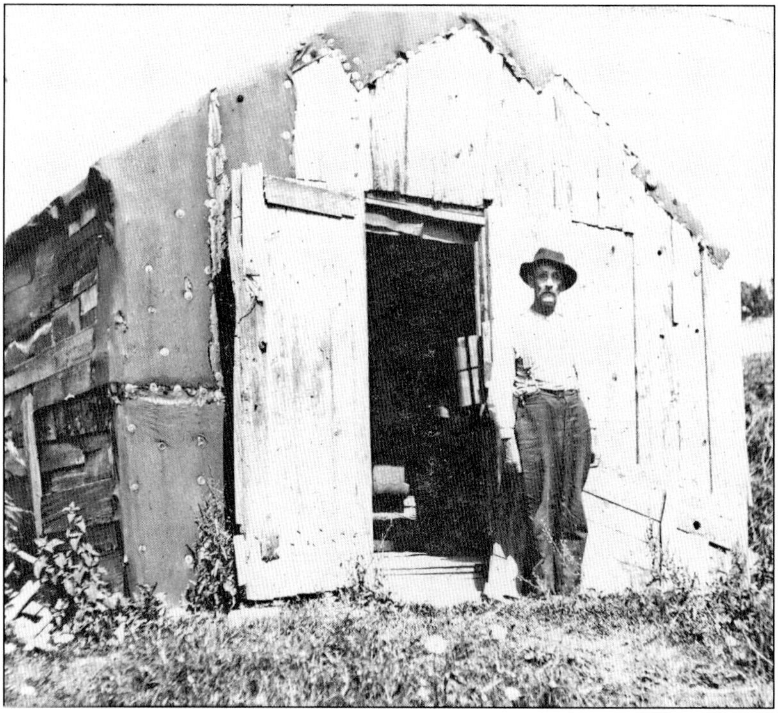

Fisherman Sam Danford is standing in front of his modest dwelling, located at Nine Mile Point, southwest of the bridge. He made his living as a sailor aboard ships plying Lake Ontario. These were seasonal homes. This picture was taken on June 20, 1909. (Courtesy of the Webster Museum and Historical Society.)

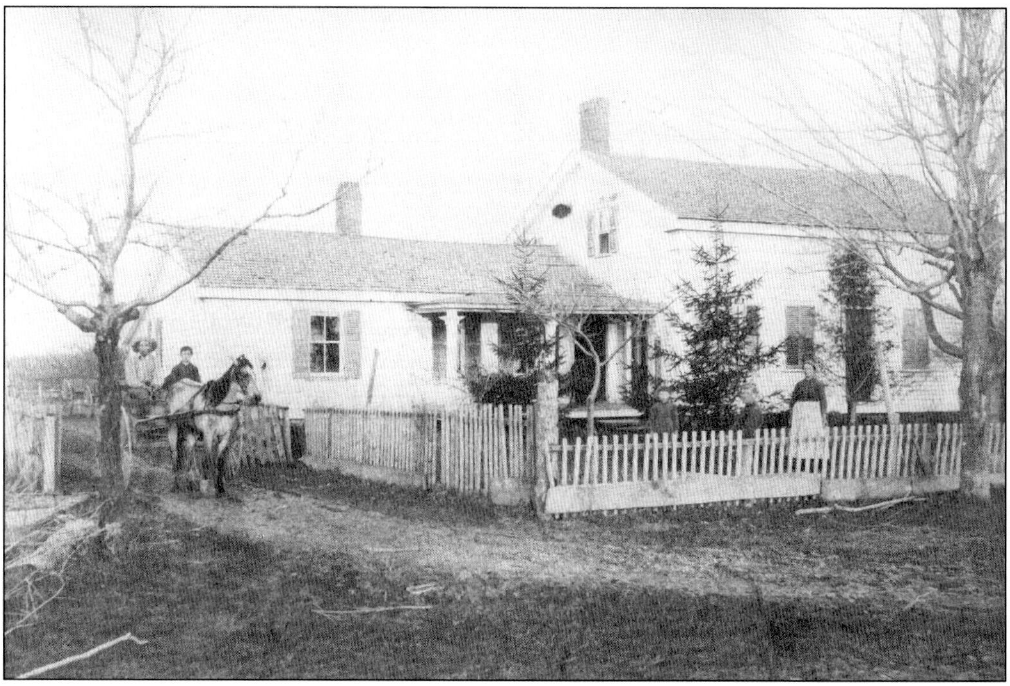

Ludwig and Carolina Brucker came to Webster from Baden, Germany, and purchased the farm at 280 Phillips Road in 1884. Their sons Philip and Charles are pictured in the wagon. Carl Brucker, Charles's son, was well known for his tours of the trains, puzzles, and Rube Goldberg machines that filled his outbuildings and his stories of early farm life in Webster. (Courtesy of the Brucker family.)

Eight

Churches, Schools, and Organizations

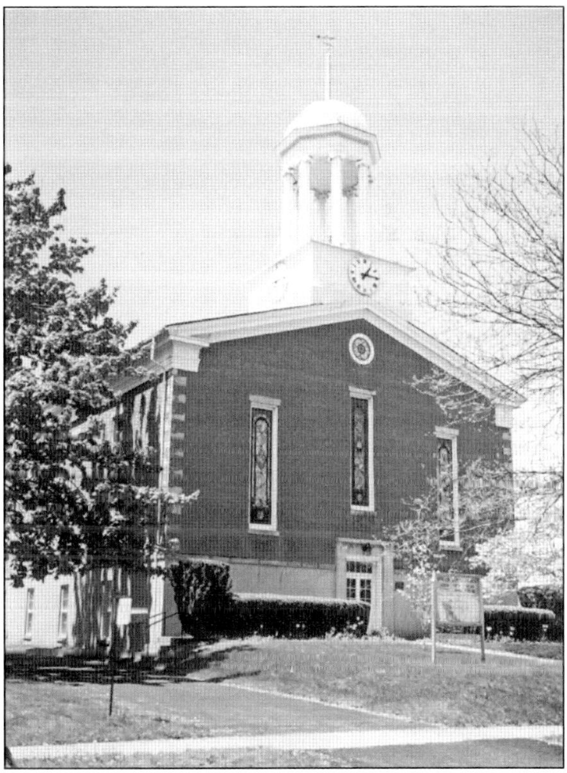

The Webster Baptist Church, listed on the State and National Register of Historic Places, is located on South Avenue. This beautifully constructed cobblestone was dedicated on January 1, 1857. It was built on the site of the original frame structure constructed in 1832 by the congregation. Church members worked together to gather cobblestones from the Lake Ontario shore.

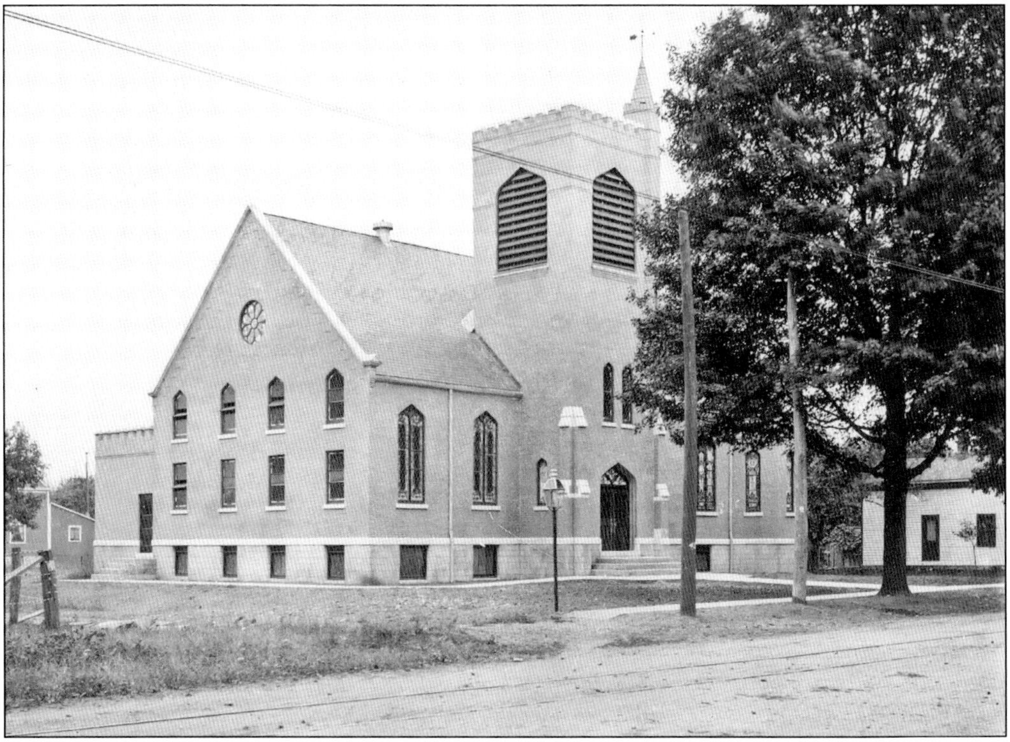

The original congregation was known as German Methodist with a small church built on Salt Road in 1861. A new church was built in 1906 on the corner of East Main Street and Hefner Lane, now Curtis Park, seen above. It is veneered with yellow brick and has beautiful stained-glass windows memorializing early church families. Today it is known as the United Methodist Church of Webster.

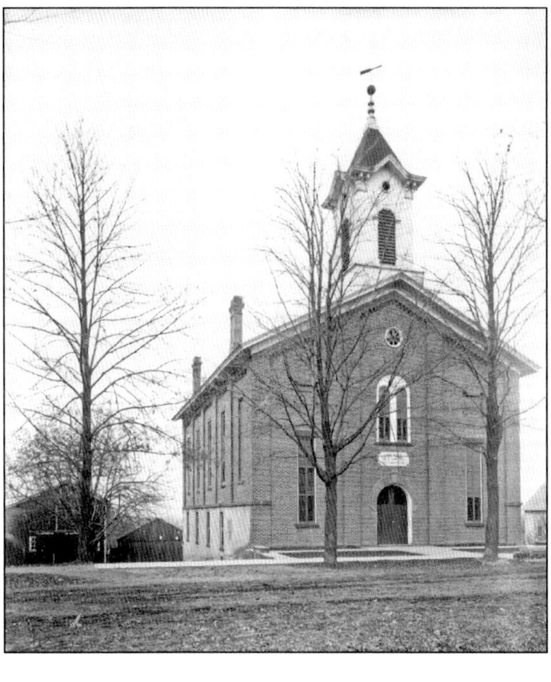

The United Methodist Church, located on West Main Street, was dedicated in 1860. The cost of construction was about $8,000. The church began as "the Second Society of the Methodist Episcopal Church," with eight members, in 1830. Today the building is called the Old Church Mall and houses businesses, including Maria's Mexican Restaurant and the Village Mall Video.

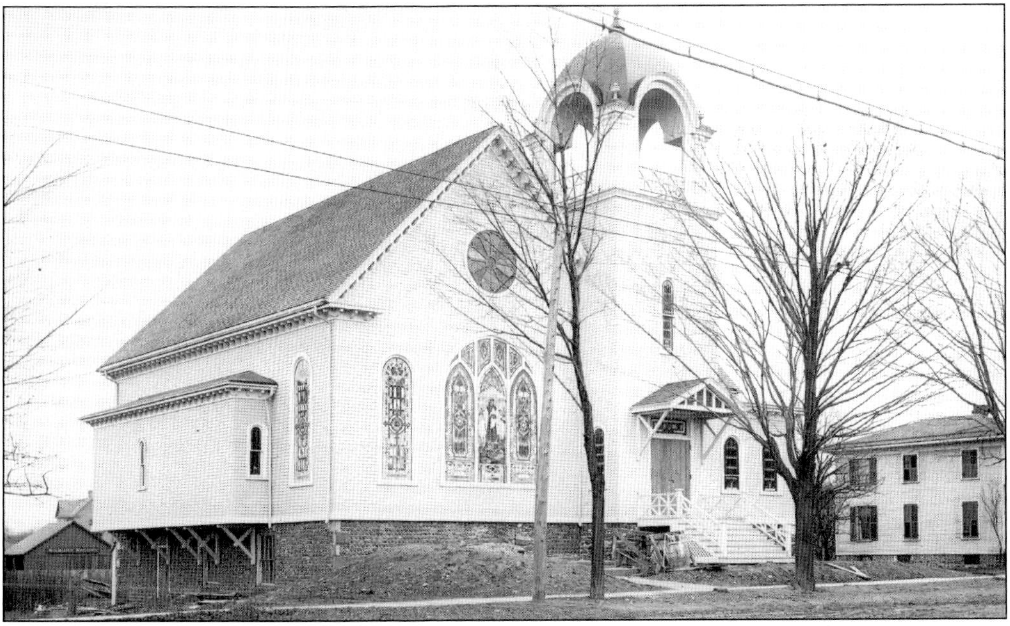

The Presbyterian Church of Webster began as a Congregational Society, organized in 1825. Early members of the church were primarily farmers. Sunday worship began in the morning with a sermon, followed by lunch, then Sunday school at noon, and another afternoon sermon. In 1855, a new church was built on East Main Street, as seen in this picture.

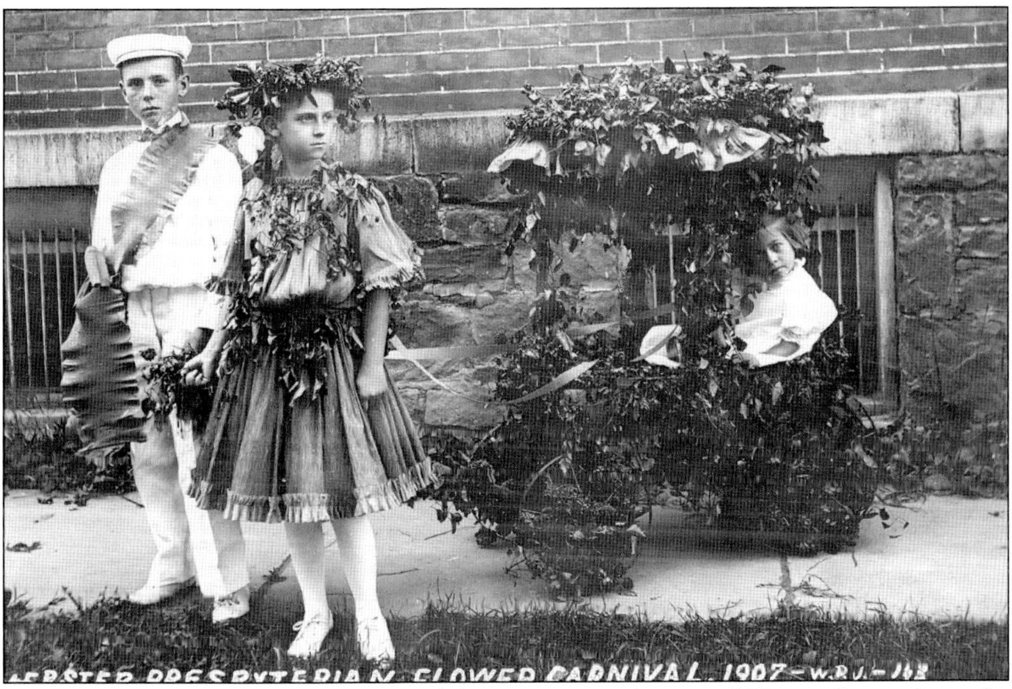

This postcard, dated 1907, shows one of the entrants in the annual Flower Carnival parade, sponsored by the Webster Presbyterian Church. The entrants are seen waiting for the parade to begin at the Webster High School on South Avenue. (Courtesy of the Robert Holtz family.)

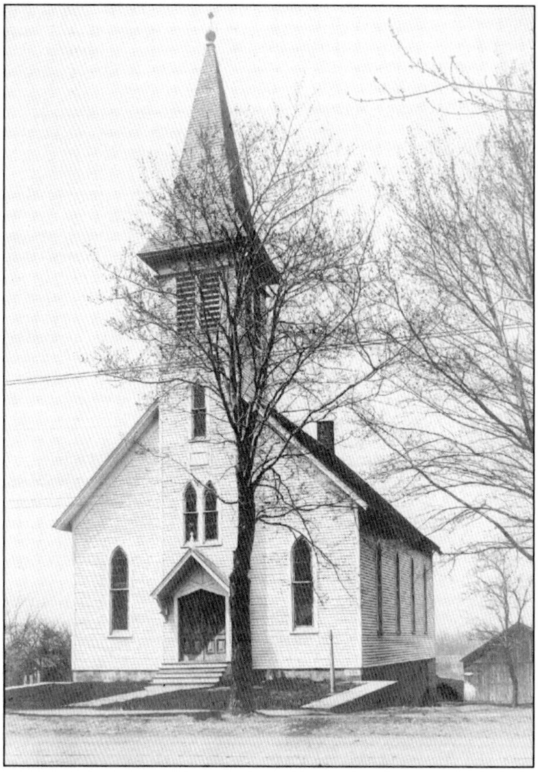

In 1860, a group of people formed a congregation called the Evangelical Church. The first building was constructed on the northwest corner of Five Mile Line Road and Ridge Road in 1868, shortly after they adopted a new constitution in favor of the Lutheran confession. The church today, which was built in 1888, is located on West Main Street in the village, as seen in this picture. (Courtesy of the Immanuel Evangelical Lutheran Church.)

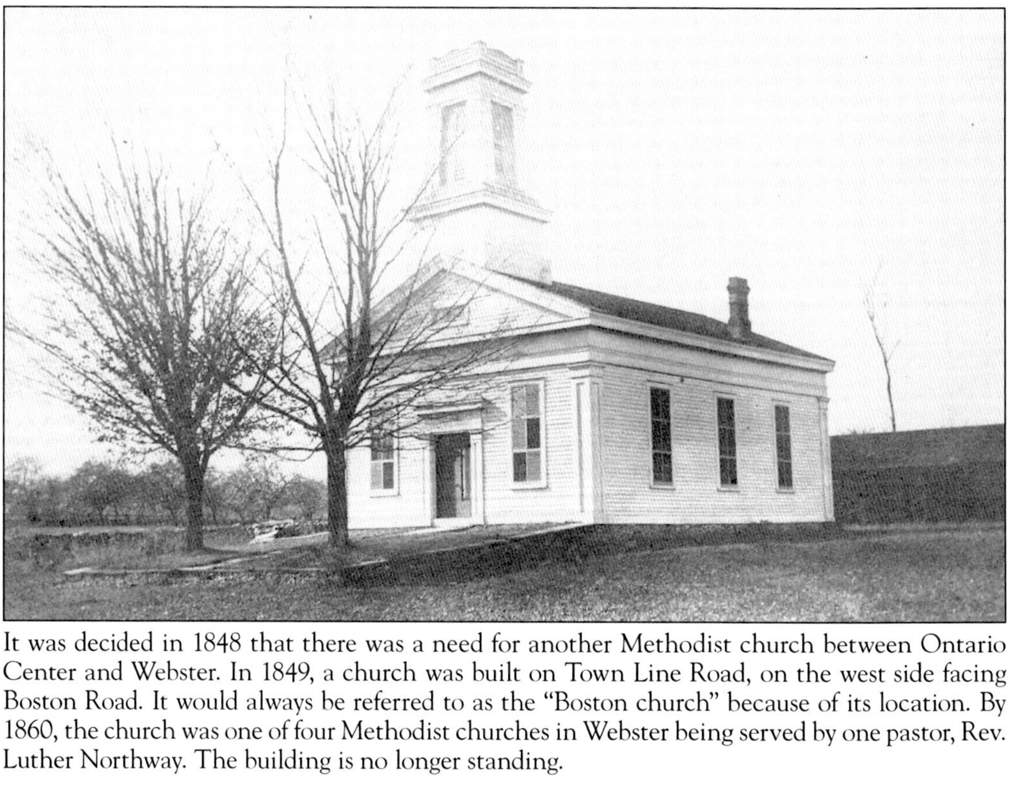

It was decided in 1848 that there was a need for another Methodist church between Ontario Center and Webster. In 1849, a church was built on Town Line Road, on the west side facing Boston Road. It would always be referred to as the "Boston church" because of its location. By 1860, the church was one of four Methodist churches in Webster being served by one pastor, Rev. Luther Northway. The building is no longer standing.

The Romanesque-style redbrick Catholic church, located east of the village, was dedicated on the Feast of the Most Holy Trinity, June 2, 1901. The church architect was Joseph Oberlies, and the contractor was August Pappert—both of Rochester—and it cost approximately $19,742 to build. The Holy Trinity Cemetery is located behind the church, where a large, 20-foot-high Celtic cross was erected in 1899.

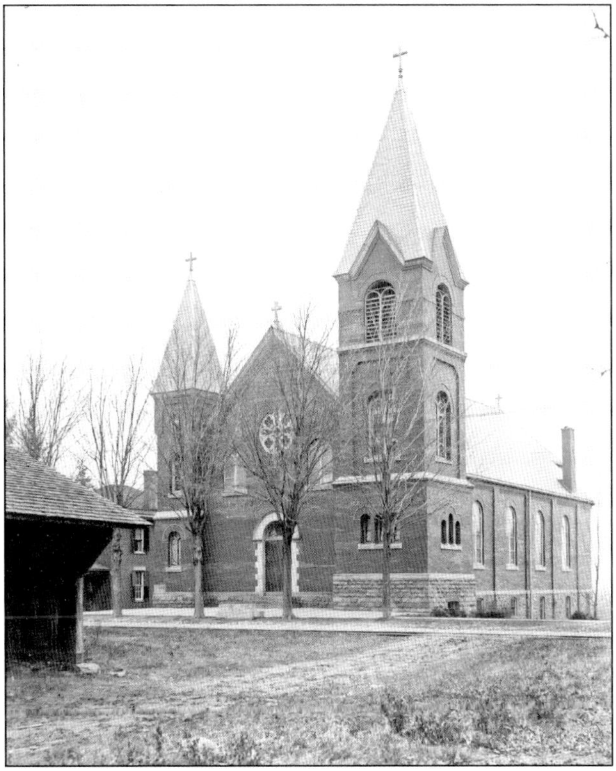

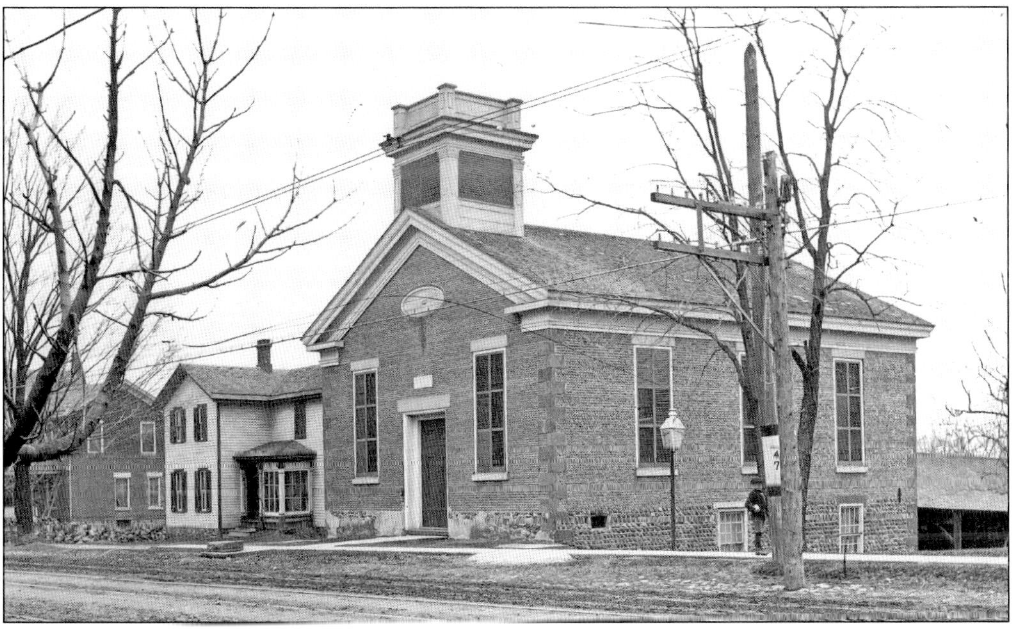

The First Universalist Society of Webster, New York, was located on West Main Street in the village. The cobblestone church was constructed by John Farr, a member of the society, and it was dedicated in November 1845. The church was active in the community until the 1920s when, because of the minister's failing health, the congregation decided to close the church. Today it is the location of Webster Automotive.

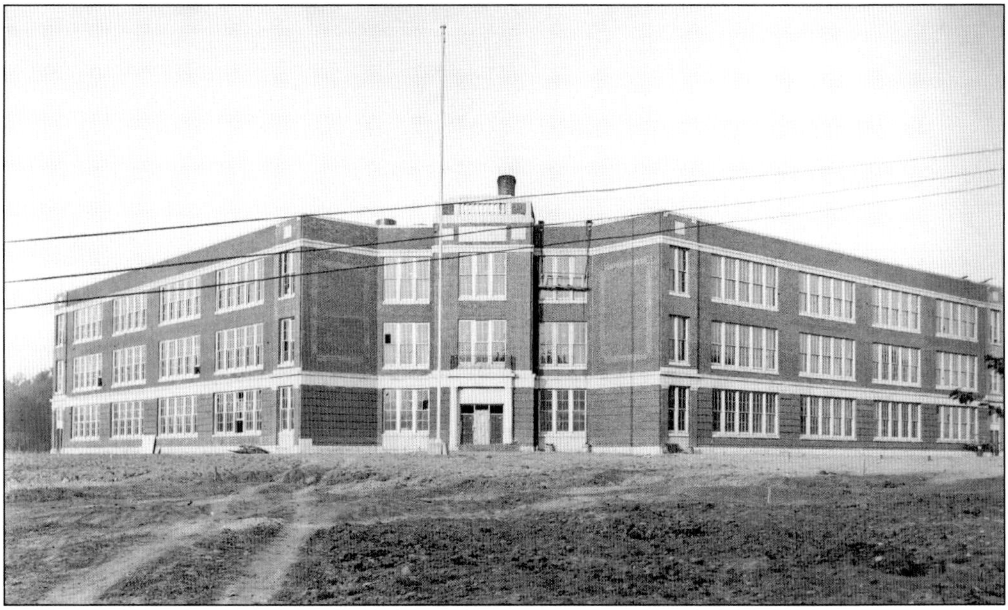

This photograph is of a yet-to-be-completed Webster High School. The building was laid out in the form of a letter W. Webster High School opened September 1925. The new school had many modern conveniences: a gymnasium, auditorium, an office for principal Edward W. Spry, a cafeteria where warm lunches were served, a large library, and a kindergarten room. Even though it was called Webster High School, grades kindergarten through 12 attended there.

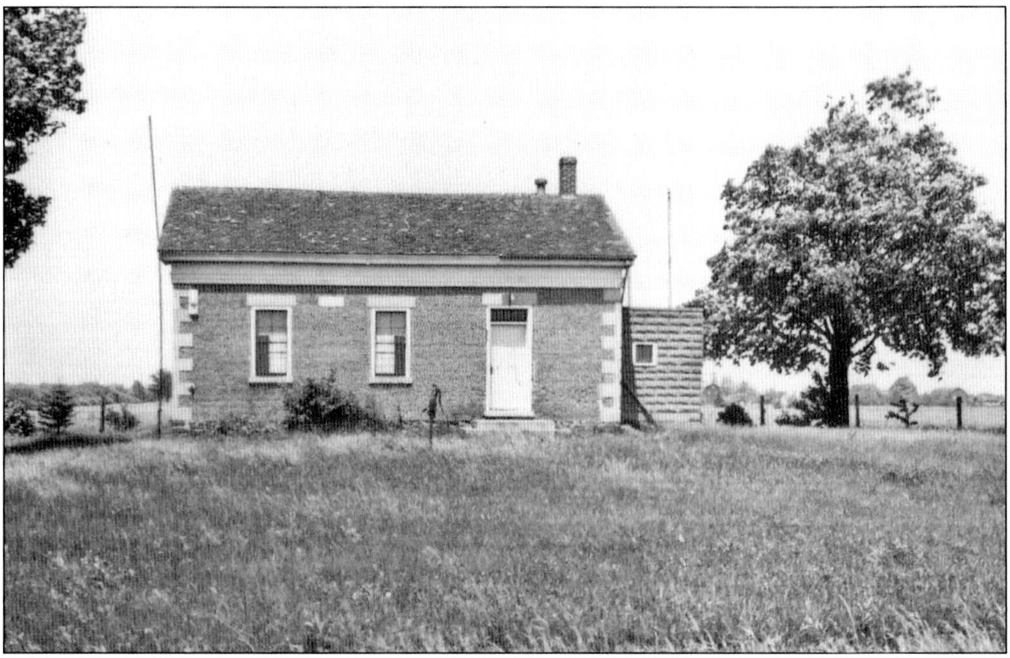

The cobblestone District No. 7 school located at 1352 Schlegel Road was constructed in 1846. It was used as a district school until 1943. When centralization of the school district took effect, the District No. 7 school was auctioned off and has been used as a private home since that time.

The Webster Union Free School was built in 1876 on the corner of South Avenue and Sanford Street. It could accommodate 250 students. There were four classrooms, two on each floor. The first graduates in 1881 were Howard Curtice and Estella Peacock. Two more additions were added over the years as attendance grew. Students Bess Hawley Gaffney, in the white hat, and Laura Gelser, on her left, are pictured in 1896.

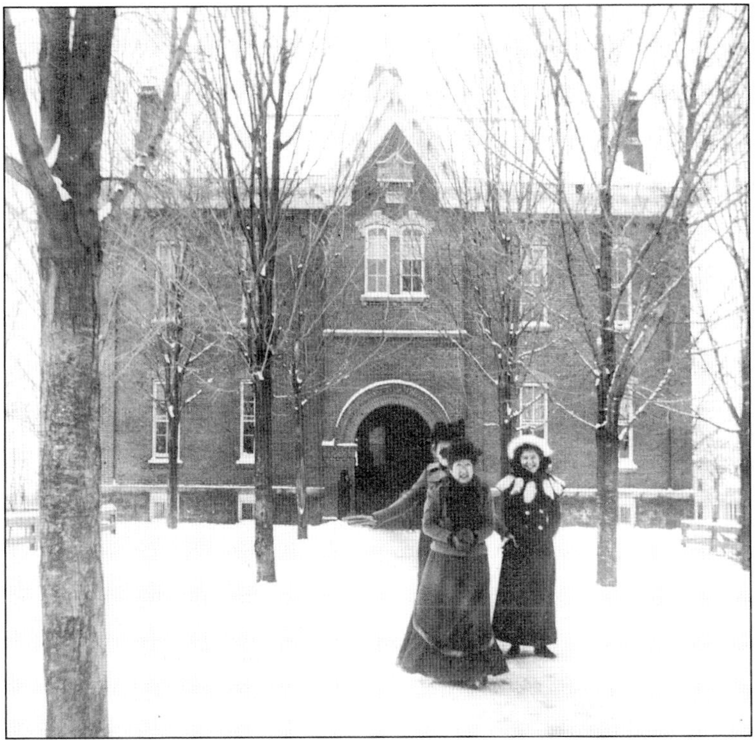

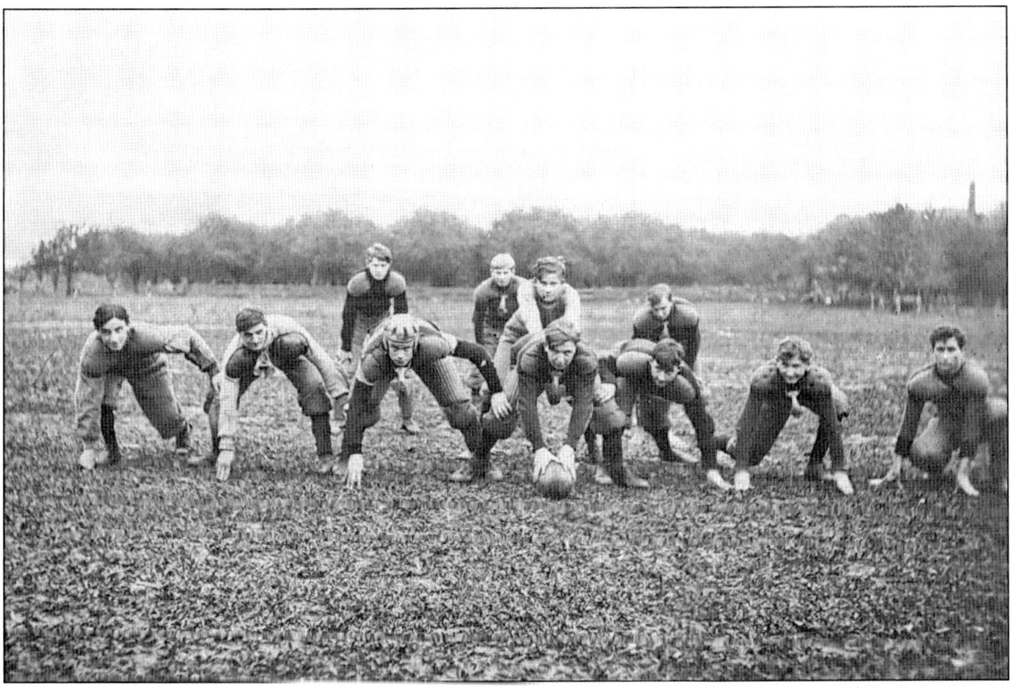

This is a picture of the first Webster High School football team, dated 1906. The photograph belonged to Carl G. Wooster, a member of the team. The playing grounds were on the west side of Kircher Park. Some of the other teams they played in their league were Sodus, Ontario, Williamson, and Fairport. (Courtesy of John VanAlstyne.)

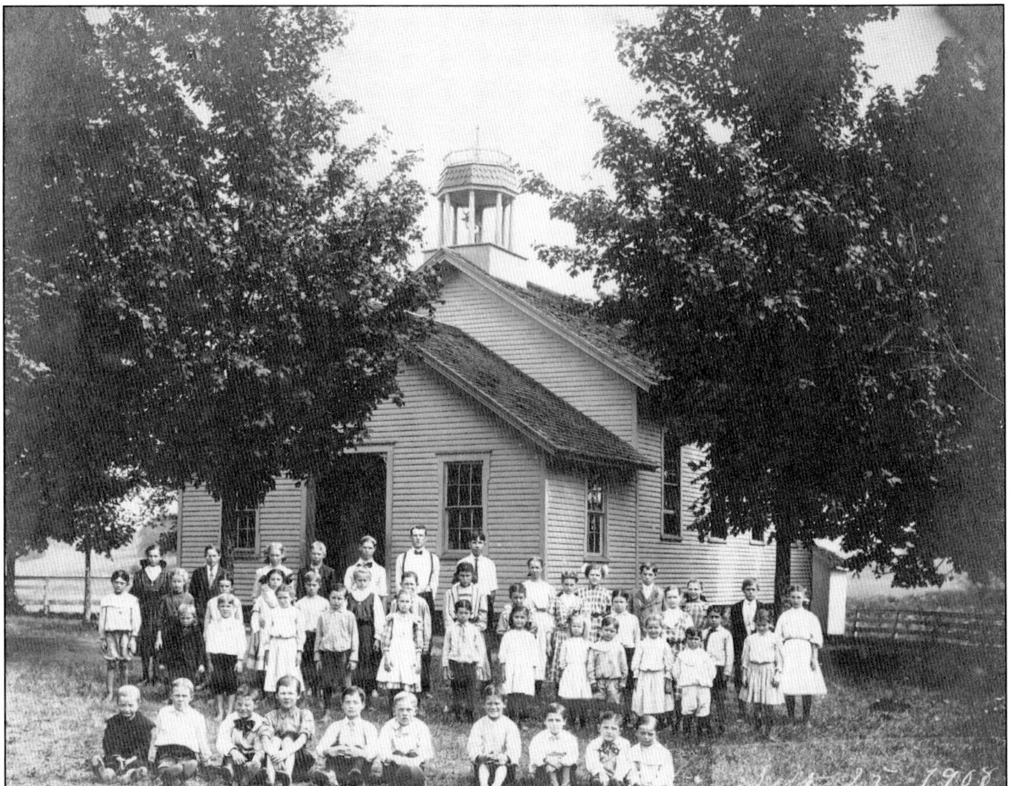

Located at 336 Basket Road, on the corner of Woodard Road, is the District No. 8 schoolhouse. It was built *c.* 1883 at the cost of $1,500. All the schools at that time were heated by woodstoves. Betty Frank, Webster resident, recalls that she and her siblings carried raw potatoes to school every day and placed them on the woodstove and had cooked potatoes for lunch. Wood needed for the year was furnished by the parents whose children attended the school. A family could arrange to have the teacher board at their home in lieu of supplying wood or paying the $1.50 fee per student. Below is the District No. 8 class of Mildred Hosenfeld. (Photograph above courtesy of Dolores Maas Zimmer and Teresa Young.)

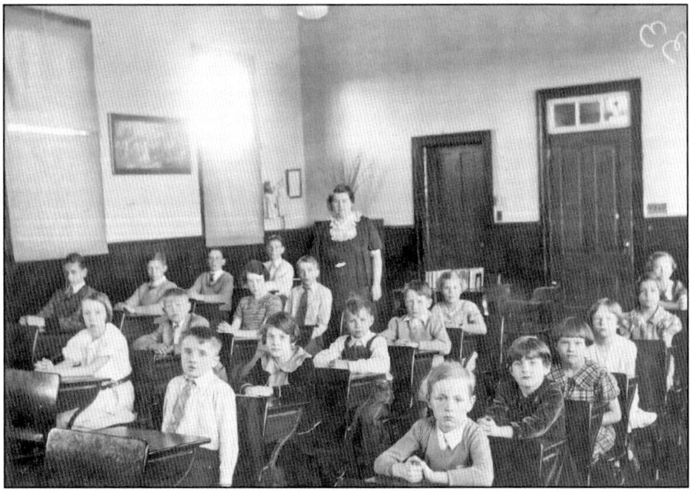

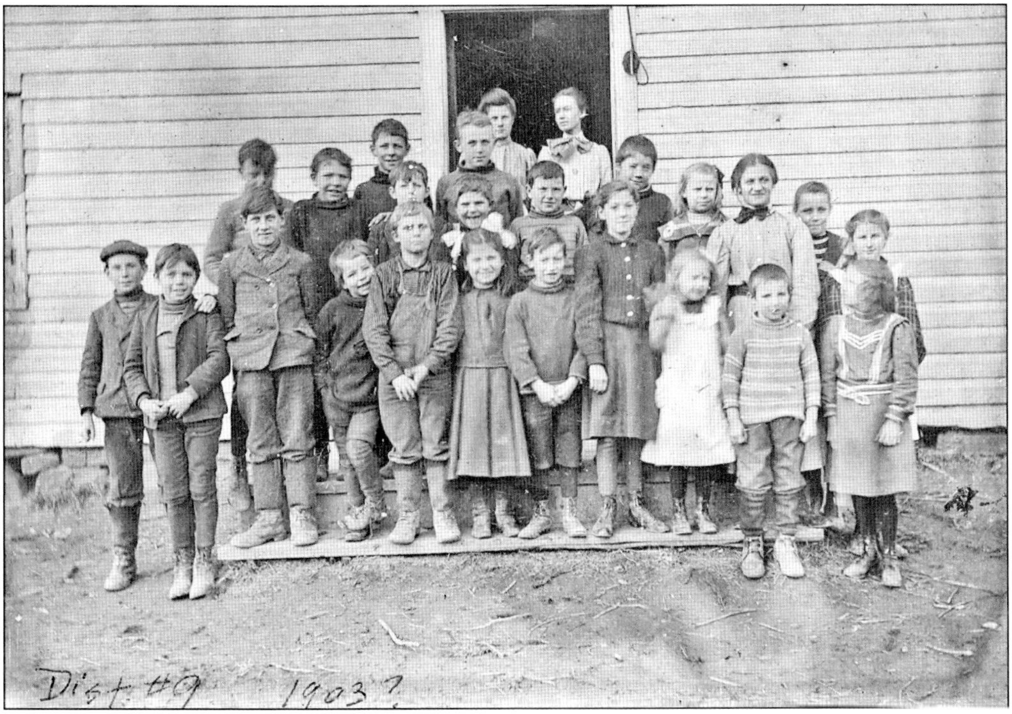

In 1912, trustee George Dunn received notice from the education department at Albany Education Department that District No. 9 school on Lake Road had been condemned. The building was too small and not up to date with sanitary rules. After meetings with district members, it was decided that they would build a new school. The old District No. 9 building was moved to adjoining grounds, was lovingly remodeled, and today is the Chapel of Saint Andrew by the Lake. (Courtesy of the Webster Museum and Historical Society.)

The new District No. 9 was completed in 1913 for a total cost of about $3,000. The new school was heated by hot air, had a well-equipped playground, and a basement that could be used as a lunchroom or for meetings. When finished, the state inspector declared that it was the most perfectly ventilated, best-arranged, and best-built one-teacher school in the state.

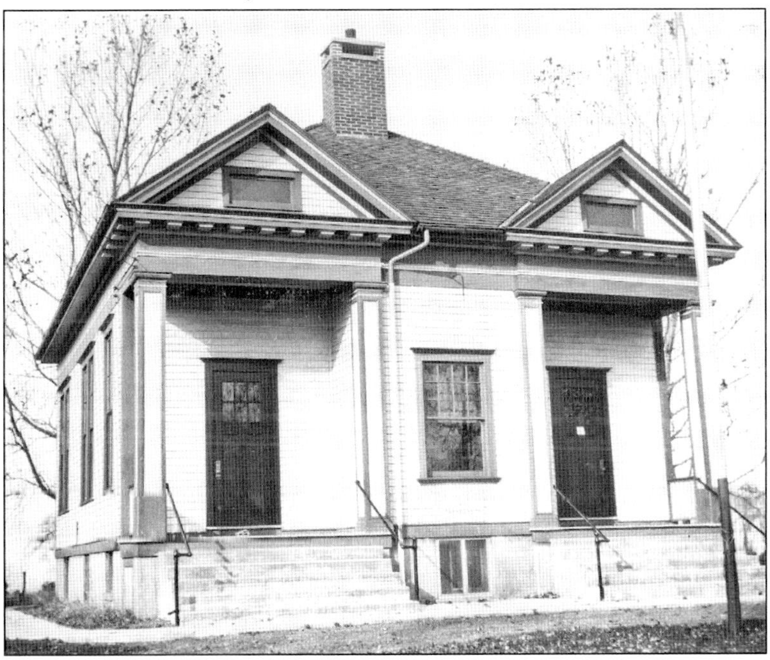

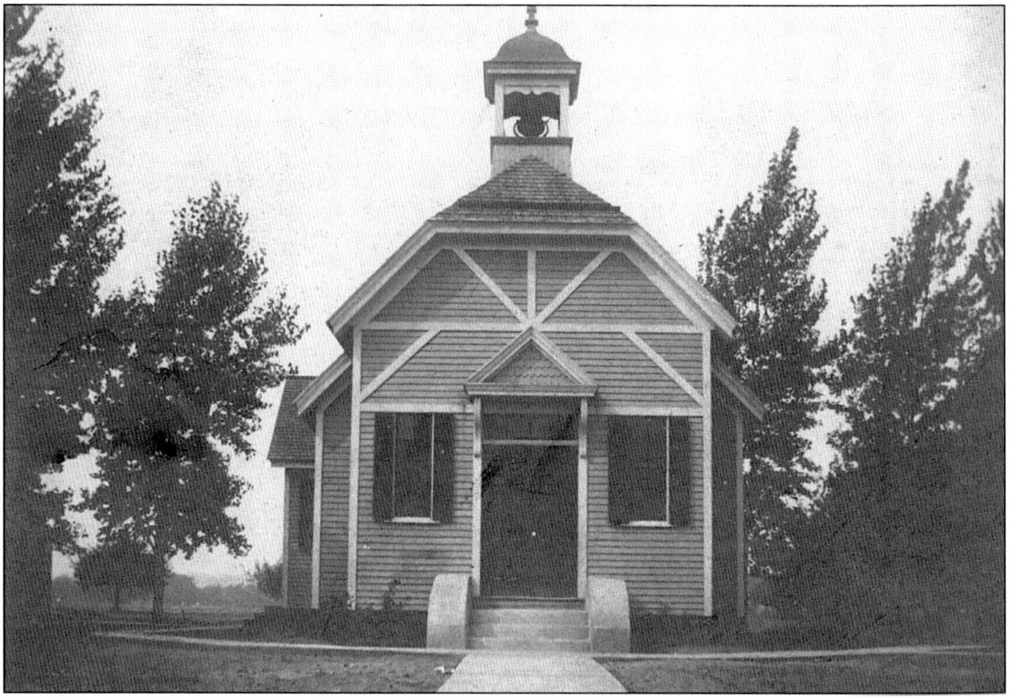

District school No. 4 on Bay Road was built *c.* 1879 and enlarged in 1902. Webster schools had winter and summer terms. The summer term began on June 1, with a female teacher, and it was attended by girls and young children. The older boys attended through the winter months when they were not needed on the farms. This school building today is the Holy Cross Anglican Church.

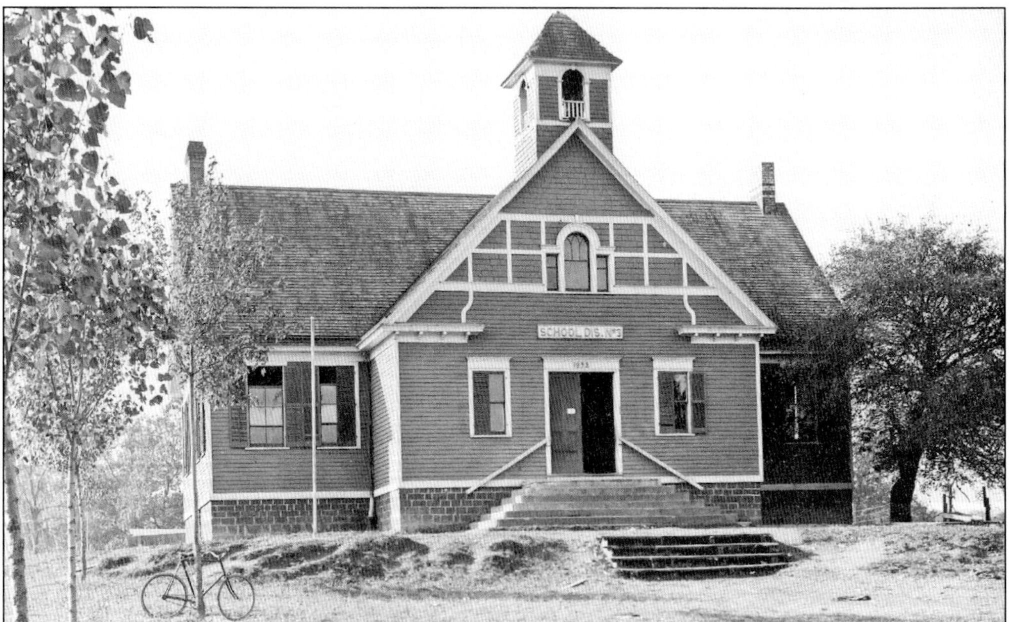

A fondly remembered school, District No. 3, is located on the south side of Ridge Road, in West Webster. It was built in 1892. The district population had increased, making it necessary for a larger building and another teacher.

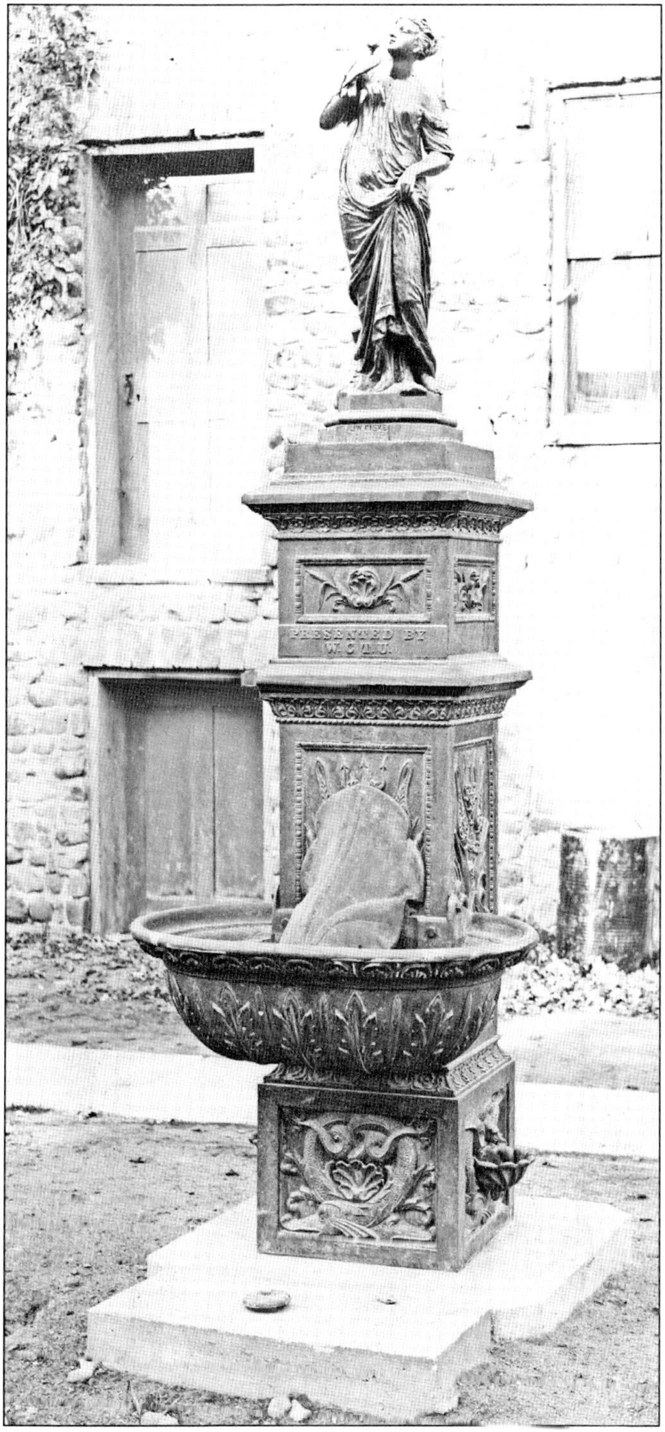

Dedicated to helping Webster residents live healthy, sober lives, the Webster Women's Christian Temperance Union was founded in 1880. The group donated this fountain to the village on July 19, 1913, to replace the old town pump. The new fountain was made of cast iron by the Brooklyn, New York, firm J. W. Fiske. It stood on the west side of South Avenue near the four corners.

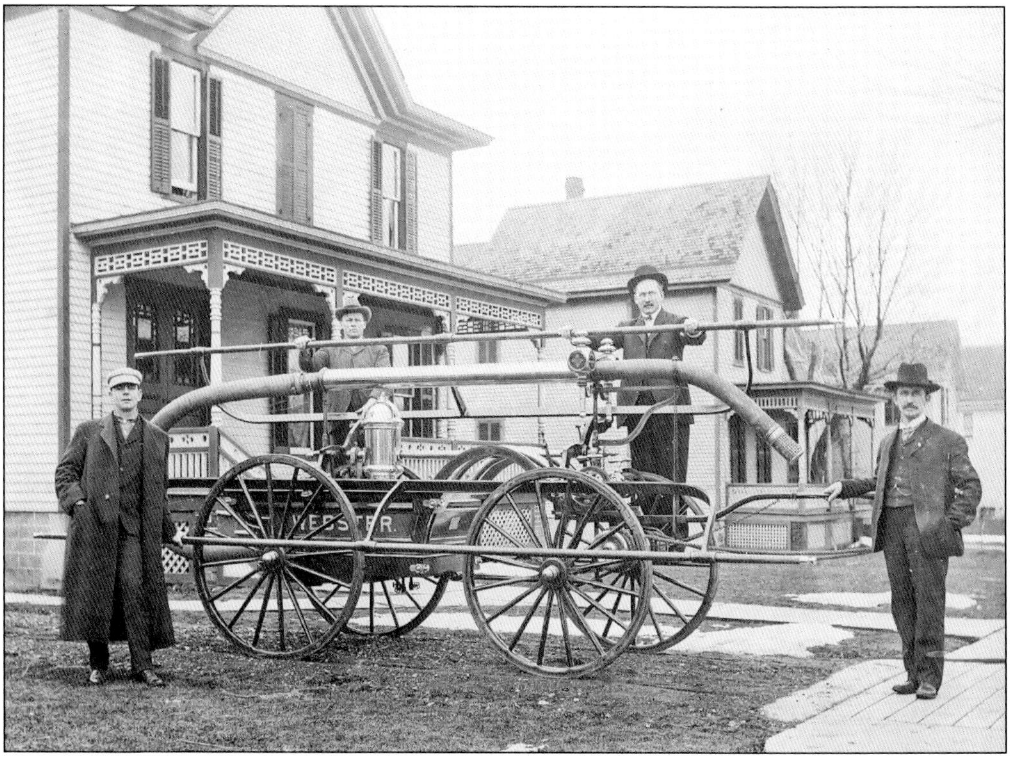

In 1906, the Webster Fire Department was formed, one year after the incorporation of the village of Webster. One of the first purchases made occurred in 1908 with the acquisition of a used hand pumper. This is a picture of the pumper in the front yard of George Mason's home on Dunning Avenue. The pumper is on display at the Fire Hall on South Avenue.

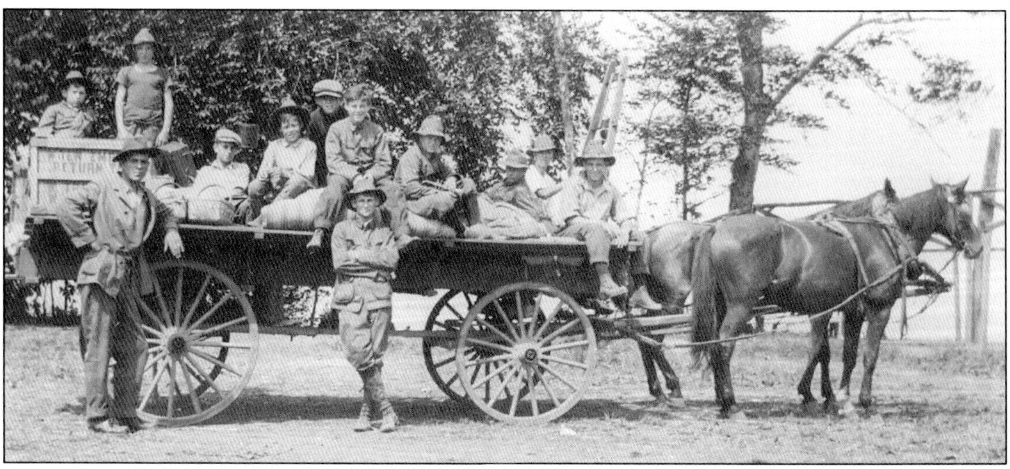

An early Webster Boy Scout Troop is shown camping at the Dunn Farm on Lake Road in 1912. Shown here are, from left to right, (standing) Scoutmaster Carl Grabb and his assistant James Johnson; (in the wagon) unidentified, Ralph Witmer, Ronald Hawley, unidentified, George Curtice, three unidentified, Immanuel Arndt, and Gordon Witmer.

The Webster Grange No. 436 was organized in 1880, and by 1900, had built its new hall located at 58 East Main Street. The grange stood for home development, public service, honest government, highway improvement, conservation of water and wildlife, protection of our forests, health, and education. The grange was instrumental in helping to get rural free delivery of mail for Webster in 1900, along with a telephone exchange in 1901.

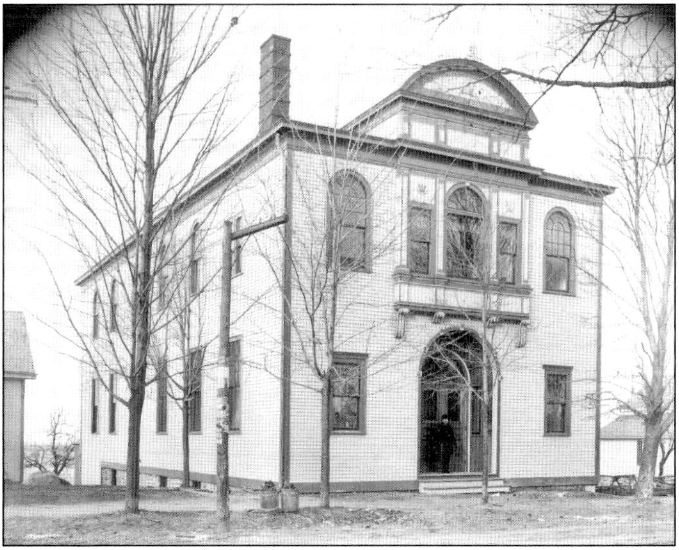

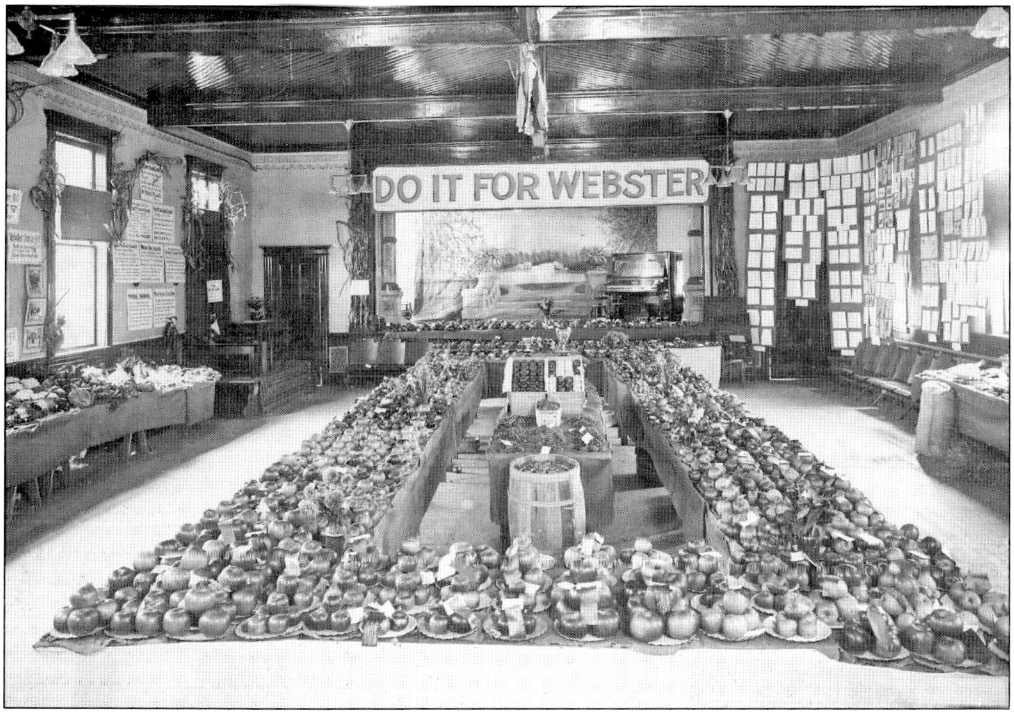

The main floor of the grange building has a large, elegant hall and a stage equipped with beautifully hand-painted scenery. The hall is remembered for the many minstrel shows, fairs, and other community entertainments that have taken place through the years. This photograph shows a Webster Grange fruit exhibit. In 1909, the grange began collecting awards at the state fair for fruit and vegetable exhibits.

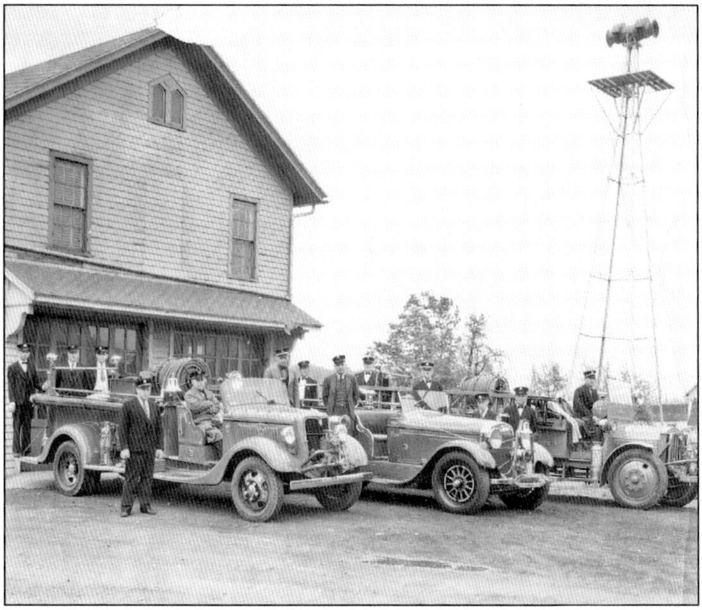

The first meeting of the West Webster Volunteer Firemen's Association was on May 3, 1926. The photograph at left, c. 1939, was taken in front of the fire station purchased in 1934, on the southeast corner of Ridge and Gravel Roads. Displayed in front of the station is, from left to right, a 1935 Ford pumper, a 1937 Lincoln emergency car, and the first pumper, a 1926 Federal. Standing far left is Chief Louis Vogt. (Courtesy of the West Webster Fire Department.)

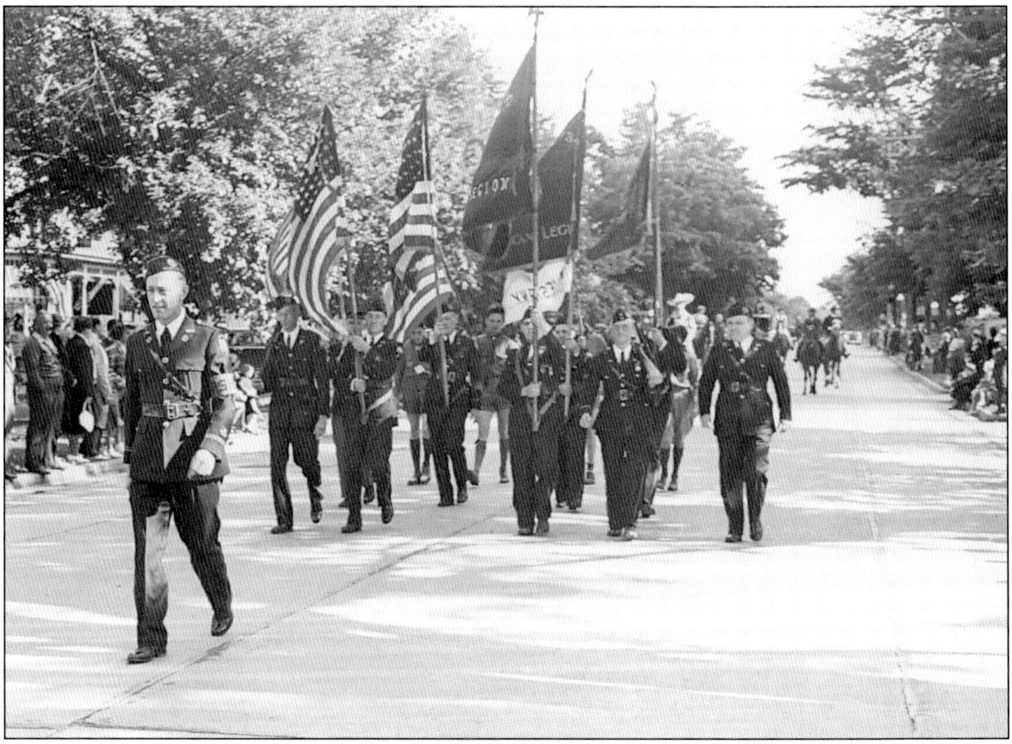

This photograph from the 1940 centennial parade shows the color guard and members of the American Legion Cottreall-Warner Post. This organization was founded in 1921. Dr. James B. Foster was elected its first commander. The post was named in memory of two Webster soldiers from World War I. Joseph Cottreall was killed in action July 15, 1918, in the Champagne Marne defensive, and Basil Warner was killed in action on September 29, 1918, on the Hindenburg Line.

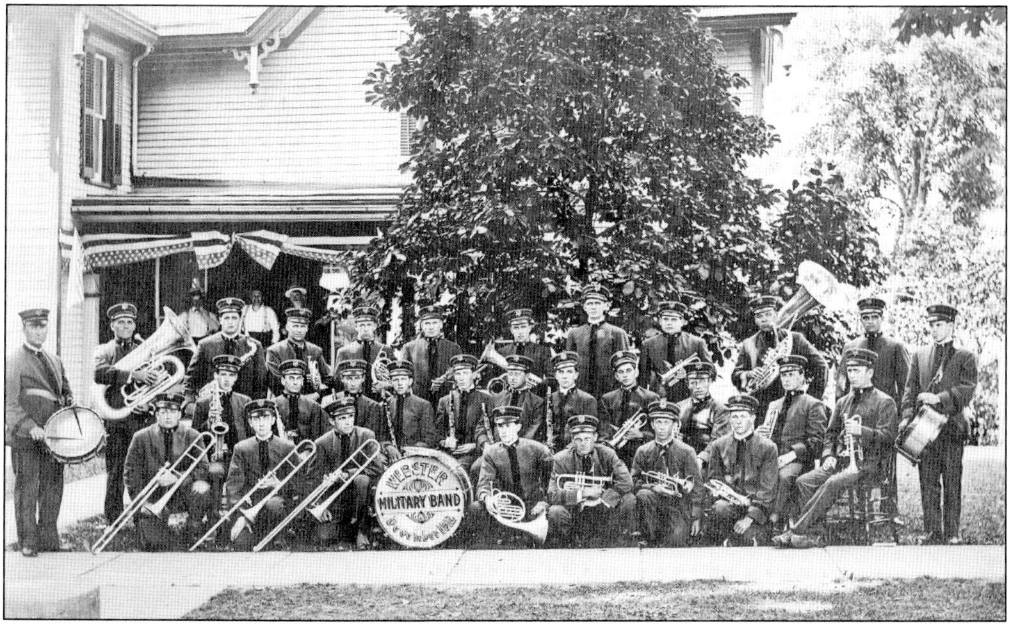

The Webster Military Band posing in front of Dr. Whittleton's home on West Main Street around 1912. The band was organized by the Webster Fire Department and financed by local merchants. During the summer months, they could be heard playing on the balcony of the Webster Hotel or in local parades. Corbin Crittenden is seen sitting on the ground at the right.

Early in 1863, Webster men who belonged to the Penfield Lodge of the Free and Accepted Masons raised $178.75 to establish a lodge in Webster. There were 13 members who petitioned the Grand Lodge of New York to organize the Webster Lodge No. 538. On June 13, 1863, the first meeting was held with H. Nelson Curtice, seen at right, elected as the first master. (Courtesy of the Webster Masonic Lodge No. 538.)

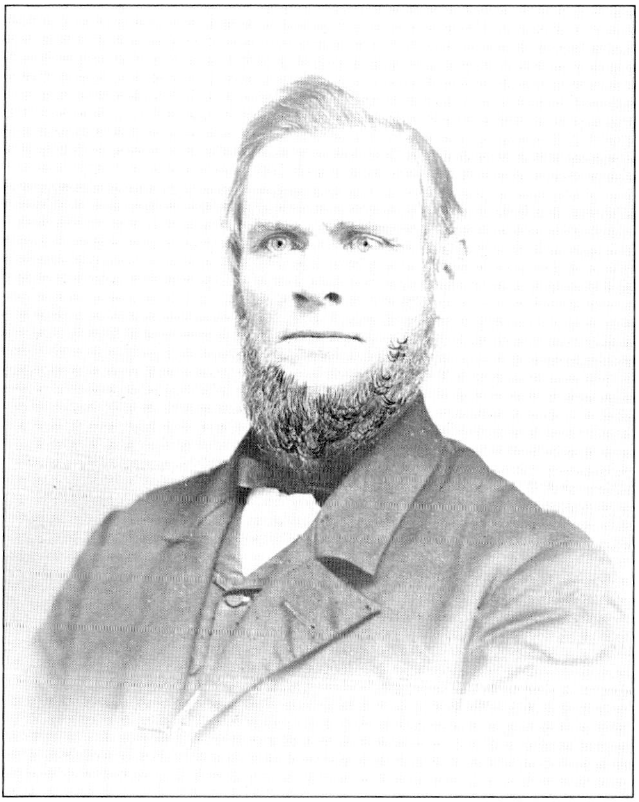

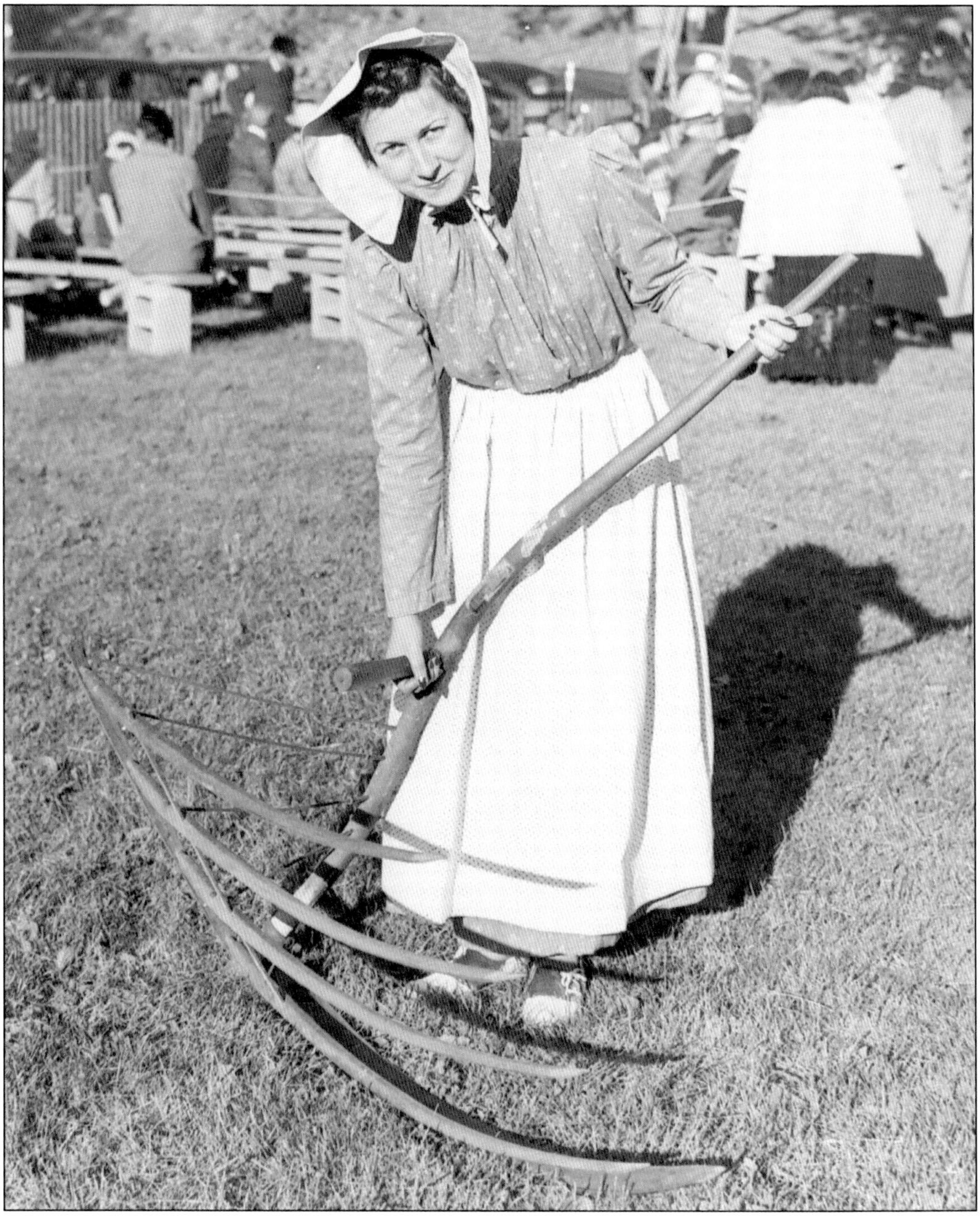

The town of Webster celebrated 100 years as an incorporated town in 1940. The centennial committee organized many celebrations, including a parade and a pageant. Hilda Krenzer Kaler was part of the "Fruits of the Forest" pageant, dramatized by hundreds of local residents and held at the Nine Mile Point. She is shown demonstrating a grain cradle used to harvest grains such as wheat.

BIBLIOGRAPHY

Atlas of Monroe County, New York. New York: F.W. Beers and Company, 1872.

Duffus, R. L., and L. Emmett Holt Jr. *L. Emmett Holt: Pioneer of a Children's Century*. New York: D. Appleton and Company, 1940.

Dunn, Esther A. *Webster through the Years*. Rochester, NY: Webster Town Board, Inc., 1971.

Foreman, Edward R., ed. *The Rochester Historical Society Publication Fund Series, Volume IV*. Rochester, NY: self-published, 1925.

Forsyth, C. Benn. *Forest Lawn Centennial Book 1888–1988*. Webster, New York: self-published, 1988.

Gleason, Lawrence J., and William R. Schlegel. *The West Webster Volunteer Firemen's Association: the first 50 years, 1926–1976*. Webster, New York: self-published, 1976.

Greeley, Adolphus. *Report on the Proceedings of the U.S. Expedition to Lady Franklin Bay Grinnell Land*. Washington D.C.: U.S. Government printing office, 1888

History of Monroe County, 1788–1877. Philadelphia: Everts, Ensign and Everts, 1877.

Lodge, Henry Cabot. *Daniel Webster*. Boston, NY: Houghton Mifflin Company, 1911.

Merrill, Arch. *Land of the Senecas*. New York: Stratford Press, Inc., 1949.

———. *The Ridge*. Rochester, NY: Louis Heindl and Son, 1944.

National Geographic Magazine. "Little Citizens of the World." DC: The National Geographic Society, February 1917.

Rochester Democrat and Chronicle. "Kislingbury's Ghastly Fate Unveiled." January 12, 2009: B1.

Rochester Post Express. Town Archives, Webster, NY: October 10, 1896.

Ross, Mae. *The First 100 Years of the Webster Grange*. Webster, NY: self-published, 1999.

Wright, Thomas E. *History of Webster, New York: Vols. I–III*: Papers unpublished. Webster, NY: 1945.